RESEARCH METHODS IN EDUCATION

By

MAHAVEER SINGH
M.Sc., M.Ed., M.Phil., Ph.D.

UDAIVEER SINGH
M.Ed., Ph.D.

UNIVERSITY SCIENCE PRESS
(An Imprint of Laxmi Publications Pvt. Ltd.)
BANGALORE • CHENNAI • COCHIN • GUWAHATI • HYDERABAD
JALANDHAR • KOLKATA • LUCKNOW • MUMBAI • PATNA
RANCHI • NEW DELHI

Published by :
UNIVERSITY SCIENCE PRESS
(An Imprint of Laxmi Publications Pvt. Ltd.)
113, Golden House, Daryaganj,
New Delhi-110002

Phone : 011-43 53 25 00
Fax : 011-43 53 25 28

www.laxmipublications.com
info@laxmipublications.com

Price : ₹ **295.00** *Only.* *First Edition* : 2012

OFFICES

© **Bangalore**	080-26 75 69 30	© **Chennai**	044-24 34 47 26
© **Cochin**	0484-237 70 04, 405 13 03	© **Guwahati**	0361-251 36 69, 251 38 81
© **Hyderabad**	040-24 65 23 33	© **Jalandhar**	0181-222 12 72
© **Kolkata**	033-22 27 43 84	© **Lucknow**	0522-220 99 16
© **Mumbai**	022-24 91 54 15, 24 92 78 69	© **Patna**	0612-230 00 97
© **Ranchi**	0651-221 47 64		

URM-9605-295-RESEARCH METHODS IN EDU-SIN **C—3801/011/07**
Typeset at :
Printed at Mehra Offset Press, Delhi.

CONTENT

SYLLABUS

EDM-104
Course-4: RESEARCH METHODS IN EDUCATION

Maximum Marks :100
Time Allowed :3 Hrs.

Note: There will be nine questions in the question paper. Students are required to attempt five questions in all. All questions shall carry equal marks.

Question no.1 shall be compulsory which will comprise of eight short answer type questions/parts and students are expected to answer any five parts.

There will be eight other questions comprising of two questions from each of the four units. Students are expected to attempt one question from each unit.

UNIT-1

Methods of acquiring scientific knowledge- Tradition-experience-reasoning-inductive- and deductive-Nature and scope of educational research-Meaning- Nature and Limitation-Need and Purpose-Scientific enquiry and theory development-Fundamental, applied and action research-Quantitative and qualitative research-Some emerging trends in educational research-Formulation of research problem-Criteria and sources for identifying the problem-Delineating and operationlizing variables-Review of related literature: Importance and various sources including internet-Developing hypothesis in various types of research.

UNIT-2

Collection of Data-Types of data-Quantitative and qualitative-Tools of techniques: Characteristics of a good research tool-Questionnaire-Observation- Projective-and-Sociometric techniques-Sampling- Concept of population and sample-Steps and characteristics of a good sample- Various methods of sampling- Probability and non-probability-Sampling errors and how to reduce them.

UNIT-3

Major Approaches to Research -Descriptive Research-Ex-post facto Research-Laboratory Experiments-Field studies-Historical Research-Research Designs

UNIT-4

Qualitative Research- Ethnographic-Developmental- documentary analysis-Validity and limitations of findings- factors influencing Validity of research findings-Research Report - Developing a research proposal (synopsis)- Writing research report and evaluation of research report.

UNIT-1

LEARNING OBJECTIVE

Methods of acquiring scientific knowledge- Tradition-experience-reasoning-inductive- and deductive-Nature and scope of educational research-Meaning- Nature and Limitation-Need and Purpose-Scientific enquiry and theory development-Fundamental, applied and action research-Quantitative and qualitative research-Some emerging trends in educational research-Formulation of research problem-Criteria and sources for identifying the problem-Delineating and operationlizing variables-Review of related literature: Importance and various sources including internet-Developing hypothesis in various types of research.

METHODS OF ACQUIRING SCIENTIFIC KNOWLEDGE

The Scientific Approach to Research

In any form of research a phenomena can be studies with two approaches:

(1) Longitudinal Approach - Under this approach the phenomena is studied from its gensis to upto its facts. It is the *time approach* to research. We have to wait for next data and observation.

(2) Cross-sectional Approach-Under this approach any aspect of the phenomena can be studied of any time, we have not to wait for time.

(3) The Scientific Approach -The scientific approach is a special systematized form of all reflective thinking and inquiry. *Dewey,* in his famous analysis of reflective thinking. *How We Think* has given a general paradigm of problematical inquiry. The present discussion of the scientific approach is based on Dewey's analysis. Dewey's treatment, however, is altered somewhat to suit the scientific framework in which we are working.

(1) Problem-Obstacle-Idea-The scientist will usually experience an obstacle to understanding, a vague unrest about observed and unobserved phenomena, a curiosity as to why something is as it is. His first and most important step is to get the idea out in the open, to express the problem in some reasonably manageable form. Rarely or never will the problem spring full-blown at this stage? He must struggle with it, dry it out, and live with it. *Dewey* says, "There is a troubled, perplexed, trying situation, where the difficulty is, as it were, spread throughout the entire situation, infecting it as a whole."

Sooner or later, explicitly or implicitly, he states the problem, even if his expression of it is inchoate and tentative. Here he intellectualizes, as Dewey puts it, "what at first is merely an *emotional* quality of the whole situation," In some respects, this is the most difficult and most important part of the whole process. Without some sort of statement of the problem, the scientist can rarely go further and expect his work to be fruitful.

2. Hypothesis Verification-After intellectualizing the problem, after turning back on experience for possible solutions, after observing relevant phenomena, the scientist may formulate a hypothesis. A hypothesis is a conjectural statement, a tentative proposition, about the relation between two or more phenomena or variables. Our scientist will say, "If such-and-such occurs, then so-and-so results."

3. Reasoning-Deduction-This step or activity is frequently overlooked or underemphasized. In some respects it is perhaps the most important part of Dewey's contribution to the analysis of *reflective thinking.* The scientist how deduces the consequences of the hypothesis he was formulated. *Conant,* in talking about the rise of modern science, says that the new element added in the seventeenth century was the use of deductive reasoning. Here is where experience, knowledge, and perspicuity are important. Often the scientist, when deducing the consequences of a hypothesis he has formulated, will arrive at a problem quite different from the one he started with. On the other hand, he may find that his deductions lead Min to believe that the problem cannot be solved with present technical tools. For example, before modern statistics was developed, certain behavioural research problems were insoluble. It was difficult, if not impossible, to test two or three interdependent hypotheses at one time. It was next to impossible to test the interactive effect of variables. And we now have reason to believe that certain problems are insoluble unless they *are* tackled in a multivariate manner. An example of this is teaching methods and their relation to achievement and other variables. It is likely that teaching methods do not differ much if we study only their simple effects. Teaching methods probably work differently under different conditions, with different teachers, and with different pupils.

4. Observation-Test-Experiment-It should be clear by now that the observation-test-experiment phase is only part of the scientific enterprise. If the problem has been well state the hypothesis or hypotheses adequately formulated, and the implications of the hypotheses carefully deduced, this step is almost automatic-assuming that the investigator is technically competent.

The essence of testing a hypothesis is to test the *relation* expressed by the hypothesis. We do not test the variables, as such; we test the relation between the variables. All observation, all testing all experimentation is for one large purpose: putting the problem relation to empirical test. To test without knowing at least fairly well what and why one is testing is usually to blunder. Simply to have a vague and poorly stated problem such as "What effect does the *core* curriculum have on students?" and then to test students for their achievement in say social studies is an inadequate procedure that can lead only to ignorance and, worse to misguided information. Similarly, to say one is go to study grouping practices (grouping children by intellectual level, reading level, and the like) of teachers without knowing really, why one is doing it or without stating a relation between grouping practices and some other variable or variables is research nonsense.

Another point about testing hypotheses is that we do not test a hypothesis directly. As indicated m the previous step on reasoning. We test the deduced implications of the hypothesis. Our hypothesis might be. "Writing remarks on student papers will improve future papers," which was deduced, say from a broader hypothesis. "Reinforcement of response leads to an increment in the response rate and strength." We are not testing "writing remarks on student papers" nor "the improvement of future papers." We are testing the relation between them.

The scientific approach is a continuous process in research. It can be illustrated with following paradigm of theory and hypothesis.

Dewey emphasized that the temporal sequence of reflection thinking or in query is not fixed. We can repeat and reemphasize what he says in our own framework. The steps of the scientific approach are not neatly fixed. The first step is not neatly completed before the second step begins. Further, we may test before adequately deducing the implications of the hypothesis. The hypothesis itself may seem to need elaboration or refinement as a result of deducing implications from it.

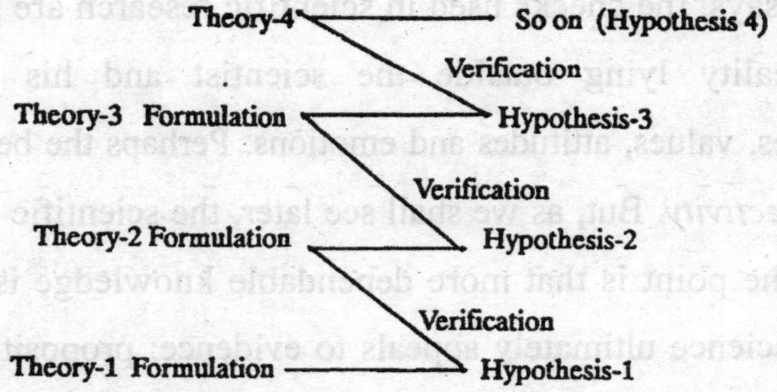

Paradigm of relationship between theory and hypotheses.

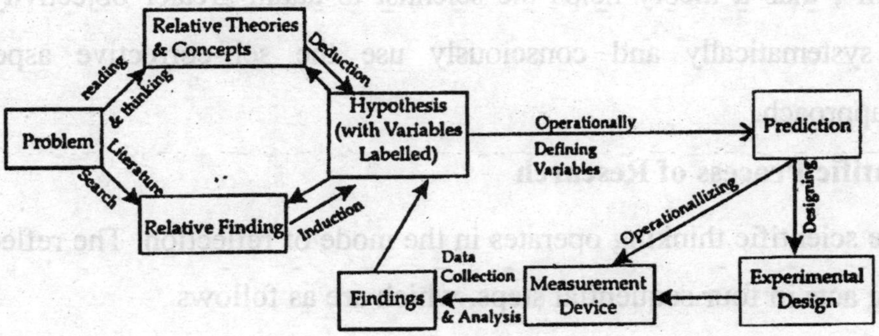

The Research Spectrum

controlled rationality of scientific research as a process of reflective inquiry, the interdependent nature of the parts of the process, and the paramount importance of the problem and its statement.

The *scientific approach* has one characteristic that no other method of attaining knowledge has: *self-correction.* There are built-in checks all along the way to scientific knowledge. These checks are so conceived and used that they control and verify the scientist's activities and conclusions to the end of attaining dependable knowledge outside himself. Even if a hypothesis seems to be supported in an experiment, the scientist will test alternative hypotheses' hat, if also supported, may cast doubt on the first hypothesis. A scientist does not accept a statement as true, even though the evidence at first looks promising. He insists upon testing it. He also insists that any testing procedure be open to public inspection.

As *Peirce* says, the checks used in scientific research are anchored as much as possible inreality lying outside the scientist and his personal beliefs, perceptions, biases, values, attitudes and emotions. Perhaps the best sin g1a word to express this is *objectivity.* But, as we shall see later, the scientific approach involves more than this. The point is that more dependable knowledge is attained through science because science ultimately appeals to evidence: propositions are subjected to empirical test. An objection may be raised: Theory, which the scientist uses and exalts, is part of man himself. But, as *Polanyi* points out, "A theory is something other than myself"; thus a theory helps the scientist to attain greater objectivity. In short, scientists systematically and consciously use the self-corrective aspect of the scientific approach.

The Scientific Process of Research

The scientific thinking operates in the mode of reflection. The reflective mode of thinking acts in four sequential steps, which are as follows

1. Felt need occurrence,
2. Tentative solution of the problem,
3. Testing the tentative solution and
4. Conclusions.

These four steps of reflection have been further developed into six workable forms. Thus the scientific process is based on the reflective mode thinking. These steps are as follows which involve the scientific process of Research -

Step-1. Selection of a problem or establishment of a problem, which may grow through a review of literature and related research studies.

'Step-2. Formulation of testable hypotheses and establishment of general assumption.

Step-3. Developing design and procedure of research. It includes method, sample tools and techniques.

Step-4. *Collection of data* or evidences, which employs the process of measurement of variables.

Step-5. *Analysis of data* for testing null hypothesis. The statistical analysis techniques are used.

Step-6. Conclusions and formulation of generalization, recommendations and implementation of findings.

METHODS OF ACQUIRING SCIENTIFIC KNOWLEDGE

The methods by which man from the earlier times sought answers to his problems can be classified under the following categories: (1) authority, (2) tradition, (3) experience. (4) deductive reasoning, (5) inductive reasoning, and (6) scientific method.

Authority

Appeal to authority and seeking its advice was a well-established method of solving problems even in -the earliest civilizations. We can find examples of reliance upon authority for truth, particularly during the ancient times, when floods, famines, or disease terrified man. He used to appeal to his elders and accepted their ancestral explanations for such incidents. At moments, he prayed to supernatural powers for help. During the Middle Ages, ancient scholars such as Plato and Aristotle, the early Fathers of Church, and others, were accepted as sources of truth than firsthand experience and analysis of facts. The modem man, sometime, also seeks advice from authorities for the solution of the problem faced by him. The authorities may be the persons who have had long experience with that problem and who have studied and thought much about it. In a court testify the sanity of the defendant, or ask a handwriting specialist to compare signatures. When factual evidence cannot be obtained to solve a problem, one may have to rely upon authoritative opinion temporarily as he only possible method for solution. In such a situation, care must be improved in choosing authorities and evaluating their claims to knowledge. One should check not only the credentials of authorities but also the arguments and evidence upon which they base their judgements.

Tradition

Closely related to authority is tradition, upon which man depends for solutions to many of his problems. He unquestioningly accepts many traditions of his forefathers or culture, such as the customary styles of dress, food, speech, and worship. In school settings, teachers often rely on tradition or past experiences as a dependable guide. Although automatic acceptance of tradition and custom is often necessary, one should not always assume that everything that has customarily been done is right and valid. If we examine the historical records, we will find that many theories based upon tradition, which prevailed for years, were later found to be erroneous and had to be rejected. One should, therefore, evaluate custom and tradition carefully before he accepts them as truth.

Experience

Our own personal experience or that of others is the most primitive, and yet most familiar and fundamental, source of knowledge. In ancient times, nomads and various tribes from their personal experience probably remembered that certain wild fruits always made them ill, that grains ripened at particular times of the year, and that sudden floods in the rivers during the rainy season were due to the fact that water does not generally stay on hills. When confronted with a problem, modem man often tries to seek its answers from his own personal experience or from others who are familiar with the problem. Children often consult their teachers, parents or even their older siblings to derive answer to their questions.

Turning to personal experience or to that of others is a useful method to obtain knowledge, but its uncritical use may lead to incorrect conclusions. According to Van Dalen (1973, p. 5):

> A person may make errors when observing or when reporting what he has seen or done. He may (1) omit evidence that does not agree with *his* opinion, (2) use measuring instruments that require many subjective estimates, (3) establish a belief on insufficient evidence, (4) fail to observe significant factors relating to

a specific situation, or (5) draw improper conclusions or inferences owing to personal prejudices.

In the light of these remarks, one should cautiously and critically use experience as an avenue for obtaining reliable knowledge.

Deductive Reasoning

The ancient Greek philosophers like Aristotle and his followers made a significant contribution towards the development of a systematic method for obtaining reliable knowledge. Aristotle developed the *syllogism,* which can be described as a thinking process in which one proceeds from general to specific statements by *deductive reasoning.* It provides a means of testing the validity of any given conclusion or idea by proceeding from the known to the unknown. The syllogistic reasoning consists of (1) a major premise based on a self-evident truth or previously established fact or relationship; (2) a minor premise concerning a particular case to which the truth, fact, or relationship invariably applies; and (3) a conclusion. If the major and minor premises can be shown to be true, the conclusion arrived at is necessarily true. To use a simple example; consider the following proposition:

1. All animals are mortal;
2. Dog is an animal;
3. Therefore, dog will die.

The method of syllogism or deduction, however useful, has the following limitations;

1. The conclusion of a syllogism is always derived from the content of premises. Therefore, if the premises are unrelated or if one of the premises is erroneous, the conclusion arrived at will not be valid.

2. Another serious limitation of the deductive reasoning is its dependence upon verbal symbolism.

3. Deductive reasoning can systematize what is already known and can identify new relationships as one proceeds from known to unknown, but it cannot be relied upon as a self-sufficient method for securing reliable knowledge.

Inductive Reasoning

The conclusions derived from generalities and from statements of presumed authorities by deductive reasoning are true only if they are based upon true premises. To determine whether the premises are true, Francis Bacon stressed the need for basing general conclusions upon specific facts gathered through direct observations. This is what is known as *inductive reasoning,* that is, going from the particular to the general. Rather than accepting premises laid down by authorities as absolute truths, Bacon advised man to observe nature closely, to experiment, to tabulate all the facts, to study these facts in order to reach minor generalizations, and then to proceed from minor generalizations to greater ones. He, however, cautioned against formulating any hypothesis or any probable solution to a problem until all the facts had been gathered.

In deductive reasoning, the premises or generalizations must be known before a conclusion can be reached. On the other hand, in inductive reasoning, a conclusion is reached by observing instances and generalizing from instances to the whole phenomenon. In order to be absolutely certain of an inductive conclusion, all instances must be observed. Under Baconian system of reasoning it is known as perfect induction. In practical situations, however, it is not possible to examine every instance of a phenomenon to which a generalization refers. When examining all the instances of a phenomenon under study is not practical, one may arrive at a generalization by observing only some instances that make up the phenomenon. This is known as *imperfect induction.*

Although imperfect induction does not help man to arrive at infallible conclusions, it can provide him reliable knowledge upon which he makes reasonable decisions.

Both inductive and deductive methods have advantages and limitations. If premises are true, deductive reasoning helps to arrive at absolutely true conclusions. These conclusions, however, do not probe beyond that, which is already known-already present, at least implicitly, in the premises. The conclusions reached by imperfect inductive reasoning do contain information that is not present, even implicitly, in one of the premises (the observed instances). If all the premises (observed instances) are true the probability of conclusions arrived at may be of varying degrees.

THE MEANING AND CHARACTERISTICS OF RESEARCH

Research may be defined as the application of the scientific method in the study of problems. At times, the terms *research* and *scientific method* are used interchangeably.

Research is a systematic attempt to obtain answers to meaningful questions about phenomena or events through the application of scientific procedures. It is an objective, impartial, empirical and logical analysis and recording of controlled observations that may lead to the development of generalizations, principles or theories, resulting, to some extent in prediction and control of events that may be consequences or causes of specific phenomena. Research is scientific, and as such, is not satisfied with isolated facts, but seeks to integrate and systematize its findings. It is concerned with the objective verification of generalizations. Such verification requires logical analyses of problems and devising of appropriate methodologies for obtaining evidence.

Best and Kahn (1992, pp. 18-20) have summarized the main characteristics of research as under:

1. Research is directed towards the solution of a problem. It may attempt to answer a question or to determine the relation between two or more variables.
2. Research emphasizes the development of generalizations, principles, or theories that will be helpful in predicting future occurrences. Research usually goes beyond the specific objects, groups or situations investigated and infers characteristics of a target population from the sample observed. Research is more than information retrieval, the simple gathering of information. Although many school research departments gather and tabulate statistical information that

may be useful in decision-making, these activities are not properly termed research.

3. Research is based upon observable experience or empirical evidence. Certain interesting questions do not lend themselves to research procedures because they cannot be observed. Research rejects revelation and dogma as methods of establishing knowledge and accepts only what can be verified by observation.
4. Research demands accurate observation and description. The researcher uses quantitative, numerical measuring devices, the most precise means of description. The researcher selects or devises valid data gathering instruments or procedures and employs appropriate mechanical, electronic, or psychometric devices to refine human observation, recording, computation, and analysis of data.
5. Research involves gathering new data from primary or first-hand sources or using existing data for a new purpose. Teachers frequently assign a so-called research project that involves writing a paper dealing with the life of a prominent person. The students are expected to read a number of encyclopedias, books, or periodical references, and synthesize the information in a written report. This is not research, for the data are not new. Merely reorganizing or restating what is already known and has already been written, valuable as it may he as a learning experience, is not research. It adds nothing to what is known.
6. Although research activity may at times be somewhat random and unsystematic, it is more often characterized by carefully designed procedures, always applying rigorous analysis. Although trial and error are often involved, research is rarely a blind, shotgun investigation-trying something to see what happens.
7. Research requires expertise. The researcher knows what is already known about the problem and how others have investigated it. He has searched the related literature carefully. He is also thoroughly grounded in the terminology, the

concepts, and the technical skill necessary to understand and analyse the data that he has gathered.

8. Research strives to be objective and logical, applying every possible test to validate the procedures employed, the data collected, and the conclusions reached. The researcher attempts to eliminate personal bias. There is no attempt to persuade or to prove an emotionally held conviction. The emphasis is on testing rather than on proving the hypothesis. Although absolute objectivity is as elusive as pure righteousness, the researcher tries to suppress bias and emotion in his or her analysis.
9. Research involves the quest for answers to unsolved problems. Pushing back the frontiers of ignorance is its goal, and originality is frequently the quality of a good research project. However, previous important studies are deliberately repeated, using identical or similar procedures, with different subjects, different settings, and at a different time. This process is *replication,* a fusion of the words *repetition* and *duplication.* Replication is always desirable to confirm or to raise questions about the conclusions of a previous study.
10. Research is characterized by patient and unhurried activity. It is rarely spectacular and the researcher must accept disappointment and discouragement as he pursues the answers to difficult questions.
11. Research is carefully recorded and reported. Each important term is defined, limiting factors are recognized, procedures are described in detail, references are carefully documented, results are objectively recorded, and conclusions are presented with scholarly cautions and restraint. The written report and accompanying data are made available to the scrutiny of associates or other scholars. Any competent scholar will have the information necessary to analyze, evaluate, and even replicate the study.
12. Research sometimes requires courage. The history of science reveals that many important discoveries were made in spite of the opposition of political and religious authorities. The Polish scientist Copernicus (1473-1543) was condemned by church authorities when he announced his conclusion concerning the

nature of the solar system. *His* theory that the sun, not the earth was centre of the solar system in direct confiict with the older Ptolemaic theory, angered supporters of prevailing religious dogma, who viewed his theory as a denial of the story of creation as described in the book *of Genesis.* Modern researchers in such fields as genetics, sexual behaviour, and even business practices have aroused violent criticism from those whose personal convictions, experiences, or observations were in conflict with some of the research conclusions.

From the examination of the above characteristics, it is evident that the knowledge gained by research is of highest order. It is not based on assumptions, beliefs, and untested generalizations. To seek such knowledge, a researcher must develop scholarship, accurate observation, integrity, willingness to spend long hours to collect and study all forms of evidence before arriving at conclusions, scholarship and ability to recognize causal relationships, and originality and objectivity in thinking. However, it must be recognized that such ideals serve as goals for which researchers should strive. Being human beings, it is difficult for researchers to realize all ideals completely

THE NATURE OF EDUCATIONAL RESEARCH

Educational research refers to a systematic attempt to gain a better understanding of the educational process, generally with a view to improving its efficiency. It is an application of scientific method to the study of educational problems. Travers (1958, p. 5) states:

> Educational research ....represents an activity directed towards the development of an organized body of scientific knowledge about the events with which educators are concerned. Of central importance are the behaviour patterns of pupils, and particularly those to be learned through the educational process. A scientific body of knowledge about education should enable the educators to determine just what teaching and other learning

conditions to provide in order to produce desired aspects of learned behaviour among young people who attend school.

Since education is a behavioural science, the major concern of educational research is to understand, explain, and to some degree predict and control human behaviour. It is an activity directed towards the development of organized and useful body of scientific knowledge about the events with which educators are concerned.

Needs and purpose for Research in Education

Research in education as in the other fields is essential for providing useful and dependable knowledge through which the process of education can be made more effective. There are various considerations, which emphasize need for research in education.

1. Education has strong roots in the fields like philosophy, history, economics, psychology, and sociology. It is, however, based on a conceptual frame of theory. It is through an intensive process of scientific enquiry about the philosophical, historical, economic, psychological, and sociological impact on various aspects of education that sound theories can be established.

2. Education is considered as much a science as an art. As a science, it has a corpus of knowledge concerning the nature of human mind, its growth and development; theories of administration and supervision; educational programmes and practices prevalent in different countries and their results. The quantum of knowledge is indicated by the courses in education prescribed by various organizations and institutions for earning degrees in this field and also by the research material, which is being produced and continuously reported in different educational research journals. Since education depends on a corpus of knowledge, there is need to add scientific knowledge to it for enrichment and improvement. This will facilitate making adjustments in educational programmes accordingly. As an art, education seeks to impart knowledge effectively. For example, "How the teacher can play an effective role in the classroom and outside?" is a vital

question before educationists, and needs careful research efforts to enhance teacher's effectiveness.

3. The slogan of democratization of education since 1870 resulted in the expansion of education. It has given rise to numerous problems like the problems of individual differences, expansion, buildings, discipline and so on. Solutions of such problems by trial and error or by experience from tradition and authority often yielded erroneous results. Moreover, growth by experience is very slow and accidental. We need solutions based on research so that the coming generation is not left to the mercy of errors of outright sins of tradition, ignorance and prejudice.

4. There is need for educational research because of the changing conception of education. The International Commission on the Development of Education in its report "Learning to Be," (Unesco, 1972, p. 143) emphasizes:

> Education from now on can no longer be defined in relation to a fixed content which has to be assimilated, but *must* be conceived *of* as a process in the human being, who thereby learns to express himself, to communicate and to question the world, through his various experiences, and increasingly-all the time-to *fulfill* himself. It *has* strong roots, not only in economics and *socio*logy, but also in findings from psychological research, which indicate that man *is* an unfinished being and can only *fulfil* himself through constant learning. If this *is so,* then education takes place at all ages of life, in all situations and circumstances *of* existence. It returns to its true nature, which *is* to be total and life long, and transcends the limits of institutions, programmes and methods imposed on it down the centuries.

In the context of the above nature of education, the limits of educational research have to be extended from the formal and conventional modes of education to the non-formal and innovative systems based on ecological and cybernetic models.

5. During the last two decades, great changes have taken place as a &result of the rapid scientific and technological developments. Education has to play an important role so that we can accept the change in a smooth way. It can do so by

bringing improvements in the existing curriculum, textbooks, methods of teaching, and evaluation.

Scope of Educational Research

At the outset it will be useful to present to the research scholar a few areas of educational research. On the basis of one's interest, expertise and inclination, one has to choose the appropriate area:

- Teacher education
- Pre-primary (early childhood) education
- Universalization of education
- Secondary education
- Higher education
- Vocational education
- Special education
- Adult education
- Open and distance education
- Non-formal education
- Education of deprived section of society (SC/ST/Minorities, etc.)
- Education of girls
- Educational technology
- Educational and vocational guidance
- Educational management, planning and finance
- Economics of education
- Curriculum development
- Evaluation
- Textbooks and learning material
- Life in classrooms (classroom interaction, classroom climate, Sociometric Studies, etc.)
- Environmental education
- Population education

- Comparative education
- Physical and health education
- Science education
- Mathematics education
- Language teaching
- Social science education
- Value education
- Art education and aesthetics
- Teaching methods, strategies and models of teaching
- Historical studies in education
- Philosophical studies related to education
- Sociological studies in education
- Creativity and education
- Innovations in education
- Correlates of achievement
- Psychological studies in education

Thrust Areas

For the benefit of a research scholar, a few thrust areas have been picked up and some concrete themes are being suggested.

Teacher Education, Training and Extension

- Duration of teacher education courses
- Curriculum components of teacher training courses
- Strengthening of teaching practice/student teaching
- Efficacy of teacher training in classroom situation
- Development of instructional material for training courses
- Multi-grade teaching methodologies
- Admission criteria for different teacher education courses

- Teacher's ability (/ies) to handle children with different disabilities
- On the job support required by teacher educators and teachers
- Needs of teachers in dealing with special groups of learners
- Gender-sensitive teacher training
- Training modules
- Organization of teacher education institutions, i.e., IASE, CTE, DIET, SIERT, STC, etc.
- Revitalizing teacher education in the light of changing scenario at national and global levels
- In-service education of teacher educators and teachers
- Organizing education extension services for teacher education institutions and schools
- Comparative teacher education (both at the intra- and inter-institutional level)
- Evaluating teacher performance
- Teacher competence and accountability
- Teacher education in the light of' NPE
- Manpower planning and unit cost study in teacher education

Curriculum

- Curriculum policy
- Translation of curriculum into specific learning tasks
- Analysis of curriculum in the light of NPE and national goals
- Interaction between learner and curriculum
- Curriculum in action/transaction
- Curriculum change
- Curriculum transaction in varying social contexts
- Analysis and evaluation of curriculum material (i.e., textbooks, etc.) with reference to learning load
- Activity-based/child-centred curriculum
- Evaluation of instructional material

- Methodology of evaluation
- Different methods and approaches of teaching (including models of teaching)

Innovations and Experiments

- Innovations and change in education
- Futurology
- Environmental education
- Population education
- Vocationalization of education at school level/school-industry linkage and related problems
- Global and international education
- Open education and distance learning
- Alternative systems of education

Educational Technology

- Educational technology and the instructional process
- Systems approach in education
- Developing instructional material for teaching and training
- Teacher behaviour and educational technology
- Computer and/in education
- Multi-media learning and training packages
- Mass-media for education
- Simulation and games in teaching and training
- Computer-assisted instruction (CAI)

Planning and Management

- Constitutional provisions
- Federal and state level framework and the impact on educational administration, planning and finance

- Policy, pronouncements, planning for all children specifically girls, SC/ST children
- Decision-making in educational institutions
- Communication
- Manpower planning in education and in teacher education
- Organizational behaviour in educational institutions
- Leadership behaviour
- Organizational climate
- Unit-cost studies and financing of education
- Institutional planning and micro planning
- Organization of institutions of higher education, distance education and open education
- Supervision
- Comparative study of various educational systems
- Training needs of educational managers, administrators and planners
- NGOs and their role in educational management

Universalization of Elementary Education

- Critical appraisal of the programme of UEE
- Drop-out and retention
- Use of mother tongue and local environment in primary schools
- Rationale of MLL
- Interaction between learner and curriculum in primary classes
- Development of new strategies of UEE
- Role of voluntary agencies
- Management of elementary education
- Operation blackboard
- Multi-grade teaching
- Non-formal education

Society and Education

- Demands for education among different socio-economic groups
- Learning styles of hoes, girls and adults
- Gender-sensitive education
- Value education
- Educational needs of different regions
- Socializational and social change
- Vocationalization of education
- NPE' 86 and education
- Education of minorities
- Education of special groups
- Educational status, needs and problems of different special groups such as SC/ST, girls, handicapped, gifted/slow learners.
- Education of special learners and implications for curriculum transaction and teacher training
- Training needs of teachers in dealing with special groups
- Development of instructional material for children with special needs

Limitations of Educational Research

In spite of the application of scientific method and refinement of research techniques, tools and designs, education, like other social and behavioural sciences, has not attained the perfection and scientific status of physical sciences.

It has not been able to establish generalizations equivalent to the theories of physical sciences in the scope of explanation, prediction and control. Frequently, there is lack of unanimity among researchers in the field, as to what the established facts are or what explanations are satisfactory for the assumed facts. Ary *et al.* (1972. pp. 18-20) have pointed out several limitations, which are involved in the application of scientific methods in education. They are of the opinion that it is because of these limitations that education like other social sciences can hardly realize the objectives of science as completely as the physical sciences.

1. Complexity of subject matter. The researcher in the field of education deals with the complex nature of human subjects. He is not concerned with a limited number of variables as is the case with a scientist who deals with physical or biological phenomena. To understand the complex nature of human subjects, he has to deal with a number of variables, acting independently and in interaction. Each individual is unique in the way he grows, in his mental, social and emotional behaviour, and in his total personality. The researcher in the field of education, therefore, has to study the individual in groups and the impact of the behaviour of group members on an individual.

2. Difficulties in observation. Observation of human behaviour is more subjective than the observation of physical or biological phenomena. The subjectivity on the part of the observer has a direct impact on the interpretation and findings on which he bases his conclusions.

3. Difficulties in replication. The physicist can find objectively and accurately resistance of a wire in the laboratory. He can report others can easily replicate his findings and the experiment. This is not easily possible in education. A teacher in India may not be able to reproduce the conditions of an American teacher's experimental teaching method with the same precision of replication as that with which an Indian physicist can reproduce an American physicist's experiment. Educational phenomena are singular events and can hardly be replicated for the purposes of observation with the same degree of precision and objectivity.

4. Interaction of observer and subjects. The researcher in the field of education is also a human being. His presence as an observer in a situation may change the behaviour of his human subjects. For example, the school children may not exhibit their natural behaviour when they know that they are being observed for a particular type of behaviour.

5. Difficulties in control. The rigid control of experimental conditions is possible in the laboratory of physical or biological sciences. It is not possible in educational studies in which the researcher has to deal with the human subjects and many variables simultaneously.

6. Measurement problems. The tools used for measurement and data collection in the educational studies are much less valid and reliable than the tools of the natural scientist

Scientific Enquiry and Theory Development

The exclusive use of Bacon's inductive method resulted in the accumulation of isolated bits of information, and therefore, it made little contribution to the advancement of human knowledge. Moreover, inductive reasoning alone could not solve many problems. In view of these limitations, it was superseded by the *inductive method or the scientific method.* This method, generally attributed to Charles Darwin, integrates the most important aspects of the inductive and deductive methods. The scientific method, therefore, is a back-and-forth movement of thought in which man first operates inductively from partially known or sometimes confused information learned from experience, previous knowledge, reflective thinking, observation and so on, towards a meaningful whole or hypothesis, and then deductively from suggested whole or hypothesis to the particular parts in order to connect these with one another in a meaningful pattern to find valid relationships. In the words of Dewey 1933, p. 87):

> While induction moves from fragmentary details (or particulars) to a connected view of situation (universal), deduction begins with the latter and works back again to particulars, connecting them and binding them together.

Although, in practice, scientific method involves a double movement of reasoning from induction to deduction, in its simplest form, it consists of working inductively from observations to hypotheses and then deductively from the hypotheses to the logical implications of the hypotheses in relation to what is already known

Steps in the Scientific Method

Scientific method, as pointed out earlier, differs from other methods of acquiring knowledge on the basis of generalizations from authority, tradition, experience, and syllogism. It also differs from the methods of chance, of trial-and-error, and of intuition. When using the scientific method, man engages himself in a thinking process called reflective thinking. The five stages of reflective thinking furnished by Dewey (1911) may be summarized as under (Van Dalen 1973, p. 13; Whitney *1964,* p. 3):

1. The occurrence of a felt difficulty. Man comes across some obstacle, experience, or problem that puzzles him.

(a) He lacks the means to achieve the end desired.

(b) He feels difficulty in identifying the character of an object.

(c) He is unable to explain an unexpected event.

2. Identification and definition of the difficulty in terms of a problem statement. Man makes observations and gathers facts so that he is able to define his difficulty more precisely.

3. Suggested solutions of the problem-hypotheses. Man makes intelligent guesses about possible solutions of the problem from the preliminary study of the facts. Such guesses that he makes to explain the facts about the cause of difficulty are called hypotheses.

4. Deriving consequences of the suggested solutions with the help of deductive reasoning. With the help of deductive arguments, man reasons that if each hypothesis is true, certain consequences should follow.

5. Experimental verification of the hypotheses. Man verifies each hypothesis by searching for observable evidence that mill confirms whether or not the consequences that follow actually occur. This process enables him to test which hypothesis is in conformity with observable facts.

The stages involved in reflective thinking presented above suggest a pattern that is employed in the scientific method. It will be seen that the pattern describing this method runs parallel to the stages involved in reflective thinking.

The scientific method also consists of five definite steps:

1. Identification and definition of the problem. A scientific inquiry starts with the identification of a problem that is in need of solution. The problem identified must be defined in such a manner that observation or experimentation in the natural world can provide a solution.

2. Formulation of a hypothesis. Once the problem is defined, the next step is to formulate the hypothesis, which provides an intelligent guess for the solution of the problem. It requires a critical review of the knowledge or information related to the problem.

3. Implication of hypothesis through deductive reasoning. The next step after the formulation of a hypothesis is to deduce the implications of the suggested hypothesis, that is, what would be observed if the hypothesis is true?

4. Collection and analysis of evidence. Collecting relevant evidence related to them through observation, testing, and experimentation tests the deduced implications of the hypothesis.

5. Verification, rejection, or modification of hypothesis. Once the evidence has been collected and analysed, the results are analysed in order to verify whether the evidence support the hypothesis. It may be noted that the characteristic of scientific method is not to prove the hypothesis in terms of absolute truth but to conclude that the evidence does or does not support the hypothesis.

THE NATURE OF SCIENCE

From the earlier times man has been curious about anything he could not understand. Slowly and gradually he developed the scientific method of thinking and of investigating his problems, which, today is producing astonishing results. It is an orderly system of searching for truth which, by basing conclusions upon factual evidence, and by using reasoning as a means of showing relationship between ideas, has given him better and more accurate answers to his many problems, not only in physical and biological sciences, but also in behavioural and social sciences. By attempting to apply this method of inquiry to behavioural and social sciences, the fields of psychology, economics, political science, sociology, anthropology, and education have become recognized as sciences. The term *science,* therefore, is now thought of as a method or attitude rather than a field of subject matter. It is described as a method of inquiry that permits man to examine the phenomena of interest to him.

Science is based on certain beliefs and assumptions, which are briefly described as under:

1. All events in nature are, at least to a degree, lawful or ordered, predictable and regular. This order, predictability and regularity of nature can be discovered through the activities of the scientific method.

2. Truth can ultimately be derived only from observation. Scientist does not depend upon authority as a source of truth, but relies upon empirical observation. Thus the phenomena that can actually be observed to exist are within the domain of scientific method.

3. The scientist maintains a doubtful attitude towards data. He regards findings as tentative unless they are verified. Verification of the findings requires that other scientists must be able to repeat the observations and get the same results.

4. The scientist is objective, impartial and logical in collecting and interpreting data or making observations. His personal bias does not in any way influence the truth and facts even when they are not in conformity with his own opinions.

5. Scientist does not bother about the moral implications of his findings. He always deals with facts and does not consider what finding is good or what is bad for us.

6. The ultimate goal of science is to integrate and systematize findings into a meaningful pattern or *theory*. The theory, however, is regarded as tentative and not the ultimate truth. It is subject to revision or modification as new evidence is found.

The Role of Scientific Theories

Theories are statements that explain a particular segment of phenomena by specifying certain relationships among variables. According to Kerlinger (1978, p. 9):

> A theory is a set *of* interrelated constructs (concepts), definitions, and propositions that present a systematic view *of* phenomena by specifying relations among variables, with the purpose *of* explaining and predicting the phenomena.

This definition emphasizes three things:

First, a theory is a set of statements comprising of interrelated constructs, definitions and propositions.

Secondly, a theory sets out the relations among the set of constructs, definitions or propositions in order to present a systematic view of the phenomena.

Thirdly, a theory explains a phenomena by specifying what variables are related to what variables and how they are related, thus enabling the scientist to predict from certain variables to certain other variables.

A teacher, for example, has a theory of low academic achievement. His variables might be home environment, intelligence, verbal and numerical aptitudes, anxiety, economic factors and achievement motivation. The phenomenon to be explained is low academic achievement. It is explained by specified relations between each of the seven variables and low academic achievement, or by combinations of the seven variables and to academic achievement. The teacher seeks to understand low academic achievement with the help of this set of relations or constructs. He is the able to-'explain' and to some extent at least `predict' it. Moreover, he can also to some extent 'control' the low academic achievement by making changes in the environment or manipulating some of the variables.

Scientific theories serve as means and ends in the development o science. As means, they provide a framework, which guide scientist's ii making observation and discovery. Theories summarize knowledge and put in order the knowledge within a given field. They also clarify and provide meaning to this summarized knowledge comprising of isolated empirical findings. As ends, theories provide scientists explanations for observed events and relationships for specific phenomena with maximum objectivity. They do so by showing what variables are related and hoi' "they are related. On the basis of such relationships, scientists make deductions and predict about what will happen in certain situations under specified conditions. In this way, theories help in the development of new knowledge.

Characteristics of a Sound Theory

A sound theory must meet the following criteria if it is to serve its purpose in the development of science.

1. A theory must be stated in simple and precise terms. A theory that explains the most in a simple form is preferred to one that has more complexities and assumptions. This is the *Law of Parismony*.

2. A theory must be in conformity both with the observed and with the previously established body of knowledge or validated theories.

3. A theory must provide means for its own interpretation and verification. In other words, it must provide deductions, which can be tested empirically.

4. A theory must guide new discoveries and identify areas, which are in need of investigation. It can do so if it is based on empirical facts and relationships.

Theories often offer a crude and general explanation of phenomena. They are refined and modified as knowledge in the form of facts accumulates. The discovery of pertinent facts is essential in order to determine whether a theory can be confirmed or should be rejected or reformulated. For example, if the facts found do not substantiate the theory, a scientist must reject or reformulate the theory to fit the new facts

Fundamental, Applied and Action Research

Classification of Educational Research: Educational research may be classified under three categories: 'basic research', 'applied research' and 'action research'. It must, however, be remembered that there are no clear-cut lines that differentiate these types of research. Basic research has been primarily the activity of psychologists rather than educators. Most of the educational research is applied research. Action research, usually, is the domain of classroom teachers.

Vielle (1981) classifies educational research as

(a) Status Research seeking to study the existing educational system with the view of examining its efficacy, diagnosing its problems and suggesting radical modifications.

(b) Prospective Research undertaken to design, predict and suggest models for educational systems.

(c) Creative Research undertaken for creating, developing or establishing new or alternative educational systems.

Basic or Fundamental Research

Meaning: Basic or fundamental research is sometimes also called 'pure research'. It is aimed at the discovery of basic truth or principles and is not immediately concerned with direct field application. Basic research emphasizes control and precision and gives less attention to direct application of the results in a field situation. According to Travers, "Basic research is designed to add to an organised body of scientific knowledge and does not necessarily produce results of immediate practical value."

Main Characteristics of Basic Research: These are given below:

1. Laboratory approach: Basic research is usually carried out in the laboratory and a good deal of equipment and apparatus is needed to carry out experiments.

2. Researchers use animal subjects: As research workers are concerned with fundamental principles of behaviour, research with animals permits a much higher level of control than is possible with human subjects; basic research usually uses animal rather than human subjects.

3. Research done by workers in other fields: A lot of basic research bearing implications on education has been done by workers in the other behavioural sciences such as sociology.

Applied Research

Meaning: Applied research or often called 'field research' is concerned primarily with establishing relationships and testing theories in the field setting and applying to other samples of the population from which the research subjects are taken. For example, a study of the friendship pattern of eighth class students is very valuable if the sample has been chosen in such a way that the results may be expected to apply reasonably well to other samples of the same population.

Main characteristics of applied research: These are given below Travers observes that applied research is undertaken to solve an immediate problem and the goal of adding to scientific knowledge is secondary.

Applied research sacrifices control and precision to some extent as compared with fundamental research. Basic Research and Applied Research Compared.

Meaning: In basic research, the researcher attempts to control a situation by the use of laboratory techniques or other techniques. In applied research, the researcher is engaged in conducting enquiries in the complicated psycho-sociological climate of on-going educational activities. There are a large number of variables in applied research, which limit control and precision.

Applied research is of course, conducted in real situations, which provide motivation to the researcher, who is interested in the immediate solution of the problem. In basic research, motivation is intrinsic and the value of research is in its contribution to the advancement of knowledge.

Both the basic research as well as applied research is committed to the high standards of scientific objectivity and scholarship. In each type of research, the researcher tries to define the problem being studied with precision, derives his hypotheses from a rich background of information related to the problem, designs the study so that it results in a genuine test of hypothesis, collects and analyses facts or evidence carefully and attempts to draw generalisations objectively. However, the conditions under which the two researchers conduct their studies may differ as observed earlier in terms of the control and precision.

Action Research

Meaning: Action research sometimes called on-the-job research involves the application of the steps of the scientific method to classroom problems. Action research is similar to applied research in many ways. Applied research, usually involves a larger number of samples as compared with action research. In action research a single teacher carries out many research projects in a single classroom, while all teachers in a school or even a school district may carry others on.

In the words of Jane Franseth of the U.S. Office of Education, "Action research is a systematic examination conducted by individuals or groups studying their own practices in search of sound answers to unresolved problems in their work and aimed at improving their own performance on their own jobs." Stephen M. Corey, a pioneer in the field says of action research, "One of the best ways to enable people to improve their curricular practices is to make it possible for them to study what they are doing to experiment with ideas that seem to be more promising and to get evidence to find out if they are better."

The same author describes action research as: "Most of the study of what should be kept in the schools and what should go and what should be added must be done in hundreds and thousands of classrooms and thousands of communities. Those who may have to change the way they do things as a result of the studies must undertake the studies. Our schools cannot keep up with the life they are supposed to sustain and improve unless teachers, pupils, supervisors, administrators and school patrons continuously examinet what they are doing. Single and in groups, they must use their imagination creatively and constructively to identify the practices that must be changed to meet the needs and demands of modern life, courageously try out those practices that give better promise, and methodically gather evidence to test their worth.

This is the process I call action research. I hold no special brief for the name, but it has some currency and is sufficiently descriptive."

Lehmann and Mehrens (1971) point out: "Action research is a type of applied or decision oriented research, but with the stipulation that the researcher is the same person as the practitioner who will make and live with the decision."

According to Best, "Action Research is focused on the immediate application, not on the development of theory, nor upon general application." Action research places its emphasis on a problem, 'here and now'. It is applicable in local setting.

Action research is not mainly concerned in obtaining generalisead scientific knowledge about educational problems but in obtaining specific knowledge concerning the subjects involved in the study.

Practitioners and Action Research

In action research in education, the researchers are usually teachers, curriculum workers, principals, supervisors or others whose main function is to help provide good learning experiences for pupils.

The fundamental point is that teachers, supervisors, and administrators would make better decisions and engage in more effective practices if they, too, were able and willing to conduct research as a basis for these decisions and practices. The process by which practitioners attempt to study their problems scientifically in order to guide, correct, and evaluate their decisions and actions is what a number of people have called action research.

A publication entitled *Research in Education* published by National Institute of Basic Education stated as:

"Action research is the research a person conducts in order to enable him to achieve his purposes more effectively. A teacher conducts action research to improve his own teaching. A school administrator conducts action research to improve his administrative behaviour.

Action research represents an attempt to be more disciplined, more objective, more scientific. It results in a more careful problem diagnosis and more objective evaluation of the consequences of action. To the degree an action intended to solve a practical problem results from objective, disciplined inquiry into the problem and its causes, the problem is more apt actually to be solved. The customary commonsense approach leads to action but afterwards the problem is often still there. Action research is a procedure that tries to keep problem solving in close touch with reality at every stage."

Scope: The action research approach to deal with practical problems seems to be appropriate and promising for all kinds of professional workers in education so long as their desire is to improve their own professional behaviour. An administrator who is dissatisfied with his efforts to develop good morale in his staff could approach this problem with action research, for example. He would only do so, however, if he accepted some responsibility for the morale situation and was willing to effect some changes in his own behaviour to improve it.

Characteristics of Action Research

(i) It is focused on the immediate problem.

(ii) It is applicable in a local setting.

(iii) It aims at improving classroom and school practices.

(iv) It aims at the improvement of professional efficiency.

(v) It involves very little finances.

(vi) The researcher and the practitioner is the one and the same person.

Advantages of Action Research

1. A person improves if he remains active in the process and programme he is engaged in.
2. Action research emphasises a desirable decentralisation of decision making and action taking.
3. Action research broadens and deepens the general as well as specific fund of knowledge of the worker.
4. Facts and evidences are stressed which keep the changed process anchored more continuously to reality.
5. Action research approach is experimental rather than dogmatic.
6. Action research helps the teacher acquire new interests, new motives and new insights.
7. One's own findings are willingly implemented and in this context, action research is very useful.
8. After having involved himself in action research, the teacher can play a better role in translating various research findings into action.
9. Action research has a great stimulating effect upon the teacher for finding better ways of doing things.
10. The entry of the teachers into the world of research will enable them to read reports or summaries of research findings more intelligently.
11. Action research introduces experimental outlook among teachers.
12. Action research enables the teacher to organise instructional procedures on a more reliable and sound basis.
13. Action research on the part of the teacher helps students acquire skill in problem solving and scientific methods.

Limitations of Action Research

1. Action research is relatively of poor quality. According to Georg G. Maouly, "Action research can become a case of the blind leading the blind, and the problem is further aggravated by the fact that teachers generally are too close to their problems and too untrained in scientific objectivity to be vigorous and objective in their approach."

2. The applicability of the findings to another school or class in the event of teacher transfer is even questionable. Action research, by and large, is a localised affair.

3. Action research is frequently added to the shoulders of already but busy teachers who have only limited freedom to say 'no'.

4. On account of several limitations, action research may result in unverifiable and deceptive conclusions.

Action Research Design

The following steps may be followed in preparing an action research design:

1. Identification of problem area: It is important to identify the problem area first. Some of the problem areas are: Teaching of different school subjects such as English, Hindi, Science, Mathematics, History, Geography, etc., and problems like student indiscipline, human relations; etc.

2. Selection of the problem: When the problem area has been identified, the teacher differentiates a more specific (pin-pointed) problem for which he wants to do something. For example, in the area of 'Teaching of Hindi', the pinpointed problem may be 'Improving the Hindi Pronunciation of 5th Class Students'.

3. Problem analysis: Problem analysis is of great importance in action research. When the problem has been pinpointed, probable causes should be outlined.

4. Action hypothesis: From the probable causes, those most relevant to the situation in the school where action research is to be conducted are selected and these form the action hypothesis.

5. The Experiment-data to be collected: After deciding upon an action hypothesis the teacher designs an experiment. At this stage, sources of data collection and the nature of data to be collected are explored.

6. Tools to be used: The teacher decides about the research tools to be used.

7. Action programme: The teacher works out the programme for conducting experiment.

8. Evaluation: The teacher finds out the difference in the result.

Action Research and the Teacher.

Generally people think that educational research is the job of specialists only. It may be remembered that educational research is just an attitude of mind, which is to be developed by all and not merely by the specialists. Such an attitude, which may rightly be called a scientific attitude, is needed not only by specialists but also by teachers.

A schoolteacher can easily take up action research. The idea of 'Action Research' is to enable the teacher to tackle everyday problems that he faces in the classroom. It aims at developing in the teacher an attitude of inquiry rather than making him a research scientist. There is no theorizing here as in fundamental research. During the course of classroom teaching, the teacher starts with certain expectations or aspirations. In actual practice when he finds that those are not fulfilled, he feels dissatisfied. This dissatisfaction leads him to take up action research. The teacher then tries to focus his attention on the problem and clearly apprehends it. Suppose, he finds that the children in his class do not have a good handwriting and he is eager to improve the handwriting of his children. First he finds out the causes of bad handwriting of the children. This may be designated as diagnosing the problem. Then the teacher carefully analyses the causes and tries to pick up those, which he can remove. For example, he finds out that the following are the causes of bad handwriting:

(i) The children do not have enough good specimens of handwriting to copy.

(ii) The children do not have comfortable seats; and

(iii) They do not have proper pens to write.

He may now start his experiment. He evaluates the handwriting of some children before the start of the experiment. Then he provides good specimens of handwriting and good writing material to a group of children during their writing periods and again evaluates their handwriting after say three months. Then he makes a comparison of the results achieved in the improvement of the handwriting of the children experimented upon with those not subjected to the experiment. From this he draws his conclusion. This is an example of simple 'Action Research'.

All teachers can try out experiments of this type. The main point in 'Action Research' is that the approach of the teacher is more careful, disciplined and objective rather than haphazard and slipshod.

This type of research, *i.e.* 'Action Research' is necessary for all types of teachers. This will help them in achieving objectivity in their life and also enable them to grow professionally. The school will benefit from such programmes of 'Action Research', because they will go a long way in improving the existing school practices.

The purpose of action research is not only to improve school practices but also at the same time to improve those who are to improve the practices.

It is unrealistic to assume that every teacher can carry on a continuous programme of research. Not every one who is a good teacher wants to carry on a continuous research programme. What is important is that every teacher is sympathetic to the spirit of research.

Summer research programmes: There are a good many research programmes in which teachers may participate away from their schools. For most teachers these would be limited to summer programmes some of which provide good incentives. Many universities are in a position to provide space and supervision in the summer time for teachers and students from other schools without interfering with their own regular programme.

Limitations of the Teachers in Undertaking Research

1. Lack of background and formal preparation in the statistical and measurement procedures in education.

2. Certain limitations in time and/or ability to pursue studies that go beyond the confines of the classroom, i.e. follow up studies.

3. Heavy teaching loads and extra-curricular responsibilities.

Assets of the Classroom Teachers

1. Their direct contact with the pupils and knowledge of their problems, their intellectual potential, their socioeconomic development and the like.

2. Ability to record happenings in the classroom and put them in proper perspective as they affect the teaching-learning process.

3. Some capacity to manipulate the educational environment and observe the corresponding reactions of the pupils.

Need and Importance of Action Research in Indian Schools

The need and importance of action research in Indian schools is being felt by all concerned to keep pace with the latest developments in the field of education. A teacher while teaching his students comes across numerous problems. Sometimes he tries to tackle them with great patience and other times being in an angry mood, he scolds the students, turns them out of the class, gives punishment of one form or the other and still at some other times, be overlooks them. If the teachers are encouraged to come out with their problems and are provided necessary facilities in the form of guidance and help in conducting action research, *they* can solve their problems themselves with great satisfaction to themselves and consequently leading to their professional growth and development.

J.W. Best suggests, "If classroom teachers are to make an active research contribution, it will probably be in the area of action research. Studies will be made for the purpose of improving school practices. Many educational observers see in action research one of the most promising avenues of teacher growth, professional improvement and the development of better curriculum".

W.C. Radford discusses the functions of the school as: "What is the function of the school in educational research? Should it be doing research, and if so, are there any limits to it? I think that there is a limitation-what I call a geographical one. I do r believe we can expect a school, established to serve a particular community, to go beyond that community in its research. Ea school is an entity with its own setting, and its own particular complex of factors affecting its operation. I believe that the school should be doing research but within that setting and on its of complex. Every aspect of the educational process is there for stud learning experiences, pupil-teacher relationships, and administration. Nothing inside the school is more important than what is going on within it. All, or almost all aspects of the process can I examined, studied, appraised and the conclusions drawn used affect the process immediately."

Difference between Fundamental Research and Action Research

Area	*Fundamental Research*	*Action Research*
1 Objectives	Its purpose is to develop and test educational theories and to obtain principles that will be applicable to a broad population.	Knowledge obtained is intended to be applied in local setting and to provide a sort of in-service training to participating teachers and administrators.
2 Training	Expert training is needed in measurement, research methods and statistics.	Only a limited training is needed. Even if the research skills of a teacher are low, action research can be done

			under the guidance or assistance of a consultant.
3	Locating the research problem	A wide range of methods is used to locate the research problem.	The participating teachers identity problems, which hinder their classroom teaching-learning process.
4	Involvement	The research worker is not usually involved in the problem he selects for research.	The teacher is invariably involved in the research problem.
5	Hypothesis	Highly specific hypotheses are developed.	Usually a specific statement of the problem serves as a hypothesis.
6	Review of the literature	An exhaustive and thorough review of the literature is done to have a thorough under-standing of the accumulated knowledge in the research area.	There is no need for such a thorough and intensive review. A glance at the review will serve the purpose of developing general understanding of the area.
7.	Sampling	Research worker is required to obtain a random or otherwise unbiased sample of the population being studied.	Pupils studying in the class of the teacher are used as subjects.
8.	Experimental design	Careful attention is given to maintain comparable conditions	Bias is usually present because participating teachers are egoinvolved

		and reducing error and bias.	in the research situation. Procedures are planned only in general terms.
9.	Analysis of data	Complex analysis is often called for.	Simple analysis procedures are usually sufficient.
10	Statistical treatment	Statistical significance is usually stressed.	Subjective opinion of participating teachers is often weighted heavily.
11	Application of results	Lack of coordination between research workers and teachers generate a serious practical problem. The generalisations usually remain confined to books and research reports	Findings are applied immediately to the classes of participating teachers and lead to far-reaching improvements in the teaching learning process.

Qualitative Research

Characteristics

- The approach is inductive
- Its focus is on specific situations, institutions, communities, groups of people, etc.
- Its emphasis is on causes, interpretations, and implications rather than quantitative scores, measurement and statistical analysis.
- Its emphasis is on personalized experiences rather than structured tools.
- It is based on smaller number of cases.

Purpose

- Understanding the meaning of broad terms like attitude, prejudice, organizational climate, etc.
- Understanding the context In Which some behaviour finds expression or some phenomenon take place.
- Identifying an anticipated phenomenon
- Understanding the process
- Developing causal explanations
- In-depth study to find out the constellation of factors that determine a particular type of behaviour or lead to a particular phenomenon
- Studying inter-relationships between various factors responsible for a phenomenon or a behaviour. Freud developed his theory of psychoanalysis through qualitative research; Piaget developed theory of cognitive development by initially starting the study Id language development in his own children.

Practical Uses

- Generating theories that arc understandable
- Conducting formative evaluation, intended to improve the existing practices rather than to simply assess the value of programme product being evaluated
- Engaging in collaborative research with practitioners

Types of Qualitative Research

- Phenomenological (see Chapter V);
- Ethnographical (see Chapter V);
- Heuristic (see Chapter V);
- Case Studies;
- Historical Studio; and
- Philosophical Studies.

Case Studied

In qualitative approach, in order to understand a phenomenon some cases are selected and an in-depth study of these cases is undertaken. A case or unit may be a person or an institution, a social group, a community, or a village. The case study unfolds the interaction between the various factors influencing the phenomena. Case studies of some juvenile delinquents can be undertaken for gaining an understanding of the phenomenon of delinquency. Jean Piaget conducted case studies of some children in order to propound his theory of cognitive development. Since the case study involves deeper study over a longer span of time involving personalised techniques of data collection such as observation, interview, etc., the sample in this approach has to be kept small. The researcher has to be *very* cautious to avoid bias in favour or against the subjects studied.

Historical Studies

Historical research is undertaken to understand the present in the light of past events. Such investigations aim at studying the growth and development of educational institutions; rise of educational movements and may be their decline, evolution of new techniques and methods in the field of education and contributions of educators and other thinkers to varying fields of education. Some problems for historical studies could be: education of women in post-Independence India; rise and fall of basic education, etc.

The data for historical studies are collected from two sources:

1 Primary sources: These are an actual witness to the events, such as objects of the past, relics, photographs, artifacts, original letters, parliamentary proceedings, documents, etc.

2. Secondary sources: These are the sources which are not actual witness to t he event I lilt are the reports of the person observing the event, for example, books on history, description of accounts, statements made by a witness

As far as possible, the primary sources should be used because they are more reliable. In the circumstances when primary sources are not available, the researcher can make use of secondary sources.

Internal and External Evaluation

Before making use of any historical source, it should be subjected to internal and external criticism in order to establish its authenticity, genuineness, accuracy and worthwhileness. External criticism and the other two by internal criticism establish the first two characteristics.

Difficulties

Historical research has its own difficulties because it involves location of authentic sources and a time-consuming process of their scrutiny and study. This research may involve visiting distant places involving a lot of tinge and heavy financial implications.

Philosophical Studied

In educational research, philosophical studies occupy, an important place. These studies are important because they seek to examine the basic assumptions about man, life and the world around him. Philosophy influences the policies related to education and also to educational practices. An individual has his own philosophy which influences his views about education, formulation of policies and practices related to education. Similarly, a nation believing in democratic philosophy will lay great emphasis on universalisation of education, human rights in education, rights of students, freedom and autonomy in education, equality of educational opportunity, and so on.

Since philosophical studies are based on reasoned analytical thinking about the relationship between mind and reality, a philosophical research worker has to have an analytical insight and the ability to synthesize ideas. The research worker has to bank heavily on a library, which provides an understanding of what eminent philosophers have to say about educational reality. The method of a philosopher is not totally different from that of a scientist. Although the philosopher does not use the tools commonly used in scientific studies, he does test and verify logical consistency of his hypothesis and draws a conclusion after careful scrutiny of the ideas.

Quantitative Research

Characteristics

- The approach is deductive.
- The sample studied is larger.
- The emphasis is on precision in describing events.
- The emphasis is on numbers rather than words.
- A relationship between variables is anticipated (hypothesis), which is tested on the basis of data collected.
- An attempt is made to convert the data into mathematical form.
- Tools used are to be such as to yield data in numerical form.
- The conclusions drawn from the sample are applicable to the total population, which the sample represents.
- It helps in objective study of phenomena.
- Data is available for analysis on a computer and hence inferences can be easily drawn.
- Demand on personalized ingenuity and skill is less for data collection.
- These can be easily replicated and results verified.

Purposes

- Standardization of tests
- Identifying characteristics of a group in quantitative terms
- Measurement of the effect of the experimental variable
- Comparison of the characteristics of groups
- Studying the relationships between the variables

Types of Quantitative Research

Under quantitative research, the main *types* are:

Experimented: A hypothesis is propounded stating a relationship between the dependent and independent variables. Then the relationship is verified by making observations under controlled conditions. The control over intervening variables is exercised either by physical manipulations or through statistical methods.

Quasi-Experimental: These studies do not apply to vigorous criteria of pure experiments. In these studies the experimental and control groups are not exactly equivalent, and control over all intervening variables is sometimes not possible. Such designs are generally used in educational experiments conducted in classrooms. The class groups are kept intact presuming that they are similar. One group is taken as the control group and in the other group experimental variable is introduced; this will be the experimental group. Pre-test and posttest scores of both the group's are used for studying the differences. Since the design does not have full check over all the intervening variables, the results of such studies need to be accepted cautiously. In some quasi-experimental studies only one group is taken. In this group an experimental variable is introduced and its effect is observed by comparing the pre-test-post-test results.

In the less refined form of quasi-experimental study, no pre-test is conducted. The experimental variable is introduced in a group and the post-test is administered. If the results in the post-test are positive, the experimenter attributes it to the experimental variable.

Surreys: Some trends in the field of education are studied quantitatively such as the dropout rate, enrolment rates, literacy percentage, unit cost of higher education, etc.

Correlational Studies: A complex phenomenon is analysed into its components and each component is defined in measurable terms. Then instruments are developed to measure each component. The relationship between the components and other variables can be studied. For example, classroom interaction can be separated into teacher and students' behaviour. Each behaviour is specifically defined. In a given time, the interval frequencies of occurrence of these behaviours can be plotted. The relationship between teacher behaviour or teacher personality traits with other variables such as students' achievements, classroom climate, etc. can be determined

UNIT-2

LEARNING OBJECTIVE

Collection of Data-Types of data-Quantity and qualitative-Tools and techniques: Characteristics of a good research tool-Questionnaire-Observation- Projective-and-Sociometric techniques-Sampling-Concept of population and sample-Steps and characteristics of a good sample- Various methods of sampling- Probability and non-probability-Sampling errors and how to reduce them.

SOME EMERGING TRENDS IN EDUCATIONAL RESEARCH

5.1 Heuristic Research

5.2 Phenomenological Research

5.3 Interdisciplinary Research

5.4 Ethnographical Studies

5.5 Policy Research

5.6 Intervention Studies

5.7 Baseline Studies

A more appropriate perspective is to consider educational research as cross disciplinary in nature, cutting across and transcending or working at the interfaces between a variety of disciplines in the social and behavioural sciences and the humanity.

During the twentieth century most developments in educational research have taken place as a result of thinking about educational problems from the perspective of social sciences, humanities and the behavioural sciences. Each disciplinary field in these areas can contribute to an examination of educational questions.

TORSTEN HEUSEN AND T.N. POSTETRTWAITE, 1994, PP. 5034

There are many approaches to educational research. Some of these are very common such as survey, historical, experimental, etc. These are given in almost all the books on educational research. There are some approaches, which are relatively new and are not commonly found in the books on research methodology. These are being described here.

Objectives

After going through this unit, you will be able to :

- Identify new approaches of research;
- Understand the main features of the different approaches of research;

- Explain the utility of new approaches or research in the area of education;
- Identify the relationship between pure and policy research;
- Differentiate between status and intervention research;
- Suggest research problems related to different approaches.

Heuristic Research

The word heuristic has its origin in the Greek word "heuriske in meaning "to search discover" or "to find". It refers to a process of internal search through which one discovers the nature and meaning of experience and develops methods and procedures for further investigation and analysis.

The self of the researcher is present throughout the process while understanding the phenomenon with increasing depth. The researcher also experiences growing self-awareness and self-knowledge. The heuristic process incorporates creative self-process and self-discoveries.

Heuristic inquiry is a process that begins with a question or a problem which the researcher seeks to answer or illuminate. The question is one that has been a personal challenge and puzzlement in the search to understand one's self and the world in which one lives. The heuristic process is autobiographic, yet with virtually every question that matters, there is also a social and perhaps universal significance.

Six phases of heuristic research guide unfolding investigations and comprise the basic research design. They include:

- the initial engagement
- immersion into the topic and question
- incubation
- illumination
- explication

- culmination of the research in a creative synthesis

Heuristic inquiry also differs from hermeneutic thinking. In heuristic, the focus is exclusively and continually aimed at understanding human experience. The research participants remain close to depictions of their experience, telling their individual stories with increasing understanding and insight. The depictions themselves achieve layers of depth and meaning through the interactions, explorations, and elucidations that occur between the primary researcher and the other research participants.

Phenomenological Research

Phenomenology is the contribution of Edmund Husserl. Martin Heidegger has also contributed in this area. It is a philosophical pursuit. Phenomenology makes human experience its object of research. In this method the investigator reflects upon his/her way of experiencing the universe in which he/she is living.

In this method, participants are invited to reflect on their experiences about a phenomena, then the researcher tries to analyse to what extent the perception of the participants is similar to his/her own and in what way it differs. A related area to phenomenology is phenomenon grab by which is the empirical study of different ways in which people experience, perceive, understand and conceptualize phenomena around then); for example, children experience, perceive, understand and conceptualize some mathematical concepts-say the number system in different ways. It would be interesting to make an empirical study of these variations. Even in languages, students understand sonic literary text in different ways. The difference in perception, understanding and conceptualization is due to the difference in relating different components of phenomena with each other and with totality. The main methods of collecting data in this type of research are interviews, participant observations, analysis of interactions and written responses of subjects, study of drawings and analysis of historical documents.

Many times a question arises about the reliability of this method, that is, whether the different persons analysing the responses would conic to the same conclusions. The proponents of this method have a very good argument about this criticism. They say that this method is not a measurement procedure but an attempt to discover a phenomena and a discovery need not have to be replicable.

Difference Between Phenomenological Research and Heuristic Research

Clark Moustakas (1994) clarified the difference between the two methods:

- In phenomenological research, the focus is on a situation, in which t-he experience under study occurs whereas in heuristic research, there is an attempt to undertake a wider investigation which is more open;
- In the heuristic research, the description of the phenomena is supplemented by diaries, journals, self-dialogues, stories or other personal documents, whereas in phenomenological research, the main stress is only on description of an experience;
- Whereas phenomenological studies end with a general description, the heuristic investigations culminate in creative synthesis;
- In the phenomenological studies, the co-research workers have a negligible role in the analysis and interpretation of data, but in heuristic research, they remain actively involved even at the stage of examination and analysis of data.

Inter Disciplinary Research

With the fast explosion of knowledge, the boundaries of disciplines are getting thinner. Any problem in one discipline can be bettered understood and solved by looking at it in its entirety. In doing this, we will find that we have to transgress the boundaries of one discipline. To be specific, any educational phenomena can be understood correctly if it is viewed comprehensively in its socio-cultural-economic-geographical-psychological contexts. Hence, in gaining an understanding of an educational phenomena or for finding out real solutions to educational problems, it would be necessary to recognise that these problems are linked with other disciplines. Thus, educational research in modern times has to develop close links with other related disciplines. This realisation has led to the origin of interdisciplinary research.

Interdisciplinary research is not merely taking help of some disciplines in solving an educational problem. It should be a genuine multi-disciplinary approach. In interdisciplinary research, an attempt has to be made for integration at conceptual as well as methodological levels across disciplines. Ecological researches or management researches are good examples of interdisciplinary research. Ecological research draws heavily on disciplines of Biology, Chemistry, Geography, etc.

Yadav and Mitra (1989) have given `our ways in which educational research can be made interdisciplinary

(i) Conceptual integration -Skinner's theory of operant conditioning led to the development of programmed instruction in different subject areas.

(ii) Adoption of a conceptual structure of other disciplines as a model for building conceptual framework of educational research, for example, the Cybernatic model which was meant for explaining information processing in the auto-regulating system has become the basis of systems approach and systems analysis in educational research.

(iii) Adoption of methodology originally evolved in other disciplines Educational research has widely used the tools developed in the area of psychometric. Clinical interviews, a gift of psychoanalysis, is widely used in educational research. The technique of participant observation used in anthropology is also a popular technique in the field of educational research. Many more examples can be quoted to show that educational research has adopted the methodological contributions from other disciplines.

(iv) Studies on pedagogical aspects of various disciplines and technology of transmission of their discipline are also an area of interdisciplinary research. In this type of research, the method and content are integrated. This has given rise to new areas like Science education, Mathematics education, Language education, etc.

Two ways of promoting interdisciplinary research

(i) Experts from different disciplines can work together for solving a problem.

(ii) Educational research workers can try to gain expertise in other disciplines and then use that knowledge for tackling a research problem in the field of educational research.

Ethnographical Studies

Ethnographic research has emerged from the discipline of Anthropology. These aim at studying a social group and giving its cultural description. The researcher enters a group or a setting that already exists intact and has its own history. He/she establishes intimate relationship with that cultural group over a long period of time and also takes residence in that social setting. He/she tries observing various actions and events of the members of the group and tries understand the meanings of such actions and events, finally resulting in define the roles and relationships of the members of the group. When the research spends considerable time with the group he/she is also able to observe ho these relationships undergo change over a period of time. This type of research lays many demands on the research worker. He/she has to first learn the language of the group, has to reside in that social setting, participate in the activities of the social group, and finally has to locate some members of that group with whom to develop a close rapport who in turn provide him/her with rich information about the cultural group.

One important precaution to be taken in ethnographic studies is maintenance of objectivity. Many times, when one is associated with a group for- a long duration, one's observations get coloured. And some significant features may completely escape notice.

In educational research, the ethnographic studies can help in describing the aspirations related to education, expectations from the educational set-up of a social group. These studies can also describe the physical attributes, the relationships and other features of an educational setting.

The steps in an ethnographic research are:

- Initial exploration;
- Study of the geographical setting;
- Planning for the observations;
- Getting into the social setting;
- Making observation about the setting;
- Finally drawing conclusions about it.

Policy Research

In pure research the problems are posed from inside a discipline and the solutions lead to progress of the discipline. Its impact on educational practices may be incidental.

In policy research the problems emerge from outside the discipline from the field of action. The research is undertaken for providing a relevant information base for policy framing. The policy research findings are not meant for enhancing the boundaries of knowledge of a discipline. They have a bearing on the way educational programmes are to be implemented.

The policy research may be further classified in two types:

(i) Research flowing out of some policy decisions such as universalisation of elementary education. It is a policy decision and has given rise to a number of research studies.

(ii) Research taken up for formulating a policy. Research which revealed that a large number of school children are malnourished, gave rise to a policy decision of providing mid-day meals to school children.

The Flow Chart given in Figure 5.1 clearly explains the two types of researches, which can be included under the heading Policy Research.

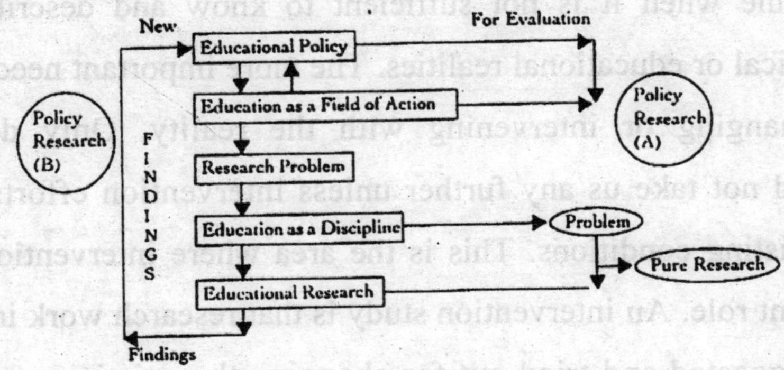

Figure. ***Relationship between Pure and Policy Research***

The route A depicts the policy researches, which flow out of implementation of an educational policy or for evaluating the impact of an educational policy. For this, one has to see the impact of the policy in the field of education and come to some conclusions, which could be useful for making necessary changes - in the policy itself or the ways of its implementation.

The route B depicts the policy researches, which lead to an educational policy. Education as a filed of action gives rise to many research problems which when investigated, taking help of education as a discipline, result in crucial findings which can form the basis of formulation of an educational policy.

Intervention Studies

Generally research studies are conducted for describing a reality, that is, what are the existing conditions. For example, studies have been conducted for knowing the problems of scheduled caste or scheduled tribe students. Studies have also been conducted for finding out dropout rates or stagnation at primary stage. These are known as status studies.

NCTE recently launched State Level studies to find out the status of teacher education in each state. These studies were launched in collaboration with SCERTs/SIERTs/SIEs. These are illustrations of 'Status studies.

A time has come when it is not sufficient to know and describe the social, economic, political or educational realities. The more important need is to find out methods of changing or intervening with the reality. Only describing the problems would not take us any further unless intervention efforts are made to improve the existing conditions. This is the area where intervention studies can play an important role. An intervention study is that research work in which some methods are suggested and tried out for changing the existing condition. These studies are generally experimental in nature and on the basis of experimentation come out with some strategies or models, which are helpful in improving the existing conditions. For examples, it is a general practice to enumerate the weaknesses in the existing teacher education programme, but an intervention study in this area would attempt to develop a new model of teacher education programme, which is likely to be more effective. The model has to be tried out and, if found really more effective, would be helpful in changing the existing state of teacher education programme. Such intervention studies are needed in the area of eradication of illiteracy, improving the retention of children in schools, diminishing the stagnation rate, etc. Care should be taken while evolving models through intervention studies that the models are replicable on a wider scale.

For effective conduct of intervention studies, a research team should be formed comprising practicing teachers, leaders from the community, administrative heads or their representatives from the departments related to the area of study and research workers. The experiences of all these persons can go a long way in evolving a model, which is practicable and down to earth.

Examples of Status and Intervention Research

	Status Research	Intervention Research
1	Study of dropout rate of children	Reducing dropout rate among tribal by providing midday meal.
2	Study of the competencies of Primary School Teachers	Developing training packages for competency based in-service programme for Primary School Teachers.
3	Study of Organizational Climate in Schools	Improving Organizational Climate through special training.
4	Study of causes leading to drug addiction	Rehabilitation of students falling prey to drug addiction.

Baseline Studies

For taking any administrative decision or framing a policy we need some basic data. The studies, which provide such basic data, are known as baseline studies.

Some examples follow:

- Location of the school (average distance from learner's homes)
- Infrastructural facilities available (building, drinking-water, toilets, furniture, black boards etc)
- Educational background of teachers
- Mid-day meals (quality, stability, timing, impact, general reaction)
- Enrolment (factors that promote and retard)
- Retention (factors that promote and retard)
- Wastage and stagnation studies
- A survey of literacy rate in an area
- A study of educational disparities

FORMULATION OF RESEARCH THE PROBLEM

The beginning researchers, by and large, do not know wherefrom to get research problems. The Ph.D. scholars and postgraduate dissertation writers, unduly, depend for this on their research supervisors. They should themselves know what the sources of the problems are.

There are a number of sources from which the researchers may get hints on selecting a problem. But the most important of all these is the voluminous accumulation of professional literature. The researcher should turn to be a scholar in the field in which he wants to work. By reading literature he should, through his imagination and hard thinking, try to know what the problem areas could be. A comprehensive list of publications to be consulted is given here. All these publications are in English. Unfortunately researchers in India face difficulty in reading and understanding these sources: and in their own state languages here is paucity of such literature.

If the researcher reads the literature carefully and critically (I) he may find certain thoughts, ideas or statements on which he does not agree with the author, (2) or if lie goes through some research study lie may feel that its results can be challenged in which case lie may like to replicate the study and verify its results, (3) or lie may feel that if the study is conducted elsewhere under more relevant circumstances its results may change, (4) or he may come across gaps in the knowledge. All these are situations, which may be potential sources of new research problems.

Certain research journals such as the *Review of Educational Research,* published and unpublished Ph.D. theses, *Encyclopedia of Educational Research* and several other journals in their articles give suggestions for further research. These also may be helpful in locating new research problems. The research studies published in these journals, sometimes, may suggest that the same study, quite meaningfully, may be conducted a fresh on a different population or in a different field or with a different design.

A researcher's personal experience and his environment both can be a good source of new problems to be subjected to research. For example, a teacher working in a school may be faced with various kinds of real problems. If he explores a little he may find that similar the teachers of other schools face problems. Also he may, then, think of conducting research on one of these collecting data from other schools also, For example, if lie experiences in his school that the quality of teaching is going down year after year, lie may think of exploring the various reasons for that. This may then take the shape of a research problem.

Finalizing and Stating the Problem

Having studied a lot in the area of his interest the researcher tries to ultimately decide what exactly should be his problem of research. While taking the decision and specifying the actual problem various considerations should guide the researcher. This is the stage at which he finally chooses or establishes or states the problem. He has found the problem but now lie has to make it.

One consideration should be that the problem, which is finally selected, is neither too broad nor too narrow. For example, if the problem selected is "A Study of School Effectiveness", it will require a team of workers and for just one researcher it may be too difficult to manage. It will have several aspects and will extend over a long period. Thus, the study will be too broad for a Ph.D. Student; to make it practical this will have to be limited to one or two aspects. Conversely, the problem to be selected should not be too narrow also. For example, "A study of intelligence of students of class-VIII of a school," such a narrow study will yield information, which is trivial, and an artifact, having no meaning.

Having located the problem it is not always possible for a researcher to formulate his problem clearly and completely. He has, at this stage, only a general, diffuse, even confused notion of the problem. He is not, yet, in a position to state his problem precisely and adequately. An important consideration underlying the final statement of a research problem is that it must be possible i.e.

it must be testable. A common fault on the part of the research students is to state a problem in such a way that its investigation is essentially impossible. A problem stated as "The role of the teacher in maintaining student discipline" is certainly impossible. In fact, it is not answerable problem. A good essay can be written on this. But, for the purpose of research it makes no sense. It can, however, he made researchable by restating as "A study of the relationship between teacher's competence and students' classroom discipline". The problem finally stated is rarely the same as was formulated originally. It is specific, precise and trimmed to manageable size.

The problem may be expressed in the form of a question or in the form of a statement. Whatever be the forth the objective must be to present the exact dimensions of the problem in a concrete and explicit statement. An adequate statement of the problem must include all the facts, relations and explanations that the analysis of the problem indicated as relevant.

The problem must be described by giving the background of the study, the theories on which it is based and the assumptions underlying the statement of the problem. This is what specification of the problem requires and means. The terms that occur in the statement of the problem and are not understood by all in the same way or they are used in the problem in some specific sense must be defined and explained. This clarifies the phenomenon under investigation and makes measurement of the same possible. Generally, the variables involved in the problem are defined operationally, i.e., they are defined in behavioural terms, which forth the basis of developing measuring tools, and techniques.

According to Van Dalen (10, pp. 141-143) some personal and social considerations should also be kept in mind while selecting a research problem. The personal considerations include (1) the problem should be one in which the researcher has genuine interest, (2) It should be such as the researcher has skills, abilities and background knowledge required for working on the problem, (3) it should be such as the tools needed for collecting data can be made available, (4) it should be such as da:a collection for solving the problem may be possible. Van Dalen lists a few social considerations also which should be kept in mind. These are: (I) the problem should contribute to advancement of knowledge, (2) findings of the problem, should be of practical value to educators, parents, social workers or others, (3) will the study lead to the development of further research in that area.

In the interest of the researchers, observations made by the Fourth Survey of Research in Education (I l, p. 14) about the selection of research topics are presented in this section. It was observed "Education is a practical activity contrived by the society in order to achieve certain desirable ends. Educational research has to help in improving the efficiency and effectiveness of the means of achieving these ends. Thus a research topic in order to satisfy the above criterion has to be not only theoretically sound but also pertinent to the practical aspect of organizing the educational process. This makes it clear that selection of the topic is a crucial step in the research process." To achieve this purpose the Survey considered two tasks more important - (1) to explore the already available research literature in the particular area, and (2) to explore the socio-cultural context with a view to identifying problems of practical relevance. With regard to the second task the Survey remarked, "The educational researchers seem to suffer from a sort of problem- blindness". They seem to indulge in fabrication of research topics purely based on arbitrary combination of a few aspects or variables. This way of fabricating research topics without any relevance either to theory or to practice has resulted in a large number of studies, which are neither socially relevant nor scientifically exact. Other observations made by the Survey about the selection of research topics include (I) that most of the topics selected are duplication of research already done, and, (2) that they invariably lack a long-range perspective.

Steps In the Development of a Research Problem

This is only a suggested sequence of steps:

1. Experiencing a difficulty, some phenomenon, need to be understood and explained, e.g., and teachers' alienation in some institution.

2. Collecting more facts about the problem from various sources and establishing that it is really a problem and needs solution, e.g., teachers' alienation may be a problem only in case of a few teachers of only one institution. So, to establish whether it is a widespread problem and needs explanation.
3. Exploring whether the problem has been explored earlier. If *so,* what dimensions, how, where, with what results- Deriving meaning from readings- Tentatively, deciding to make a study around that
4. Selecting variables that may be related or studied in relation to that problem. This is done after a thorough scanning of the literature
5. Building relationship between the selected variables and the problem after verifying the assumptions underlying the relationship.
6. Stating the problem finally.
7. Formulating hypotheses.
8. Defining the problem.

Criteria for Selection of the Problem

The factors are to be considered in the selection of a research problem both the criteria external and personal. External criteria have to do with such matters as novelty and importance for the field availability of data and method, and institutional or administrative cooperation. Personal criteria involved such considerations as interest, training, cost and time, etc.

Thus criteria fur the selection of the problem suggested *by Good* and *Scates* are as follows:

1. Novelty and avoidance of unnecessary duplications.
2. Importance for the field represented and implementation.
3. Interest, intellectual curiosity, and drive.
4. Training and personal qualifications.
5. Availability of data and method.
6. Special equipment and working conditions.

7. Approachability of the sample.
8. Sponsorship and administrative cooperation.
9. Hazards, penalties and handicaps.
10. Cost and returns.
11. Time factor.

1. Novelty and avoidance of unnecessary duplication The question of novelty or newness is not merely one of duplication of earlier investigations. It involves the regency of the data summarized especially in the case of survey studies made during a period of great Economic. Educational and Social change.

2. Importance for the field represented and implementation. This criterion of importance in choice of a problem involves such matters as significance for the field involved, timelines and practical value in term of application and implementation of the results. Scientific research in Education, psychology and social sciences in general have an especially urgent obligation to play a social role rendering service to society and humanity.

3. **Interest, intellectual** curiosity and drive. One of the personal motives of research most frequently mentioned by scientists themselves is pure curiosity, accompanied by genuine interest and a derived satisfaction and enjoyment.

4. Availability of data and method The data under consideration must meet certain standards of accuracy, objectivity and verifiability.

5. Special equipment and working conditions The major purpose of equipment is to define the process of observation to provide control of conditions and accuracy for permanence of recording.

6. Sponsorship and administrative cooperation It is a common practice for the thesis to be sponsored by a faculty adviser in whose area of specialization the problem lies.

7. **Costs and returns.** The candidate must consider carefully his own financial resources 0 the light of such facilities and assistance as can be provided by the institution.

8. Time facts As a general rule the minimum amount of graduate work for the master's degree is one year, and for the Doctor's degree three years.

Historical, experimental case and longitudinal genetic studies frequently require more time than the several types of normative survey work.

Hildreth Hoke Mc Ashan[7] has proposed an objective guideline for judging the merits of a problem. The following questions may be raised for this purpose.

1. Is the problem really important?
2. Is the problem interesting to others?
3. Is the chosen problem a real problem?
4. Does the problem display originality and creativeness
5. Am I really concerned with finding the solution?
6. Am I able to state hypotheses from the problem in a testable form?
7. Will I learn something new from this problem?
8. Do I understand the relationship of this specific problem to the broader problem area?
9. Will I be able to select a sample from which I can generalize to some population? Are the sample subjects approachable?
10. Will some other intelligent person be able to replicate the study?
11. Will my proposed data-gathering instruments actually give the information, which I want?
12. Is the study, including the application of its results, practical ?

The number of affirmative answers should be required for a suitable problem.

Defining A Problem

Defining a problem means, "To pin-point the problem or defining a problem means to reach the core of the problem, i.e., threadbare analysis."

(a) Need of defining a problem. The definition of a problem serves the following purposes:

1. The definition of a problem sets the direction of the study.
2. The definition reveals the methodology or procedure of the study.

3. The definition helps the researcher to control subjectivity or biases of the researcher.
4. The definition of the problem suggests and specifies the variables to betaken up into the investigation through a problem involved so many variables.
5. The definition makes the research work practicable.

(b) Precautions are to be taken in identifying the problem. The following precautions should be taken into consideration for identifying problem.

1. The words used for defining a problem would have a single meaning.
2. The statement of the problem must be a brief but comprehensive.
3. The assumptions are to be recognised for the study.
4. The problem should have practical importance in the field of Education.
5. The definition or the statement of the problem should have certain rationale.

(c) Steps in defining a problem. The following steps are to be followed in defining a problem:

1. Researcher should have to develop a conceptual framework of the problem. The conceptual framework should be such that it can be stated into verbal form.
2. Delimiting the elements of the problem.
3. Classifying the elements in the homogeneous group.
4. Locating the key-points in the conceptual framework.
5. Evaluating the theoretical security of the problem.
6. The final form of the statement can be given into verbal form to a conceptual framework of the problem.
7. Deciding the practical difficulty in conducting the study.

1. Analysis of the Problem into its Elements. The major problem is subdivided into subordinate questions or problems. The definition of the problem is really the planning of the investigation with an indication of the data and techniques needed to answer. The questions raised. The Schematic Analysis of a problem has been shown in the chart.

2. Orientation and Related literature. Avoidance of unnecessary duplication in the selection of the problems suggest library procedures that should provide the setting for the investigation under consideration and an over view of the related studies. Detailed information concerning use of the appropriate library guides and illustrative review of the literature in particular area given in fourth chapter. Even though it may not be feasible in some report of research to devote a section or chapter of earlier investigations in the same field. The worker himself is obligated to make critical examination of such related studies. Literature may come hypotheses, suggestive methods of research and comparative data useful in the interpretation of results.

Schematic Analysis of a Problem

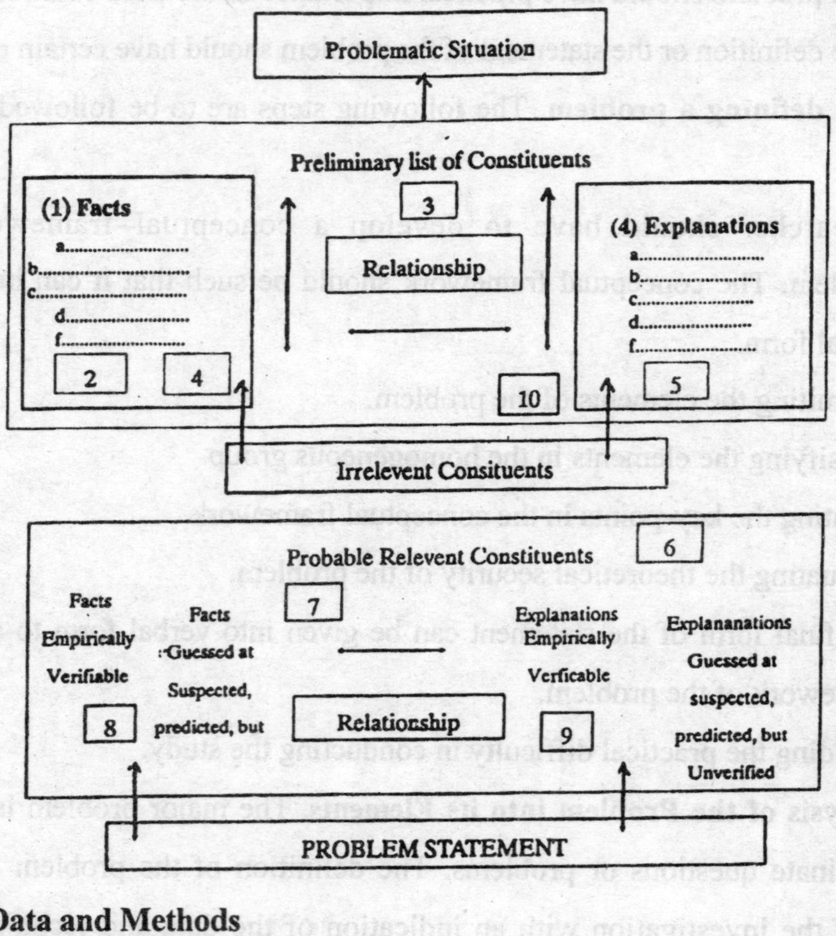

Sources of Data and Methods

For an adequate definition of the problem sources of data and methods for securing evidences must be carefully selected and clearly outlined in the introductory section of the report. Therefore as a matter of intellectual honesty and for accuracy of interpretation and reporting any limitation in source and procedure must be pointed out frankly but no apologetically.

Terminology. Technical terms and words or phrases with special meaning should be defined adequately.

Initial Assumptions Research like geometry begins with certain basic assumptions or postulates. Assumptions underlie each step of research. *They* should be stated not only in the definition of the problem and procedure, but also with the conclusions of which they are an integral part.

(d) Ways to Define the Problem The following are various ways of defining a problem

1. Analyse the major problems or problems in terms of subordinate problems.
2. Statement delimits the scope of the study.
3. Orientation of the problem in an unique direction.
    (a) A historical account, remote or recent.
    (b) A survey of previous study or related studies.
    (c) An analysis of previous studies or related subjects.
    (d) Preliminary survey or pilot work
4. Description of the general nature of the problem.
    (a) Type,
    (b) Source, and
    (c) Procedure.
5. Statement of limitations of the techniques employed.
6. Recognitions of assumptions and implications.
7. Importance or significance of the study of education.
8. Definition of terms used.

Statement of Problem

After selecting a problem, it should be stated carefully the researchers to delimit his task and isolate a specific problem before he can proceed with active planning of the study. This type of decision is culminated in the problem statement. *Kerlinger* has identified three criteria of good Problem Statements.

1. A problem should be concerned with relation between two or more variables.
2. It should be stated "clearly and unambiguously in question form."
3. It should be amenable to empirical testing.

Meeting these criteria in his problem statement will result, on the researcher's part, in a clear and concise idea of what he wants to do, this sets the stage for further planning.

Characteristics of A Problem

Although selecting a research problem is one of the most difficult step for a scholar in a research process, it is unfortunately one for which the least guidance can be given.

A problem statement must have the following characteristics

1. It should ask about a relationship between two or more variables.
2. It should be stated clearly and unambiguously, usually in question form.
3. It should be possible to collect data or answer the questions raised.
4. It should not represent a moral or ethical position.

1. Relationship between Variables: In this kind of problem the researcher manipulates a minimum of one variable to determine its effects on other variables, as opposed to a purely descriptive study in which the researcher observes, counts or in some way measure the frequency of appearance of a particular variable in a particular setting. For example, how many students in school have I. Q's in excess of 120. Since no attempts need be made to deal with a relationship between variables, this problem requires only a "book-keeping" procedure, if however; the problem has been stated;

Are boys more likely than girls to have 1 Q's in excess of 120 then it would involve the relationship between variables:

2. The Problem is Stated in Question Form: The problem should be in question form as:

1. What is the relationship between I. Q. and achievement?
2. Do students learn more from a directive teacher or a non-directive teacher?
3. Is there a relationship between racial background and dropout rate?
4. Do more students continue in training programmes offering stipends or in programmes not offering stipends?
5. What is the relationship between role learning ability and socio-economic status?

3. Empirical Testability: A problem should be testable by empirical purposes; it should lend itself to study by a single researcher, on a limited budget, within a period. The nature of the variables included in the problem is a good clue to its testability. An example of the kind of problem that is wise to avoid it: Does an extended experience in communal living improve a person's outlook on life? In addition to the magnitude and probable duration of studying such a problem, the variable themselves would be difficult to manipulate or measure.

4. Avoidance of Moral or Ethical Judgements: Questions about ideals or values are often more difficult to study than questions about aptitudes or performance, as, that would be difficult to test are: Should men define their feelings? The ethical consideration should also be taken into consideration in defining or stating a problem.

Clarifying and Stating a Problem

It is essential for a researcher before he proceeds with his study that he converts his tentative topic into a precise researchable problem. Since a problem is broad infinite therefore it is wise for the researcher to delimit or to narrow the range of the problem in terms of his interests and skills. The problem mentioned in this chapter can stated in the following way

Problem: "Analysing the potentials of teacher- effectiveness."

This statement is still vague and does not provide any direction to the researcher. It may be restated to clarify the study.

Restatement: *"A* study of relationship between predictors and criteria of teacher-effectiveness."

This statement indicates the specific task to be performed by the researcher that he has to study the relationship between predictors as independent variables and criteria as the dependent variables.

Problem: "The relation of socio-economic status to creativity."

It is also vague statement of a problem. It can be clarified and restated in the following way:

Restatement: "A comparative study of the performance of student of different socio-economic status on the items of the Baquer Mehdi creativity test.

Areas of the Research: Educational philosophy, Sociology, Educational Curriculum development, Institutional material, Learning process, Teaching methods, Teacher-education, Teacher- behaviour, Educational administration and supervision, Educational technology, Environmental education and distance education, etc.

Delimiting a Problem

Delimiting a problem is very important step. The following aspects should delimit a study:

1. A study should be delimited to certain variables that should be mentioned clearly in the problem.
2. The study is delimited to the area or level as primary level, secondary level, college or university level.
3. Again study is delimited to size of sample. Considering the time, energy and money, but it should be a representative.
4. Method of Research: - A Problem or study may be conducted by different methods but it is not possible. Therefore, the best method should be used so that the study should be delimited to the method only.
5. Measuring, Instruments: - In behavioural science number of instruments are available but all tools cannot be used to measure. Thus the best available tool will be used for measuring the variable.

6. Techniques of Research: - A number of techniques can be used for analysing data but most appropriate techniques should be used.
7. The other delimitation should vary from problem to problem as every problem has its own delimitations.

This delimitation may help the researcher for conducting the study and the findings of studies also confine to these delimitations.

Assumption s about the Problem

The following are main criteria for evaluating statement of the problem -

A good statement of a problem is based on some assumptions. An assumption is the s position that it is taken for granted to better establish the scope, frame of reference and conditions under which the study will be conducted. The following arc the major purposes of assumptions:

1. It makes the research work feasible.
2. It delimits the scope of the problem.
3. It establishes the proper frame of reference.
4. It sets forth certain conditions of the study.
5. It aids in the development of testable hypotheses.
6. It helps in establishing the population and extent of generalization.
7. It also determines the statistical limits for accepting and rejecting of hypotheses.

The assumptions are essential features in the building of scientific model, which helps inn critical analysis.

Sources for identifying the problem

The selection of a suitable problem is not an easy task. It is a serious responsibility to commit oneself to a problem that will inevitably require much time and energy and which is so academically significant. The following are the main sources to which one may proceed for a suitable research problem:

1. Personal experiences of the investigator in the field of education are the main sources for identifying suitable problem. Many of the problems confronted in the classroom, the school or the community lend themselves to investigation and they are perhaps more appropriate for the beginning

researcher than are problems more remote from his own teaching experiences.

2. The other source of problem, which is most frequently used by the investigator, as suggested by the supervisors, is the extensive study of available literature-research abstracts, journals, handbooks of research international abstracts etc. He can draw an analogy for selecting a research problem or can think parallel problem in the field studied of own country.
3. In the choice of a suitable problem, the researcher has to decide his field of investigation. He should study the field intensively in the specific area; this may enable him to identify a problem from the specific field.
4. The new innovations, technological changes and curricular developments are constantly bringing new problems and new opportunities for educational research.
5. The most practical source of problem is to consult supervisor, experts of the field and most experienced persons of the field. They may suggest most significant problems of the area. He can discuss certain issues of the area to emerge a problem.
6. It is a general practice that researchers suggest some problems in their research reports. The researcher can pick up a suitable problem for his own study.

Suggestive List for Source of Problems

NCTE organized in 1996-97 four National Workshops at New Delhi, Mumbai, Hyderabad and Pune. In these workshops, some crucial research problems related to education were worked out. After going through the list of problems, these could be regrouped in the broad areas given below: Area	**Problems**

Teacher Education	• Comparative study of objectives, materials and techniques of various training agencies. • Developing training programmes for various levels of functionaries. • Developing multiplier (cascade) model of training programme for adult education functionaries. • An investigation into the problems faced by the trainers in organizing training programmes. • Developing strategies to be adopted for mobilization of resources for effective training of functionaries. • A study of organizational and management skills needed by teacher trainers for conducting training. • Developing training programmes to cater to the psychological, vocational and community needs of learners. • Survey of learners' needs in the context of volunteer/instructors' training. • A follow-up study to evaluate the extent to which the trainees are able to translate into classroom practice the knowledge and skills acquired during training.
Teaching Learning Process	• A study of teaching-learning process in the training centre/school/college. • Analysis of the instructional process with special reference to communication skills in the training programme. • Study of teaching styles of teachers' trainers. • Study of learning styles of students/trainees. • A critical analysis of the use of learning materials and aids used by teacher/trainer. • A study of identification of the teaching skills relevant to teacher training.
Development of Teaching Competencies	• An in-depth study of the training competencies of teacher educators/adult education instructors. • An experimental study of the use and suitability of technology for improvement of teaching competencies. • A study of entry and exit behaviours of trainees. • A study of teaching behaviours (interaction analysis of teachers/trainers). • Evolving a training package for the development of competencies in trainees.
Adult Education	• A survey of characteristics of adult education functionaries. • A study of motivational phenomena in relation to people who opt for joining, continuing or dropping out of adult education. • A study of differentiates characteristics of effective versus ineffective adult education functionaries. • Evolving a training package for the development of competencies in adult education functionaries.
Non-formal Education	• Identifying parameters for assessing effectiveness of NFE

	facilitators training programme. • A study of the role of mass-media in teacher training programme for NFE. • A study of the cultural context of NFE and its implications for education of NFE facilitators. • Developing a training programme for NFE supervisors emphasizing their role as facilitators of creative teaching at NFE centres.

In addition to the above problems which emerged through the deliberations in the four National Workshops organized by NCTE', a few more problems in the area of Educational Research are being given below so as to enable a new research scholar to develop an insight into the nature of the problems.

Suggestive List of a few more Research Problems

- Study of the organizational climate of government and primary schools.
- Job satisfaction of primary school teachers, its relationship with personal, professional and organizational characteristics.
- Critical inquiry into in-service educational programmes conducted by DIETs.
- Self-concept of teachers and their emotional adjustment.
- Training of primary school teachers in, the context of education for all.
- A study of the relationship between certain psycho-sociological factors and achievement of student teachers in teacher training institutions.
- A study of the attitude of' teachers towards environmental/population education.
- A study of role conflicts of teachers.
- Secondary teacher education programme -a status survey.
- Relationship among teaching style, learning gains and teaching effectiveness.
- A comparative study of the different feedback methods for changing teacher behaviour.
- Effectiveness of inquiry training and advance organizer models for teaching social studies.

- A critical study of the Gandhian philosophy of education.
- Humanism in the educational philosophy of Sri Aurobindo.
- Educational thoughts in *Srimad Bhagwat Geeta.*
- Ethics of trade unionism in education.
- Professional ethics of teachers.
- Comparative study of the aims of education and curriculum in democracy.
- Post-Independence development of education, its impact on villagers' social life.
- Study of the growth and development of higher education during the British period in India.
- History and survey of education in a district.
- A survey of the development of school education in the state of Rajasthan.
- Cost and Benefit of Teacher Education.
- Unit cost and efficiency of certain colleges of education
- A study of parent investment on primary education in some selected schools.
- The place of distance education in Indian economy.
- A study of the characteristics of innovative educational administration.
- A study of the administrative behaviour of secondary school principals.
- Organisation, functions and problems of an open university: a case studs'.
- Inspection and supervision of primary schools.
- Psychosocial factors of wastage and stagnation among tribal students.
- Case studies of innovative institution.
- Study of the leadership behaviour of DIET principals.
- Study of the managerial styles and achievement motivation of headmasters.
- Case studies of single teacher primary schools.
- Academic leadership and student unrest.
- Astudyofintclligence, selfconceptandlevelofaspirationofadolescents.

- Study of the effect of home and school environment on the creativity of children.
- Educational/vocational aspiration of students.
- Correlational study of personality patterns, occupational choices and subject preferences of tribal learners.
- Evaluative study of students' personal sea ices in public schools.
- Educational problems of girl child.
- A study of the mental health and adjustment problems of school going girls.
- A study of the role commitments and conflicts women teachers.
- A study of occupational choices of adolescent girls and factors influencing them.
- A study of the adjustment problems of scheduled tribe students in schools.
- A socio-psychological study of adjustment of SC and ST Students.
- A study of cognitive process and motivational patterns of deprived students.
- Scheduled tribe students-their values, problems and level of frustration.
- Cognitive style and cognitive ability of tribal and non-tribal children.
- A study of the achievement motivation of tribal students.
- A study of concept learning in the disadvantaged school children
- Cognitive processes and personality characteristics of primary school children.
- A study of the curriculum for primary schools of Lok Jumbish project.
- A study of the learning disabilities of primary school children.
- A study of barriers in the primary education of girls.
- A study of the impact of midday meals programme on enrolment and retention in primary schools.
- A study of dropouts and failure in primary classes.
- A case study of model primary school.

- A study of graded basic vocabulary of I-V standards.
- An investigation into the effect of the reading improvement programme in Hindi.
- A study of the moral education of primary school children.
- A study of the acquisition of concepts in Mathematics of pupils at primary school level and its relation to some personal and environmental variables.
- A study of the effectiveness of educational television on the educational development of primary school children.
- A study of the nature and incidence of reading disability among school children.

Variables in a Hypothesis

A hypothesis is made testable by providing operational definitions for the terms or variables of the hypothesis. For a testable hypothesis there are two important things:

(1) Variables, and

(2) Operational definitions.

Variables: There are five types of variables. Among students of the same age and intelligence, skill performance is directly related to the number of practice traits particularly among boys but less directly among girls. In such a hypothesis the variables, which must be considered, are:

(i) Independent variable -number of practice trails.

(ii) Dependent variable-skill performance.

(iii) Moderator variable-sex rural and urban.

(iv) Control variable-age, intelligence.

(v) Intervening variable -learning attitude, interest.

(i) **The Independent Variable**: The independent variable, which is a stimulus variable or input, operates either within a person or within environment to affect his behaviour. It is that factor which is measured, manipulated, or selected by the experimenter to determine its relationship to observed phenomena.

If a researcher is studying the relationship between two variables X and Y. If X is independent variable, then it affects another variable Y. So the characteristics of independent variables are:

(a) It is the cause for change in other variables.

(b) Independent variables are always interested only it affects another variable, not in what affects it.

(2) The Dependent Variable: The dependent variable is response variable or output. It is an observed aspect of the behaviour of an organism that has been stimulated. The dependent variable is that factor which is observed and measured to determine the effect of the independent variables. It is the variable that will change as a result of variations in the independent variable. It is considered dependent because its value depends upon the value of the independent variable. It represents the consequence of change in the person or situation studied.

Relationship Between Independent and Dependent Variables

Most experiments involve many variables when two continuous variables are compared, as in correlational studies, deciding which variable to call independent and which dependent is sometimes arbitrary. In such cases variables are often not labelled as independent or dependent since there is no real distinction. Independent variables may be called factor and their variation may be called levels.

(3) The Moderator Variable: The term moderator variable describes a special type e of independent variable a secondary independent variable selected for study to ermine if it affects the relationship between the primary independent variable and the dependent variable.

The moderator variable is defined as that factor which is measured, manipulated or selected by the experimenter to discover whether it modifies the relationship of independent variable to observed phenomena. The sex and rural urban generally function as moderator variables.

(4) Control Variable: All the variables in a situation can not be studied at the same time, some must be neutralized to guarantee that they will not have a differential or moderating effect on the relationship between the independent and dependent variables. These variables whose effects must be neutralized or controlled are known as control variables. They are defined as those factors, which are controlled by experimenter to cancel out or neutralize any effect they might otherwise have on the observed phenomena. While the effects of the control variables are neutralized, the effect of moderator variables is studied.

Certain variables appear repeatedly as control variables, although they occasionally serve as moderator variables. For example sex, intelligence and socio-economic status are three subject variables that are commonly controlled, noise, task order and task content are common control variables in the situation.

(5) Intervening Variable: Each independent, moderator, and control variable can be manipulated by the dependent variable. Often these variables are not concrete but hypothetical, the relationship between a hypothetical underlying or intervening variable and dependent variable.

An intervening variable is that factor which affects the observed phenomenon but cannot be seen and measured or manipulated, its effects must be inferred from the effects of the independent and moderator variables on the observed phenomena. The attitude, learning process, habit and interest function as intervening variables.

Hypothesis-Teachers given more positive feedback-experiences will have more positive attitudes towards children than teachers given fewer positive feedback-experiences.

Independent Variable-Number of positive feedback-experiences for teacher.

Intervening Variable-Teacher's self esteem or habit-pattern.

Dependent Variable -Positive ness of teacher's attitude towards students.

The researcher must operationalize his variables in order to study them and conceptualize his variables in order to generalize from them. Researchers often use the labels independent, dependent, moderator, and control to describe operational statements of their variables. The intervening variables always refer to a conceptual variable-that which is being affected by the independent, moderator control and dependent variables.

Examining a hypothesis can often discover the intervening variable. They are usually abstract in nature.

Independent, moderator and control variables are inputs or causes, the first two being these that are studied while the third, control variables are neutralized or `eliminated'. At that other end, dependent variables represent effects or it is also known as criterion variable while intervening are conceptualizations, which intervene between operationally stated causes, and operationally, stated effects.

The Research Variables Combined

The variables research variables interact among themselves. The independent, moderator, and control variables arc under the researcher's control. They cause an impact within the subject. The impact is referred to as the intervening variable. In addition, those extraneous variables have an impact upon this intervening variable. Such extraneous variables are not under the researcher's control their presence weakens a study. One of the goals of a researcher is to remove as many significant factors as possible from the extraneous variables category by bringing them into the categories of moderator and control variables. Such a process of removing extraneous variables strengthens a study.

The intervening variable is merely hypothesized. It is abstract in nature. It cannot be visually observed. It is defined in conceptual terms. It is produced by some combination of the casual variables in the top row of the figure. It produces the effect on dependent variable. Every experimental study has at least one independent variable and one dependent variable. Both of these variables should be explicitly stated in the hypothesis and in the research prediction. If either the treatment or the outcome variable is too complex to be stated succinctly, further operational definitions of these variables can be included in the methods section of a report. Every study has also an intervening variable, and often there can be more than one intervening variable. The *intervening variable* is not stated in operational terms, but rather conceptual explanation for the observed results. Intervening variables are normally not stated in the hypothesis or research prediction. Sometimes intervening variables are only vaguely described or are not mentioned at all.

Every study does not contain moderator and control variables. When such variables are contained in a study, they should be operationally defined. Moderator and control variables are stated in the research hypothesis and in the research prediction. Often the operational definitions further explanation in the method section of a report.

Identify each of the research variables from the following hypothesis

High school than that who do study English for years not will develop better Hindi vocabulary, skills than those who do not study English.

Independent Variable -Studying English v s. not studying it.

The Variables in the Research Process

Causes (Operationally defined)

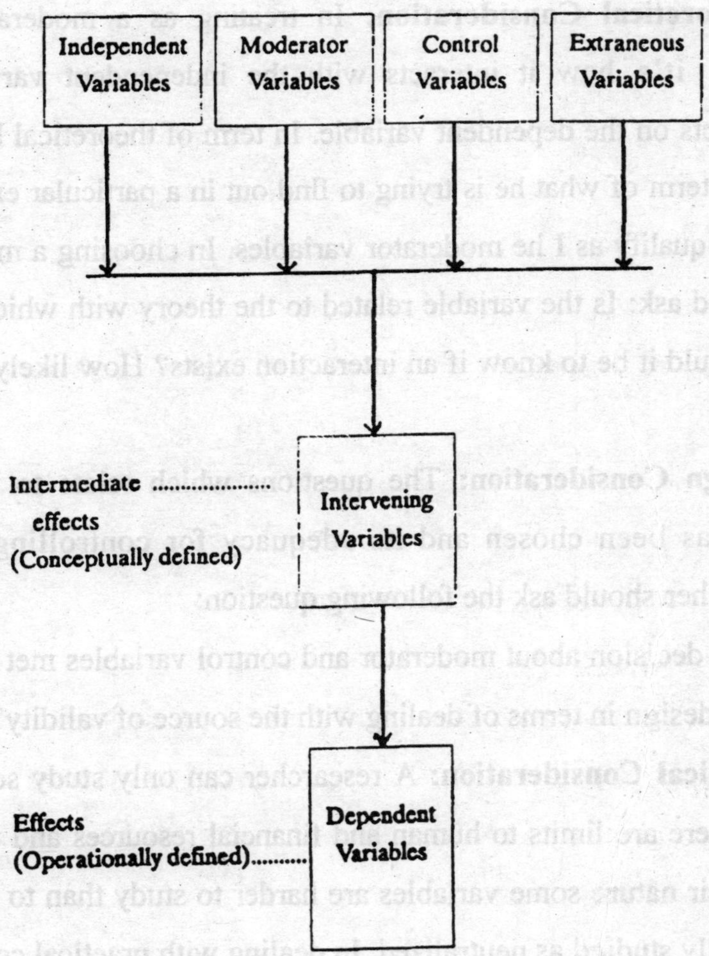

Dependent Variable -Vocabulary skills.

Moderator- Hindi class placement (advanced vs non- advanced). *Control*- High School students.

Intervening variable -Increased ability or learning style.

Some Considerations For Variables Choice

After selecting the independent and dependent variables the researcher must decide which variables are to be included as moderator variables and which are to be excluded or hold constant as control variables. He must decide how to treat the total part of the other variables (other than the independent). That might effect the dependent variables. In making these decisions which variables are 'in' and which are 'out' he should take into account three kinds of considerations:

(1) Theoretical Consideration: In treating as a moderator variable, the researcher lest, it's how it interacts with the independent variable to produce differential effects on the dependent variable. In term of theoretical base researcher is working and in term of what he is trying to find out in a particular experiment, certain variables highly qualify as I he moderator variables. In choosing a moderator variable a researcher shod ask: Is the variable related to the theory with which I am working? How helpful would it be to know if an interaction exists? How likely is there to be an interaction?

(2) Design Consideration: The questions which relate to the experimental design which has been chosen and its adequacy for controlling for sources of bias, the researcher should ask the following question:

Have my decision about moderator and control variables met the requirements of experimental design in terms of dealing with the source of validity?

(3) Practical Consideration: A researcher can only study so many variables at one t into. There are limits to human and financial resources and the dead lines he can meet. By their nature some variables are harder to study than to neutralize, while others are as easily studied as neutralized. In dealing with practical considerations, the researcher must ask question like the following:How difficult is it to make a variable a moderator as opposed to a control variable? What kinds of resources are available what kinds are required to create moderator variables?

This is highly significant one. In educational experiments researchers often have has control over the situation than design and theoretical considerations might necessitate.

Operational Definiitions

Immediately upon completion of the testable hypotheses a researcher should examine them and the problem in general to determine if there are any terms, which may be abstract or misleading. If any is found, particularly in the testing hypotheses, I hey should be defined so as to make them completely operational for the study being undertaken.

The necessity for operational definitions does not mean that the researcher can define a term to mean whatever he cares to make it mean, but does enable the researcher to limit the meaning of a word. *Operational definition* should be more specific than those used in ordinary discourse. In other words any special term, which must be used in the statement of the problem, may require an operational definition to Ensure clarity. Particular clarification should be given terms, which are used in the formulation of testable hypothesis. The term selected must be useful and make sense. Even common adjectives maybe used if you adequately explain what you mean. A point to remember is that once a researcher makes a definition, he must strick to it.

Words, which may need defining, are those which appear ambiguous, which have confusing interpretation and which might make a difference to a person attempting to replicate the study.

The Conditions for Making Final Decision

H.H. McAshan suggests that new researcher check the following conditions for operationally defining words before making a final decision:

1. The definition decides upon must withstand subjective analysis to determine if other qualified people could look at the word involved and come to the same conclusion.
2. The reliability of each word should be checked to find out if the subjective judgements are consistent.

3. The meaning of the operationally defined words must be mutually exclusive and not synonymous with other words, terms or, expressions.
4. The definition of each word chosen must fit the material researchers intent to study.
5. The definition decides upon must include all situations of use which will be included in the course of the investigation.

An operational definition is a definition based on the observable characteristics of that, which is being defined. The word *`observable'* in the significant wored in describing an operational definition.

There are three approaches to constructing operational definitions:

(i) Type A,

(ii) Type B, and

(iii) Type C.

**Type `A' Operational Definition:** The `Type A operational definition can be constructed in terms of the operations that must be performed to cause the phenomenon or state than an object or thin$. It tells what manipulation to use to induce a particular state. They are useful in defining independent variables as prescriptions carried out by the experimenter. The same variable, of course, be operationally defined by more than one type of definition but when what variable is the independent variable. It is often the most useful.

'Type B' Operational Definition: The `Type B' operational definition can be constructed in terms of how the particular object or thing being defined operates, that is, what it does or what constitutes its dynamic properties. `Type B' operational definitions seem particularly appropriate in an educational context for describing a type of person.

Though they may be used to define other variables, Type B definitions are particularly useful for defining the dependent variable when it is to be operationally based on behaviour.

'Type C' Operational Definitions: The `Type C' operational definition can be constructed in terms of what the object or phenomenon being defined looks like, that is, what constitutes its static properties. An intelligent student can be defined as a person who has good memory, a large vocabulary, good reasoning ability, good arithmetic, and skill stage. This type of operational definitions utilizes observable structural properties of the object. It describes the qualities, traits, or characteristics of people or thing. Thus, they may be used for defining any type of variable when used for defining a person's characteristics, they specify the static or internal qualities rather than his behaviour as does the `Type B' definition. Type C' operational definitions often lend themselves to measurement by tests although the ability to he tested is not a requisite part of the definition.

REVIEW OF THE RELATED LITERATURE

Meaning of the Related Study

Study of the related 'literature implies locating, reading and evaluating reports of research as well as reports of casual observation and opinion that are related to the individual's planned research project. As observed *by J.W.* Best, "Practically all human knowledge can be found in books and libraries. Unlike other animals that must start anew with each generation, man builds upon the accumulated and recorded knowledge of the past."

Importance and the Purposes of the Review

(i) The review of the literature is the basis of most of the research projects in the physical sciences, natural sciences, social, sciences and humanities.

(ii) A review of the related literature gives the scholar an understanding of the previous work that has been done.

(iii) The results of the review actually provide the data used in research.

(iv) It enables us to know the means of getting to the frontier in the field of our problem. Until we have learnt what others have done and what still remains to be done in our area, we cannot develop a research project that will contribute to furthering knowledge in our field.

(v) A review of the literature would develop the insight of the investigator.

The information thus gained will save the researcher's time and energy.

(vi) The importance of the review is quite obvious in delimiting the research problem and in defining it better.

(vii) The review of the literature will give the student the insight he needs to convert his tentative research problem to a specific and concise one.

(viii) A review of the literature can help the research worker in making him alert to research possibilities that have been overlooked.

(ix) In the process of reviewing the literature the student is on the alert for finding out research approaches in his area that have proved to be sterile.

(x) The review of the literature provides us with an opportunity of gaining insight into the methods, measures, subjects and approaches employed by other research workers. This in turn will lead to significant improvement of research design.

(xi) A careful consideration of the chapters entitled recommendations for further research in various research studies guides us regarding the suitability of a problem and in assisting us delimiting our research problems.

(xii) The review provides ideas, examinations and theories of research, valuable in studying the problem.

(xiii) Review prevents repetition of research.

(xiv) Review helps in locating comparative data interpretation of results.

In the words of Walter R. Borg, "The literature in any field forms the foundation upon which all future work will be built."

The author further observes that if we fail to build this foundation of knowledge provided by the review of the literature, our work is likely to be shallow and naive, and will often duplicate work that has already been done better by someone else.

Carter V. Good thinks, "The keys to the vast storehouse of published literature may open doors to sources of significant problems and explanatory hypotheses, and provide helpful orientation for definition of the problem, background for selection of procedure, and comparative data for interpretation of results. In order to be truly creative and original, one must read extensively and critically as a stimulus to thinking."

Various Sources of Related Literature

A researcher should be familiar with the with the regulations governing and services. He should also be a s. libraries use a printed guide that the use and circulation of material Many uses a diagram to indicate the contains helpful information. The guide location of the stacks, the periodicals section, reference section, reading, and special collections of books, microfilm or microcard equipment, manuscripts, or pamphlets. The guide lists the periodicals to which the library subscribes and the names of special indexes, abstracts, and other reference materials.

The regulations concerning the use of stacks, the use of reserve books, reference materials held by the library or those procedures for securing are also included in the guide.

Research scholars and other readers are usually issued a library card them access to the stacks. They may take the help of library staff or giving for the books and other reference may carry on the independent searching materials. After using the books, it is desirable for the readers to leave them on the tables so that the library staff will return them to their proper position on the shelves.

Sometimes a reference is not available in the library. In such a situation the reader must consult the `union' catalog, which lists references found in other libraries. Such references may be obtained in the following ways by the library:

1. By inter-library loan system. The reader requests the librarian to borrow the desired reference from other library where it is available.

2. By requesting a photostatic copy. The reader may request the librarian to obtain the photostat of a page or a number of pages of a desired reference from the source.

3. By requesting an abstract or translation of the portion of a desired reference. Some large libraries have abstracting and translating service that provides abstracts, or copied or translated portions of needed materials at an established fee.

4. By requesting microfilm or microfiche. The reader may purchase a microfilm that can be projected on library microfilm equipment. A microfiche is a sheet of film that contains micro-images of a printed manuscript or book. Its development has been one of the most significant contributions to library and information services by providing economy and convenience of storing and distribution of long runs of scholarly materials.

The size of the internationally standardized microfiche is *105* mm X *148* mm, which contains *98* images *(7* rows with *14* microimages) having a reduction ratio *24* x. The American National Micrographics Association has approved this, while the size of the British Standard microfiche is smaller which can have 60 images *(BS 4187 1973).*

A superfiche, which has been recently developed by the PCMI process of National Cash Register, has a *75* x reduction ratio and contains upto 1000 pages of printed material on a single *4"x* 6" transparent card.

An even more significant development is the *ultra-fiche.* It has reduction ratio of 150 x and has the capacity of *3200* pages per fiche (Mittal, 1979, p.10). Various types of cameras are used to record microimage on roll film.

Planetary camera is either *35* mm or 16 mm still camera which is mounted on a vertical column that can be moved up and down to change the reduction ratio between 10 *x and *50* x. At a time, it can be loaded with 100 feet of roll film. It does not cost much.

Step-and-repeat camera is a costly camera, which is used to record automatically microimages on microfiche one by one.

Rotary camera, like the planetary camera, records microimages *on roll* film and has the capacity to change the reduction ratio as desired.

Flow camera costs less than half of a planetary camera. Its reduction ratio is fixed unlike previously mentioned types of camera.

All these cameras make use of *silver, diazo* or *vesicular film* for recording microimages microfilms or generally, six types of *Readers* are used for reading microfiche (Mittal, 1979, p. 13).

(i) Cuddly Microfiche Reader is a portable reader and can be used by keeping it in one's lap. It is very cheap and can be lent to library members for home use.

(ii) Microfilm and Microfiche Readers.

(iii) Universal Machines.

(iv) Reader/Printer is a push-button machine, which not only helps in reading a microfilm/microfiche but is capable of producing a full-sized paper copy of the frame on the screen.

(v) Production Printer/Enlarge is an automatic machine and cap print the requisite number of copies of a microfilm or selected portions of a microfilm. It is used for mass production of full-sized copies of microfilms.

(vi) Xerox Copy flow Machine is a costly beyond the reach of ordinary libraries. In can print out a microfilm into a readable size, and as such, a single copy of any requisite document can be had at low cost and in less time.

The Card Catalog in the Library

The card catalog is the index to the entire library collection. It lists the details of publications found in the library, with the exception of serially published periodicals.

Generally, the card catalog contains author, title, and subject cards arranged alphabetically. A great deal of information about a book can be the found on the cards. Besides the title of the book and the name of the author, the reader will find the date of birth of the author, the edition, the publication date, the number of pages, and the name and location of the publisher. Other items listed on the cards are bibliographies, maps, portraits, illustrations, tables, series (if any) in which a book app description of the book - whether the book is a translation and who did the translation.

Library Classification Systems

Library classification systems provide ingenious ways of systematizing the placement and location of books. Every system is based upon a methodology that is logical and orderly to the smallest detail. The two principal systems of library classification in the United States are the 'Dewey Decimal' system and the `Library of Congress' system.

The 'Dewey Decimal' system is a decimal plan with the numbers running from 001 to *999.99.* The `Library of Congress' system is particularly used in large libraries. It provides for twenty main classes instead of the ten of the Dewey Decimal system. The system uses letters of alphabet for the principal headings and numerals for further sub-grouping.

In a library, 'all books have a call number or letter that appears in the upper left-hand corner of the author, subject, or title card, and on the back of the book. These call numbers or letters are used to arrange the books serially on the library shelves and within each classification; the books are arranged alphabetically by author's last name.

Library Searching Guidelines

Identifying the best available sources pertaining to a problem and extracting the essential information from them is of much importance to a researcher. For this he must develop some library searching techniques so as to save his time and effort. Van Dalen *(1973,* p.88) has suggested the following valuable guidelines for a researcher:

1. Before using a library, familiarize yourself with its layout, facilities, services, and regulations.
2. Learn how to use the microform readers, photocopiers, and other mechanical aids.
3. In the stacks and in the periodical, reference, reserved book, and rare book rooms, note where materials that you will use frequently are placed.

4. Schedule your work session in a library when you will encounter the least competition for resources and services.
5. Make out call slips for all or most *of* the books needed in one session.
6. Copy all information that the librarian needs to obtain each reference for you, and before closing the periodical index or card catalog, recheck and rectify any errors or omissions.
7. Arrange to spend a block of time in the library that is sufficient to accomplish a specific task.
8. When little time is available, clear up questions that can be answered quickly through the help of reference books that are readily available.
9. Before initiating search for materials in a library, write down questions that cover precisely the information you wish to locate and group the questions in accordance with the areas in the library where the answers may be found.
10. Compile a list of the present and any previous names of periodicals, organizations, government agencies, research agencies, collectors of statistics, libraries and museums with special collections, and outstanding authorities in your field.
11. Keep a list of the best reference books, indexes, handbooks, historical stud ies, and legal references in your area of specialization.
12. Obtain copies *of* the best bibliographies and reprints *of* significant research
13. Note which periodicals regularly or occasionally print bibliographic, reviews of literature, or such other reference material and the issues in which they appear.

Reference Material

There are a number of references that may be useful to a researcher in the field of education. To facilitate the search for such material, a researcher may consult the following carefully compiled volumes:

Constance M. Winchell, ed. A *Guide to Reference Books,* 8th edn. Chicago: American Library Association, 1967. This comprehensive work has biennial supplements to bring the up-to-date information in a number of languages. It describes and evaluates about 7,500 references and a section is devoted to education.

Albert J. Walford, *Guide to Reference Material.* This is a two volume, work which covers (1) science and technology (1966) and (2) philosophy and psychology, religion, social sciences, geography, and history (1968).

Mary N. Barton and Marion V. Bell (1962) *Reference Books : A Brief Guide for Students and Other Users of the Library.* This guide is helpful but considerably shorter.

International Guide to Educational Documentation (1955-1960), UNESCO, 1963. This is a one-volume international guide to educational books, pamphlets, periodicals, occasional papers, film and sound recordings.

Arvid Burke and Mary Burke, *Documentation in Education.* This guide provides an excellent introduction to literature in the field of education.

The Standard Periodicals Director, New York: Oxbridge Publishing Co., 1964-date. This is a directory of over 30,000 entries and covers every type of periodical, with the, exception of local newspapers. It is published every year and covers about two hundred classifications, which are arranged by subject. An alphabetical index is provided.

Christine L. Wyner, *Guide to Reference Books for School Media Centres.* Littleton, Colo: Libraries Unlimited, 1973. This guide includes 2575 entries with evaluative comments on reference books and selection tools for use in educational institutions. It is indexed by author, subject, and title.

Encyclopaedias. These serve as a storehouse of information, and usually contain well-rounded discussion and selected bibliographies that are prepared by specialists. Encyclopedias are arranged alphabetically by subject, and for each field of research, they present a critical evaluation and summary of the work that has been done. In addition, these suggest the research needed in the field and provide *a selective bibliography.*

The following list provides a sample of encyclopedias that researchers in the field of education might use:

A Cyclopedia of Education, Paul Monroe, ed., 5 vol. (New York: Macmillan, 1911-13). It is edited by Paul Monroe with the assistance of departmental editors and more than 1,000 individual contributors. It provides excellent bibliographies and is extremely useful for historical and biographical purposes.

The Encyclopedia of Education, ed., Lee C. Deighton *(New York: The Macmillan Company & The Free Press, 1971).*

The encyclopedia includes more than 1,000 articles. It offers a view of the institutions and people, of the processes and products, found in educational practice. The articles deal with history, theory, research, philosophy, as well as with the structure and fabric of education.

Encyclopedia of Modern Education, Henry D. Rivlin and H. Schueller, ed. (New York: Philosophical Library, 1943). Henry D. Rivlin and H. Schueller have edited this comprehensive work of about 200 authorities. It stresses present-day problems, trends, theories, and practices. The articles are accompanied by brief bibliographies and there is a system of cross-references.

Encyclopedia of Educational Research. Walter Scott Monroe, ed., rev. ed. (New York: Macmillan, 1950). Monroe's *Encyclopedia of Educational Research* was prepared under the auspices of the American Educational Research Association. It aims to present a critical evaluation, synthesis, and interpretation of research studies in the field of education. All the articles, arranged alphabetically, are provided with bibliographies.

Encyclopedia of Educational Research. Chester Harris, ed. 3d edn. (New York: Macmillan, 1960). Harris's *Encyclopedia of Educational Research* is also prepared under the auspices of the American Educational Research Association. It is not merely a revision of earlier editions, but it is completely a re-written volume that has attempted to put into a new, perspective.

Encyclopedia of Educational Research. Robert L. Ebel, ed., 4th edn. (New York: Macmillan, 1969). Ebel's Encyclopedia of Educational Research provides concise summaries of research and many references for further research. The articles deal with persistent educational problems and continual educational concerns.

Encyclopedia of Educational Research. Harold E. itzel, ed., 5th edn. (New York: The Free Press: A Division of Macmillan Publishing Co., Inc., 1982).

The contents of the encylopedia have been classified under eighteen broad headings, alphabetically ranging from `Agencies and Institutions Related to Education; Counselling, Medical, and Psychological services; Curriculum Areas etc. to Teachers and Teaching'. The new concepts and topics, viz., 'Computer-Based Education', 'Drug Abuse Education', Equity Issues in Education', 'Ethnography' and 'Neurosciences' are also included in this volume. These additions reflect recent events and developments in the world to which education must attend.

The International Encyclopedia of Education. Torsten Husen and T. Neville Postlethwaite, ed., (New York: . Pergamon Press, 1985).

This publication is the first major attempt to present an up-to-date overview on educational problems, practices, and institutions all over the world. The information available in this volume provides answers to three basic questions: What is the state of the art in the various fields of education? What scientifically sound and valid information is available? What further research is needed in various aspects of education?

The Encyclopedia of comparative Education and National Systems of Education. T Neville Postlethwaite, ed., (New York: Oxford Press, 1988).

This encylopedia is in two parts: the first part presents a series of articles about comparative education; the second part provides description of 159 different systems of education in various countries.

International Encyclopedia of the Social Sciences (New York: Macmillan Co., 1968). It was prepared under the direction of ten learned societies. This reference work treats topics in all of the social sciences.

Encyclopedia of Childcare and Guidance (Garden city, New York: Doubleday and Co., 1968). It is a comprehensive treatment of the nature of the problems of childhood. It also suggests the methods of dealing with such problems.

Encylopedia of Social Work. (New York: National Association of Social Workers, 1965). This reference work presents extensive articles on all aspects of social work.

Encyclopedia of Philosophy (New York: McGraw-Hill Book Co., 1971). This encyclopedia contains more than 7000 articles written by more than 2000 contributors in all areas of science and engineering.

Encyclopedia of Philosophy (New York: Macmillan-Free Press, 1967). It is an authoritative and comprehensive reference work covering both Western and Eastern thought-ancient, medieval, and modern.

Dictionaries. They serve as constant guides to the researcher. A few known dictionaries are detailed below:

Dictionary of Education. (New York: McGraw-Hill Book Co., 1973). This dictionary covers 33,000 technical and professional terms. It also includes educational terms used in various countries.

Comprehensive Dictionary of Psychological and Psychoanalytical Terms (New York: David McKay Company). It *contains* more than 13,000 terms. All these are defined in non-technical terms.

Dictionary of Sociology (Totowa, N.J.: Littlefield, Adams and Co.). In this dictionary sociological terms are defined in non-technical language.

Roget's International Thesaurus of Words and Phrases (New York: Crowell, Collier and Macmillan). A Thesaurus is the opposite of a dictionary. One turns to the Thesaurus when one has an idea, but does not yet have appropriate word to convey it. Thesaurus lists together the synonyms and antonyms of words. A researcher should use this reference in conjunction with a good dictionary to ensure precision of expression.

Yearbooks, Almanacs and Handbooks. A large amount of current in formation on educational problems, thought and practices may be found in yearbooks, almanacs and handbooks. Some yearbooks cover a new topic of current interest each year and some others give more general reviews of events. A list of some yearbooks, almanacs and handbooks is given as under:

The Handbook of Research on Teaching. N.L. Gage (ed.), (Chicago: Rand McNally & Co., 1963). This handbook presents comprehensive research information on teaching with extensive bibliographies.

The Rand McNally Handbook of Education, Arthur W. Foshay (ed.), (Chicago: Rand McNally & Co, 1963). It is a convenient source compilation of the most important facts about education in the United States. This handbook provides a quick-reference comparison of education in England, France and Russia.

Education Yearbook (New York: Macmillan Co., 1972-date). This is an annual publication. It includes statistical data on major educational issues and movements with a comprehensive bibliography and reference guide.

Mental Measurement Yearbook (Highland Park, New Jersey: Grayphon Press, 1938-date). It is compiled by Oscar K. Buros and provides a comprehensive summary on psychological measurement and standardized tests and inventories. It is published every four years and includes reviews on all significant books on measurement and excerpts from book reviews appearing in professional journals.

Indian Mental Measurement Hand Book: Intelligence and Aptitude Tests (New Delhi: National Council of Educational Research and Training, 1991).

The Handbook is one of major efforts of National Library of Educational and Psychological tests (NCERT) to present before the researchers, a review of the standardised tests, particularly in the areas of `Intelligence' and `Aptitude'. It makes available the organised information on tests developed in India and the Indian adaptations or standardisations of foreign tests. The information covers not only tests, which are commercially available to test users, and those available for restricted use, but also tests for which only specimen sets are available. Test reviews have been included in this Handbook in order to help the readers to evaluate-the tests more critically.

The Student Psychologist's Handbook: A Guide to Sources (Cambridge, Mass: Schenkman Publishing Co., 1969). This handbook describes the major content areas of psychology, with sources of information, methods of data collection, and the use of reference materials.

Data Processing Yearbook (Detroit: Frank H. Gille, 1952-date). This yearbook is published irregularly and includes articles on equipment, techniques, and developments in data processing. It also provides information about institutions offering data-processing and computer courses.

United Nations Statistical Yearbook. (New York: United Nations, 1949-date). This is an annual publication. It presents statistical data on population, trade, finance, communication, health, and education.

World Almanac-Book of Facts (New York: Newspaper Enterprise Association, 1968-date). This reference guide is published annually. 'It provides up-to-date statistics and data concerning events, progress and conditions in social, educational, political, religious, geographical, commercial, financial and economic fields.

The Standard Education Almanac. It provides a record of facts and statistics on virtually every aspect of education, *Directories and bibliographies.* A researcher to locate the names and addresses of persons, periodicals, publishers, or organizations when he wants to obtain information, about financial assistance, or research material- and equipment, uses directories. Directories may help a researcher to find people or organizations that have similar professional interests or who can answer his queries or help to solve his problems.

A few important directories in the USA and the UK are:

Guide to American Educational Directories. It lists in one volume over 12,000 educational and allied directories. The directories are listed alphabetically and are arranged under subject headings.*The Education Directory* (Washingtqn: US Office of Education, Superintendent of Documents, 1912-date). This directory is published annually in five parts. It deals with names, educational agencies, officials, institutions, and other relevant data.

NEA Handbook for Local, State and National Associations (Washington, D.C.: National Education Association, 1945-date). This is an annual publication and contains listings and comprehensive reports of state and national officers of affiliated associations and departments.

Educator's World (Englewood, Colo.: Fisher Publishing Co., 1972date). This is an annual guide to more than 1600 education associations, publications, research centres, and foundations.

National Faculty Directory. (Detroit: Gale Research Co., 1964-date). This annual publication lists alphabetically the names and addresses of more than 300,000 full-time and part-time faculty members and administrative officials of colleges and universities in the USA.

Encylopedia of Associations. (Detroit: Gale Research Co., 1964-date). This directory lists alphabetically more than 14,000 national associations of the USA. It includes information on membership, addresses, names of executive secretaries, and statement of purpose of these associations.

Directory of Exceptional Children. (Boston: Porter Sargent Publishing Co., 1962-date). This directory provides a description of schools, camps, homes, clinics, hospitals, and services for the socially mal-adjusted, men tally retarded or physically handicapped in the United States.

Mental Health Directory. (Washington_ D.C.: National Institute of Mental Health. Government Printing Office, 1964-date). This annual publication lists national, state and local mental health agencies in the USA.

American Library Directory. (New York: R.R. Bowker Co., 1923 date). This directory provides a biannual guide to private, state, municipal, institutional, and collegiate libraries in the USA and Canada. It includes information on special collections, number of holdings, staff salaries, budgets and affiliations.

Kelley, Thomas (ed.) A *Select Bibliographies of Adult Education in Great Britain* (London: National Institute of Education, 1952). Blackwell, A.M. A *list of*

Researches in Educational Psychology presented for Higher Degrees in the Universities of the United Kingdom and the Irish Republic from 1918. (London: Newnes Educational Publishing Co., 1950).

In India, a very few bibliographical guides to educational research on a national basis have appeared. *The Inter-university Board of India has published Bibliography of Doctorate Theses in Science and Arts accepted by the Indian Universities for 1946-48 and 1948-50 recently.* These are listed under the respective universities, with subject sub-headings including education.

The Index. A periodical index serves the same purpose as the index of a book or the card file of library. It identifies the source of the article or of the book cited by listing the titles alphabetically, under author and the readers should read all such directions before trying to locate the references.

A list of some important educational indexes is given below:

Education Index. (New York: H. W. Wilson Co., 1929-date). One valuable and work saving guide created for educators is Education Index. It is published monthly (September through June) cumulated annually and again every three years. It indexes more than 250 educational periodicals, and many yearbooks, bulletins, and monographs published in the United States, Canada, and Great Britain. The material on adult education, business education, curriculum, educational administration, educational psychology, educational research, exceptional children, higher education, guidance, health and physical education, international education, religious education, health and physical education, international education, religious education, secondary education and teacher education are included in this index.

*Canadian Education Index (*Ottawa, Ontario: Canadian Council for Educational Research, 1965-date). This index is issued quarterly and indexes periodicals, books, pamphlets, and reports published in Canada.

Current Index to Journals in Education (New York: Macmillian Information 1969-date). This index is published monthly and cumulated six monthly and annually. It indexes about 20,000 articles each year from more than 700 education and education-related journals, under author and subject headings.

ERIC Educational Documents Index. (Washington, D.C.: National Institute of Education, Government Printing Office, 1966-date). This index is published annually. It is a guide to, all research documents in the Educational Resources Information Centre collection.

Index of Doctoral Dissertations International. (Ann Arbor, Mich.: Xerox University Microfilms, 1956-date). Published as the issue 13 of *Dissertation Abstracts International* each year, it consolidates into one list all dissertations accepted by American, Canadian, and some European universities during the academic year, as well as those available in microfilm.

International Guide to Educational Documentation. (Paris: UNESCO) This guide is published every five years. It indexes annotated bibliographies covering major publications, bibliographies and national directories written in English, French and Spanish.

British Education Index Vol I, August 1954 to November 1958. This index is compiled by the Librarians of Institutes of Education and it includes references to articles of educational interest published during the period of four years. The index covers more than fifty periodicals.

Index to Selected British Educational Periodicals (Leeds: Librarians of Institutes of Education, 1945-date). This index is issued thrice per year and it covers 41 educational periodicals excluding those on fundamental and adult education.

Research Periodicals

Information about new ideas and developments often appear in periodicals long before it appears in books. There are many periodicals in education and in other closely related areas that are the best sources for reports on recent research studies. Such periodicals give much more up-to-date treatment to current questions in education than books possibly can. They also publish articles of temporary, local or limited interest that never appear in book form. The periodicals of proper dates are the best sources for determining contemporary opinion and status, present or past.

It has been estimated that there are about 2100 journals that are specifically related to the field of education. In all such journals one may also find articles of interest devoted to psychology, philosophy, sociology, and other subjects.

All those engaged in educational research should become acquainted with certain educational periodicals and they should also learn to use the: indexes to them. Knowledge about the editor of a periodical, the names of its contributors, and the associations or institutions publishing it may serve as clues in judging the merit of the periodical.

Ulrich's Periodicals Directory; A Classified Guide to a Selected List of Current Periodicals, Foreign and Domestic, 12th ed. (New York: Bowker, 1967) provides a comprehensive list of periodicals relating to education. In this directory, periodicals are grouped in a subject classification and are alphabetically arranged. Each entry includes title; sub-title, date of origin, frequency of publication, annual index, cumulative indexes, and item characteristics of each periodical.

In India, some associations or institutions publish many periodicals. They provide a medium for dissemination of educational research and exchange of experience among research workers, teachers, scholars and others interested in educational research and related fields and professions.

Abstracts

Abstracts include brief summaries of the contents of the research study or article. They serve as one of the most useful reference guides to the researcher and keep him abreast of the work being done in his own field and also in the related fields.

In America the most useful of these references are the following:

The review of educational research. It gives an excellent overview of the work that has been done in the field and about the recent developments. This publication, between 1931 and 1969, reviewed about every three years each of tine following eleven major areas of education: (i) Administration; *(ii)* Curriculum; *(iii)* Educational Measurement; *(iv)* Educational Psychology; (v) Educational Sociology: *(vi)* Guidance and Counselling; *(vii)* Language Arts, Fine Arts, Natural Sciences, and Mathematics; *(viii)* Research Methods; *(ix)* Special Programmes; *(x)* Mental and Physical Development; and *(xi)* Teaching Personnel.

Since June 1970, the *Review of Educational Research* has pursued a policy of publishing unsolicited reviews of and research topics of the contributor's choosing. The role played by this publication in the past has been assumed by the ***Annual Review of Educational Research***.

Research in Education (RIE). This represents the most comprehensive publication of research materials in education today. RIE is published monthly since 196-6 by the Educational Resources Information Centre (ERIC) and indexed annually. Each monthly issue of RIE is divided into three sections: (1) Document Section; (2) Project Section: and (3) Accession Numbers Section.

Psychological abstracts. The American Psychological Association publishes this useful reference since 1927. It is published bimonthly and contains abstracts of articles appearing in over 530 journals, mostly educational periodicals. The biannual issues (January-June, July-December) contain both author and subject index.

Education abstracts. This is a publication of UNESCO, which began in 1949 and has been published monthly except in July and August. Each introductory essay devoted to a particular aspect of education, is followed by abstract of books and documents, selected from various countries dealing with the topic under consideration.

In addition to the above periodicals, a researcher may also consult the following publications:

(1) Annual Review of Psychology (1950-date):

(2) Child Development Abstracts and Bibliography (1927-date);

(3) Psychological Bulletin (1904-date):

(4) *Sociological Abstracts* (1952-date);

(5) *Educational Administration Abstracts* (1966-date);

(6) *Sociology of Education Abstracts* (1965-date);

(7) *Mental Retardation Abstracts* (1964-date),

(8) *Dissertation Abstracts International* (1952-date).

In India, the Ministry of Education and Social Welfare, Government of India, (now Ministry of Human Resource Development) New Delhi, since 1955, has been issuing *Indian Education Abstracts* every three months. It abstracts the contents of books and periodicals on education published in India in English and Hindi. Most of the Indian Journals are indexed in the various issues. The abstracts appear under the following subject headings: Philosophy of Education; Educational Psychology; Measurement and Testing; Examinations; Students and Students' Organizations; Educational and Vocational Guidance; Teacher Education and Training; Curriculum; Basic Education; Health and Physical Education; Primary, Secondary, Higher, Vocational and Technical Education: and Social Education.

Many professional periodicals and yearbooks, in India and abroad, include some reviews of research and technical discussions of educational problems in one or all the issues of their series. Lists of some of the publications are:

USA; Journal of Educational Research, NE4 Research Bulletin, Educational and Psychological Measurement, Journal of Experimental Education, Research Quarterly, Journal of Research in Music Education, American Educational Research Journal, Reading Research Quarterly, Journal of Educational Psychology, Journal of Psychology, Journal of Social Psychology, Journal of Applied Psychology, Sociology of Education, American Journal of Sociology, American Sociological Review, Sociology and Social Research, Harvard Educational Review, Journal of Teacher Education, Elementary School Journal, History of Education Quarterly, and Educational Forum.

UK: British Journal of Educational Psychology

India: Indian Educational Review, Journal of Psychological Researches, Indian Journal of Applied Psychology, Indian Journal of Experimental Psychology, Journal of Education and Psychology, The Education Quarterly, Perspectives in Education, Journal of Educational Planning And Administration, University News, Journal of Higher Education.

Theses and Dissertations

The universities that award the authors their doctoral and master's degrees usually preserve theses and dissertations. Sometimes these studies are published in whole or in part in various educational periodicals or journals. Because the reports of many research studies are never published, a check of the annual list of theses and dissertations issued by various agencies is necessary for a thorough coverage of the research literature.

In the United States, references of doctoral dissertations in all fields, including education, can be found in sources compiled by various agencies. For the period 1912 to 1938, the Library of Congress issued the annual *List of American Doctoral Dissertations* for published studies. The Association of Research Libraries published the list of *Doctoral Dissertations accepted by American Universities* from 1933-1934. to 1954-1955. This service was continued by the Index to *American Doctoral Dissertations* 1956-1963, which became the *American Doctoral Dissertations,* 1963-64 to date. It lists all doctoral dissertations accepted by the American and Canadian universities and other educational institutions.

Dissertation Abstracts International, May, 1970, abstracts dissertations in the humanities, social sciences, physical sciences and engineering. It is published monthly. For each dissertation, there is a 600 word abstract that provides the researcher enough information to satisfy his needs. If a researcher wants to read a complete copy of a dissertation that is presented ***in** Dissertation Abstracts International,* he can purchase a microfilm or xerox copy from the University Microfilms. The reference number for placing an order and price are provided in the abstract.

In India, only a few universities publish abstracts of dissertations and theses that have been completed at the institution.

Kurukshetra University, Kurukshetra .(Haryana) published *Abstract of M.Ed. Dissertations* Vol. 1, 1966; *Abstracts of M.Ed Dissertations, Vol. 11.* 1967; *Abstract of M. Ed. Dissertations, Vol.* III, 1968; *Abstract o/' A I/'(/ Dissertations* Vol. IV, 1969; *Abstract of MEd Dissertations, Vol. V, 19 /*o, *Abstract of MEd dissertations and Ph.D. Theses. Vol. VI, 1973.*

M.B. Buch ed. *A Survey of Research in Education,* Centre of Advanced Study in Education, Baroda: M.S. University, 1973. This publication contains all the research studies in education completed in Indian universities upto *1972.* The break up of the studies in the said volume is *462* Ph.D. studies and *269* project research. The abstracts of all the studies have been classified into seventeen meaningful areas of education. They are (i) Philosophy of Education, *(ii)* History of Education, *(iii)* Sociology of Education, (iv) Economics of Education. (v) Comparative Education, (vi) Personality, Learning and Motivation, *(vii)* Guidance and Counselling, *(viii)* Tests and Measurement, *(ix)* Curriculum, Methods, and Textbooks: (x) Educational Technology, (xi) Correlates of Achievement, *(xii)* Educational Evaluation and Examination, *(xiii)* Teaching and Teaching Behaviour, (xiv) Teacher Education, *(xv)* Educational Administration, *(xvi)* Higher Education, and *(xvii)* Non-formal Education.

M.B. Buch, ed. *Second Survey of Research in Education (1972-1978)* Baroda: Society for Educational Research and Development *(1979).* This publication incorporates *839* research studies completed during the period *1972-1978* and follows the same pattern of organization of seventeen research areas as .4 *Survey of Research in Education (1973).* The first chapter gives a broad perspective of the place and function of research for educational development including historical account of the development of educational research in India. Each subsequent chapter includes a report based on the abstracts of research studies giving the trend of research in the area, including the gaps and high-lighting the research priorities as perceived by the author. The abstracts are arranged alphabetically for each area and continuously numbered throughout the volume. Each abstract contains the title of the study, the objectives and/or hypotheses examined, methodology including the sample, tools of research, the statistical techniques used, and the findings. A special feature of this publication is the incorporation of a large number of studies on educational problems completed in the university departments of social sciences and humanities other than the departments of education. The trend reports are based not on the research completed during the period *1972-1978,* but on the total research activities during the period *1940* to *197.8*.

M.B. Buch, ed. Third Survey of Research in Education (1978-1983) New Delhi: National Council of Educational Research and Training, 1987. The publication consists of twenty chapters beginning with a comprehensive review of the general trend of research in education in India based on a quantitative and qualitative analysis of the studies. Eminent educationists on the basis of studies conducted during the period of four decades, from have developed the trend reports in different areas of education 1943 to ' 198' . In all, 1481 research abstracts have been presented after being classified under the seventeen areas. Each research abstract reports in brief the problem, objectives of the study, research techniques adopted, and the findings and conclusion of the study. A special feature of the volume is the chapter on 'Research on Indian Education Abroad', which presents a review of *192* doctoral dissertations submitted to American and British universities, covering a period of around two decades. Another significant inclusion in the volume is the chapter on `Priorities in Educational Research'. The volume also makes available at one place a complete list of all researches in education conducted in India till *1983.*

ALB. Buch, ed. Fourth Survey of Research in Education (1983-1988) New Delhi: National Council of Educational Research and Training, 1991. This publication, published in two volumes, covers researches in education till *1988.* It comprises thirty one chapters beginning with a comprehensive review of the general trend of research followed by trend reports in different areas of education developed by eminent educationists on the basis of studies conducted during the period of about four and a half decades - *1943* to *1988*. In all, *1652* research abstracts have been presented after classification in *29* areas. The volume makes available a complete list of all the *4703* educational researches conducted in India since *1943*.The Fourth Survey has a new dimension. There is a chapter on review of research at the M.Phil level in Indian Universities.

Newspapers and Pamphlets

Many articles of particular interest to a researcher may be located through pamphlets and newspapers. Current newspapers provide up-to-date information on speeches, seminars, conferences, new trends, and a number of other topics. Old newspapers, which preserve a record of past events, movements and ideas, are particularly useful in historical inquiries. Some libraries catalog pamphlets and newspapers in their reference sections.

Government Documents

Government documents are a rich source of information. They include statistical data, research studies, official reports, laws and other material that are not always available elsewhere. These are available in national, regional, state as well as local level government offices.

Monographs

Monographs are also major sources of information on ongoing research. In the United States, universities and teachers' colleges publish many research studies in education in the form of monographs. A few examples of these are *Supplementary Educational Monographs, Educational Research Monographs,* and *Lincoln School Monographs.* In England too, the various institutes of education publish monographs from time to time. In India, only some universities and research organizations publish a limited number of monographs.

Computer-generated Reference Materials

School Research Information Service (SRIS), Direct Access to Reference Information (DATRIX), and Psychological Abstract Search and Retrieval Service (PASAR) in the United States provide a number of computer-generated reference sources that may save a great deal of time and effort of the researcher. SRIS operated by Phi Delta Kappa (Bloomington, Indiana) provides a computer printout of abstracts for a moderate fee. DATRIX, a development of the University Microfilms (Ann Arbor, Michigan) provides computerized retrieval for *Dissertation Abstracts,* from 1928 to date. The researcher can procure information on microfiche or Xerographic copy of the complete dissertation, which he needs, from *University Microfilms,* on payment. The PASAR furnishes printouts of abstracts of psychological journal articles, monographs, reports, and parts of books for a moderate fee.

THE HYPOTHESES

Once the selection and definition *of* the problem have been accomplished. The derivation of hypotheses is the most important step in the research process.

Etymologically *hypothesis* is made up of two words, "hypo" (less than) and "thesis", which mean less than or less certain than a thesis. It is the presumptive statement of a proposition or a reasonable guess, based upon the available evidence, which the researcher seeks to prove through his study. The terms hypothesis, theory, and conclusion occur frequently in research literature and need some clarification. The *hypothesis* is precisely defined as a tentative or working proposition suggested as a solution to a problem, and the *theory* as the final hypothesis, which is defensibly supported by all the evidence. The final hypothesis, which fits all the evidence, becomes the chief *conclusion* inferred from the study. According to Hilway (1964, p. 123):

> From the research scholar's point of view, the hypothesis may be conveniently considered as a tentative or working assumption, and the theory as the surviving or final hypothesis, which is most defensibly supported by all the evidence. But since knowledge arrived at through the scientific method is subject to revision in the light *of* new data, a theory is in only one sense always only a working assumption, so that the conventional distinction between hypothesis and theory (on the basis *of* increasing

adequacy of evidence and hence a greater certainty) is a relative one. For all practical purposes, the duality of the term hypothesis need not concern the research scholar except to serve, as a salutary reminder that no conclusion reached by the scientific method is necessarily a fixed and final truth.

The hypothesis is a powerful tool in research process to achieve dependable knowledge. It helps the researcher to relate theory to observation and observation to theory.

Hypotheses are formulated only as the suggested solution to the problem, with the objective that the ensuing study may lead either to its rejection or to its retention. They enable the researcher to locate and identify the variable involved in the study and suggest methodological procedures that are to be employed.

Importance of the Hypotheses

The importance of hypotheses is generally recognized more in the studies, which aim to make predictions about some outcome. In. experimental research; the researcher is interested in making predictions about the outcome of the experiment or what the results are expected to show and therefore the role' of hypotheses is considered to be of utmost importance. In the historical or descriptive research, on the other hand, the researcher is investigating the history of a city or a nation, the life of a man, the happening of an event, or is seeking facts to determine the status quo of some situation and thus may not have a basis for making a prediction of results. A hypothesis, therefore, may not be required in such fact-finding studies. Hillway (1964, p. 130) too is of the view that "when fact-finding alone is the aim of the study, a hypothesis may not be required."

Most historical or descriptive studies, however, involve not only factfinding but interpretation of facts to draw generalizations. If a researcher is tracing the history of an educational institution or making a study about the results of a coming assembly poll, the facts or data he gathers will prove useful only if he is able to draw generalizations from them. Whenever possible, a hypothesis is recommended for all major studies to explain observed facts, conditions, or behaviour and to serve as a guide in the research process. If the hypotheses are not constructed, a researcher may waste much time and energy in gathering extensive empirical data and then find that he cannot state facts clearly and detect relevant relationships between variables, as there is no hypothesis to guide him. The importance of hypotheses may be summarized as under (Ary *et al.* 1972, pp. 73-74)

1. Hypotheses facilitate the extension of knowledge in an area. They provide tentative explanations of facts and phenomena, and can be tested and validated.

   Such explanations, if held valid, lead to generalizations which help significantly in understanding a problem and thereby extend the existing knowledge in the area to which they pertain.
2. Hypotheses provide the researcher with rational statements, consisting *of* elements expressed in a logical order of relationships, which seek to describe or to explain conditions or events that have not yet been confirmed by facts. Some relationships between the elements or variables in hypotheses are known facts and others transcend the known facts to give reasonable explanations for known conditions. The hypotheses enable the researcher to relate logically known facts to intelligent guesses about unknown conditions.
3. Hypotheses provide direction to the research. They represent specific objectives and thus help the researcher to determine the type *of* data needed to test the proposition. The hypotheses tell the researcher specifically what he needs to do and find out in his study. They help in the selection *of* relevant facts and variables that the researcher needs in his study. Hypotheses provide a basis for selecting the sample and the research procedures to be used in the study. The statistical techniques needed in the analysis *of* data, and the relationships between the variables to be tested, are also implied by the hypotheses. Furthermore, the hypotheses help the researcher to delimit his study in scope *so* that it does not become broad or unwieldy.

For example, a researcher is interested in studying the effect of test anxiety on the academic achievement of sixth grade children. He hypothesizes: "There is a negative relationship between the test anxiety and academic achievement of sixth grade students." It is clear from the statement of the hypothesis that the researcher would use an experimental method in which he may compare the academic achievement of a group of sixth grade students with high test anxiety with the achievement of a similar sample of students with low test anxiety. The significance of the difference between the mean academic achievement scores of the two groups could be analyzed by using t-test or analysis of variance technique.

4. Hypotheses provide the basis for reporting the conclusions *of* the study. The researcher will find it very convenient to test each hypothesis separately and state the conclusions that are relevant to each. On the basis *of* these conclusions, he can make the research report interesting and meaningful to the reader.

Formulation of the Hypotheses

Hypotheses are guesses or tentative generalizations, but these guesses are not merely accidents. Collection of factual information alone does not lead to successful formulation of hypotheses. Hypotheses are the products of considerable speculation and imaginative guesswork. They are based partly on known facts and explanations, and partly conceptual. There are no precise rules for formulating hypotheses and deducing consequences from them -that can be empirically verified. However, there are certain necessary conditions that are conducive to their formulation. Some of them are:

1. Richness of background knowledge. A researcher may deduce hypotheses inductively after making observations of behaviour, noticing trends or probable relationships. For example, a classroom teacher daily observes student behaviour. On 'the basis of his experience and his knowledge of behviour in a school situation, the teacher may attempt to relate the behaviour of students to his own, to his teaching methods, to changes in the school environment, and so on. From these observed relationships, the teacher may inductively formulate a hypothesis that attempts to explain such relationships.

Background knowledge, however, is essential for perceiving relation ships among the variables and to determine what findings other researchers have reported on the problem under study. One finds limitless knowledge in almost any area of human pursuit, which has accumulated, in the form of literature as a result of painstaking efforts of past generations. New knowledge, new discoveries, and new inventions should always form continuity with the already existing corpus of knowledge and, therefore, it becomes all the more essential to be well versed with the already existing knowledge. The researcher may be led astray, if he does not have thorough acquaintance with and mastery of the existing knowledge.

Relevant to a particular problem, various researchers may have different hypotheses, but the soundness of the hypotheses will depend upon the quantum of knowledge that one possesses of the area of investigation. Significant researches have not taken place accidentally and if it be a mere accident to come cross some important discovery, the researcher must have the rich background knowledge which may enable him to perceive that important discovery. Closed minds tend to see problems from a narrow and biased viewpoint, but liberal and objective educated minds look at them from multiple points of view suggested by their multiple experiences. Persons who have rich experiences and academic background may formulate hypotheses correctly, but those who have poor background knowledge can never formulate them.

2. Versatility of intellect. Hypotheses are also derived through deductive reasoning from a theory. Such hypotheses are called deductive hypotheses. A researcher may begin a study by selecting one of the theories in his own area of interest. After selecting the particular theory, the researcher proceeds to deduce a hypothesis from this theory through symbolic logic or mathematics. This is possible only when the researcher has a versatile intellect and can make use of it for restructuring his experiences. Creative imagination is the product of an adventure, sound attitude and agile intellect. In the hypotheses formulation, the researcher works on numerous paths and he may be led to blind alleys and only rarely he may be led to the right path. The researcher, therefore, has to exercise great restraint and command considerable patience. He has to make a consistent effort and develop certain habits and attitudes. Moreover, the researcher has to saturate him with all possible information about the problem and then think liberally at it and proceed further in the conduct of the study.

3. Analogy and other practices. Analogies also lead the researcher to clues that he might find useful in the formulation of hypotheses and for finding solutions to problems. For example, suppose a new situation resembles an old situation in regard to a factor X. If the researcher knows from previous experience that the old situation is related to other factors Y and Z as well as to X, he reasons that perhaps a new situation is also related to Y and Z. The researcher, however, should use analogies with caution as they are not fool proof tools for finding solutions to problems.

At times, conversations and consultations with colleagues and experts from different fields are also helpful in formulating important and useful hypotheses.

Criteria of Usable Hypotheses

It is essential that hypotheses be carefully formulated. Travers (1978, pp. 76-78) has suggested seven criteria to which they should conform:

1. Hypotheses should be clearly and precisely stated. When hypotheses are clearly stated, they usually avoid the use of general terms such as personality, intelligence, social class, etc. in their statements. On the other hand, the researcher may use "personality as measured by the Sixteen Personality Factor Questionnaire," "Intelligence as measured by Raven's Progressive matrix", or "social class as defined by Socio-economic Status Scale by Jalota *et al.*" The clear statement of hypotheses generally involves concise technical language and definition of terms that are better defined than those in common language.

2. Hypotheses should be testable. Hypotheses should be formulated in such a way that they can be tested or verified. Such hypotheses enable the researcher to determine by observation whether those consequences that are derived deductively, actually do occur or not. If the hypotheses are not testable, it would be impossible either to confirm or contradict them and therefore they do not help the researcher to draw conclusions. For example, the hypothesis: "The N.C.C. programme promotes all-round adjustment of the high school students" would be hard to test because of the difficulty of defining and measuring "all-round adjustment." Moreover, it would be difficult for the researcher to isolate other factors that might contribute to the adjustment of high school students.

Since hypotheses are predictors of the outcome of the study, they must relate variables that are capable of being measured. It is essential that the tools or instruments should exist (or can be developed) which will provide measures of the variables involved. If no tools or means were available for measuring the variables, then it would be impossible for the researcher to collect the data necessary to test the validity of the hypotheses. A hypothesis, therefore, should define the variables operationally by stating the operations or procedures necessary to measure them. For example, the hypothesis: "There is a negative relationship between neuroticism and achievement in mathematics of fifth grade students' meet the criterion of testability because the variables involved in the statement can be defined operationally. Neuroticism might be defined as "the scores made on the neuroticism-stability scale of Maudsly Personality Inventory" and achievement in mathematics defined as "marks obtained in mathematics by the fifth grade students in their annual examination."

3. Hypotheses should state the expected relationship between variables. A satisfactory hypothesis should state explicitly an expected relationship between the variables. Let us consider two hypotheses:

(i) High school students who attend N.S.S. programmes show greater moral growth than those who do not attend N. S. S. programmes.

(ii) Extraversion, as measured by the Maudsly Personality Inventory, will be related positively to achievement in social studies of seventh grade students, as measured by standardized test X.

The first hypothesis is not usable because the term "greater moral growth" does not refer to a variable that is measurable at the present time, or likely to be measured in the near future. On the other hand, the second hypothesis refers to the variables 'extraversion' and `attainment in social studies' that can be measured by Maudsly Personality Inventory and the standardized test X respectively.

Moreover, the relationship assumed is that the personality variable and the attainment variable will be related positively.

4. Hypotheses should be limited in scope. Hypotheses of global significance are not usable as they are not specific and simple for testing and drawing conclusions. A beginner in research, however, is overly ambitious in his initial efforts and formulates hypotheses of global significance. It is partly because of his earnestness and partly because it takes maturity of viewpoint to realize how little can be accomplished in a specified period. It is desirable to formulate hypotheses that are simple to test, and yet are highly significant. Sometimes it is of course possible to state a rather broad research hypothesis and derive a number of operational hypotheses from it.

5. Hypotheses should be consistent with most known facts. Hypotheses should not be inconsistent with a substantial body of established facts. They should be grounded in the well-established theories and laws. Consider the hypothesis: "There is no relationship between the self concept of adolescent male students and their rate of physical growth." This hypothesis is` not worth testing because the preponderance of evidence supports the relationship between self-concept and rate of physical growth.

Hypotheses, however, cannot be consistent with all known facts, because in many areas, the facts themselves contradict one another. In such cases it is worthwhile to formulate hypotheses that resolve the contradiction.

6. Hypotheses should be stated as for as possible in simple terms. Stating the hypotheses in simple terms not only makes there meaning clear to others, but also helps in their testability. Moreover, the simplicity of statement provides a basis for a clear and easily comprehensible report at the completion of the study. Hypotheses should not make use of the vague terms or constructs. It is quite useless to formulate a hypothesis that makes use of the terms or constructs, which do not convey the intended meaning to the reader. The researcher should make use of such terms that are generally accepted for naming a phenomenon.

7. *The hypotheses selected should be amenable to testing within a reasonable time.* The researcher should not select a problem, which involves hypotheses that are not amenable to testing within a reasonable and specified time. He must know that there are problems that cannot be solved for a long time to come. These are problems of immense difficulty that cannot be profitably studied because of the lack of essential techniques or measures.

Statement of the Hypotheses

A research or substantive hypothesis must be stated in a testable form for its proper evaluation. As already stressed, this form should indicate a relationship between the variables in clear, concise, and understandable language.

Research hypotheses are classified as being *directional* or *non-directional.* The hypotheses, which stipulate the direction of the expected differences or relationships, are termed as direction hypotheses. For example, the research hypothesis: "There will be a positive relationship between individual's attitude towards high caste Hindus and his socio-economic status," is a directional research hypothesis. This hypothesis stipulates that individuals with favourable attitude towards high caste Hindus will generally come from higher socio-economic Hindu families and therefore it does stipulate the direction of the relationship. Similarly, the hypothesis: "Adolescent boys with high IQ will exhibit low anxiety than adolescent boys with low IQ" is a direction) research hypothesis because it stipulates the direction of the difference between groups.

A research hypothesis, which does not specify the direction of expected differences or relationships, is a non-directional research hypothesis. For example, the hypotheses: "There will be difference in the adaptability of fathers and mothers towards rearing of their children" or "There is a difference in the anxiety level of adolescent girls of high IQ and low IQ" are non-directional research hypotheses. Although these hypotheses stipulate there will be a difference, the direction of the difference is not specified.

A research hypothesis can take *declarative* form, the *null* form, or the *question* form.

When the researcher makes a positive statement about the outcome of the study, the hypothesis takes the declarative form. For example, the hypothesis: "The academic achievement of extroverts is significantly higher than that of the introverts," is stated in the declarative form. In such a statement of hypothesis, the researcher makes a prediction based on his theoretical formulations of what should happen if the explanations of the behaviour he has given in his theory are correct.

In the null form, the researcher makes a statement that no relationship exists. The hypothesis, "There is no significant difference between the academic achievement of high school athletes and that of non athletes," is an example of null hypothesis. Since null hypotheses can be tested statistically, they are often termed as *statistical* hypotheses. They are also called the *testing* hypotheses when declarative hypotheses are tested statistically by converting them into null form. This often happens in educational research.

A null hypothesis challenges the assertion of a declarative hypothesis and denies it altogether. It states that even where it seems to hold good it is due to mere chance. It is for the researcher to reject the null hypothesis by showing that the outcome mentioned in the declarative hypothesis does occur and the quantum of it is such that it cannot be easily dismissed as having occurred by chance. The criteria for rejecting the null hypothesis may differ. Sometimes the null hypothesis is rejected only when the quantity of the outcome is so large that the probability of its having occurred by mere chance is 1 time out of 100 or .01 time out of 1. We consider the probability of its having occurred by chance to be too little and we reject the chance theory of the null hypothesis and take the occurrence to be due to a genuine tendency. On other occasions, we may be bolder and reject the null hypothesis even when the quantity of the reported outcome is likely to occur by chance 5' times out of 100 or .05 time out of 1. Statistically the former is known as the rejection of the null hypothesis at .01 level of significance and the latter as the rejection at .05 levels.

It may be pointed out that if the researcher is able to reject the null hypothesis, he cannot directly uphold the declarative hypothesis. If an outcome is not held to be due to chance, it does not mean that it is due to the very cause and effect relationship asserted in the particular declarative statement. It may be due to something else which the researcher may have failed control. However strong inferentially the case of the declarative hypothesis becomes quite strong. The less plausible the null hypothesis is, the more plausible is the declarative one. Hayman (1968, p. 23) is of the opinion that null hypothesis should not be used as an alternative to the declarative one, but should be used in combination with it for statistical purposes.

In the question form hypothesis, a question is asked as to what a outcome will be, instead of stating what outcome expected. Suppose has researcher is interested in knowing whether programmed any relationship to test anxiety of children. The declarative form instruction hypothesis might be:

"Teaching children through programmed instruction material will have no effect on their test anxiety". This statement shows that no relationship exists between programmed instruction and test anxiety. The question form puts the statement in the form: "Will teaching children through programmed instruction decrease their test anxiety?"

A novice in research finds it relatively easy to state a hypothesis in question form. It seems easy for him to write down all of the questions that some difficulty in declarative form. However, it must be noted by the researcher that the question form is less powerful than the declarative or null form as a tool for obtaining valid information.

Testing of the Hypotheses

Hypotheses are possible explanations, which account for the factors, events, or conditions that the researcher attempts to understand. After they are formulated according to the criteria discussed, they are subjected to the empirical as well as logical testing:

1. Some hypotheses are simple and can be tested directly. In most situations, however, they are complex and cannot be so tested. They have to be tested in terms of their deduced consequences. In scientific thinking process, the hypotheses involve deduction of consequences. Suppose a researcher wants to test the hypothesis: "Affluence leads to immorality"; he cannot test this hypothesis directly and he has to proceed pro indirectly. He might deduce the consequences emanating out of the situation of affluence, reason, giving rise to greater crime rates, adultery, fast driving, etc. It would then be considerably convenient to test the hypothesis in terms of its deduced consequences. Indirect method of handling research problems involves intricate and complex procedures. Intellectual and disciplined effort is needed for the deduction of consequences. In this way the researcher does not test the hypothesis, but tests the deduced consequences of the hypothesis. Once all the deduced consequences, after testing, come out to be true, the hypothesis is confirmed. If some of the consequences are true and some others not, the hypothesis needs to be examined afresh.

In order to test the hypothesis in terms of deduced consequences, it is necessary to collect evidence by selecting or developing data collecting instruments, to analyse the data, and then to interpret results in the light of the hypothesis and its deduced consequences. Any hypothesis then will be confirmed if the evidence agrees with the deduced consequences.

The necessary conditions for confirmation are:

(a) All factual evidences collected through tests or other means should correspond with the deduced consequences.

(b) The test situations or data collecting tools should take into account all factors and conditions that are suggested by the consequences.

(c) The consequences are logically deduced from the hypotheses.

2. The absence of conflict with the other satisfactorily proved generalizations lends support to the correctness of a hypothesis.

3. A hypothesis is also confirmed to be correct if the predictions made on its basis prove to be successful.

It is important for the researcher to formulate hypotheses before data are gathered. This is necessary for an objective and unbiased study.

Hypothesis in Various Types of Research

Nevins (1962) illustrates the use of hypotheses in the historical research of Edward Chananing in answering the question, "Why did the Confederacy collapse in April 1865?" Channing formulated four hypotheses and tested each one in light of evidence gathered from letters, diaries, and official records of the army and the government of the Confederacy. He hypothesized that the Confederacy collapsed because of

1. The military defeat of the Confederate army
2. The dearth of military supplies
3. The starving condition of the Confederate soldiers and the civilians
4. The disintegration of the will to continue the war

Channing produced evidence that seemed to refute the first three hypotheses. More than 200,000 well-equipped soldiers were under arms at the time of the surrender, the effective production of powder and arm'; provided sufficient military supplies to continue the war, and enough food was available to sustain fighting men and civilians.

Channing concluded the excessive number of desertions of enlisted men and officers substantiated that hypothesis 4, the disintegration of the will to continue the war. Confederate military officials testified that they had intercepted many letters from home urging the soldiers to desert. Although the hypothesis sustained was not specific enough to be particularly helpful, the rejection of the first three did claim to dispose of some commonly held explanations. This example illustrates a historical study in which hypotheses were explicitly stated.

Hypotheses in Educational Historical Research

Hypotheses may be formulated in historical investigations of education. Several examples are listed.

1. The educational innovations of the 1950s and 1960s were based upon practices that previously have been tried and discarded.

2. Christian countries whose educational systems required religious instruction have had lower church attendance rates than those countries in which religious instruction was not provided in the schools.

3. The observation of European school systems by American educators during the nineteenth century had an important effect upon American educational practices.

4. The monitorial system had no significant effect upon American education.

Although hypotheses are not always *explicitly* stated in historical investigations, they are usually implied. The historian gathers evidence c and carefully evaluates its trustworthiness. If the evidence is compatible with the consequences of the hypothesis, it is confirmed. If the evidence is not compatible, or negative, the hypothesis is not confirmed. It is through such synthesis that historical generalizations are established.

The activities of the historian, when education is his or her field of inquiry, are no different from those employed in any other field. I he sources of evidence may be concerned with schools, educational practices and policies, movements, or individuals, but the historical processes' ate the same.

Stating of Hypotheses of Experimental Research

The stating of problem hypotheses is one of the distinguishing characteristics of experimental method. Hypotheses are the heart of experimental research. They suggest that an antecedent condition or phenomenon (independent variable) is related to the occurrence of another condition, phenomenon, event, or effect (dependent variable). To test a hypothesis, the researcher attempts to control all the conditions accept the independent variable, which he manipulates.

Then he observes the effect on the dependent variable presumably because of the exposure to the independent variable. The researcher, therefore, should not only be concerned primarily with experimental plans and statistical procedures, but should give sufficient attention to the formulation of hypotheses. The experimental plans and statistical procedures merely help him in the testing of hypotheses and contribute little in the development of theories or advancement of knowledge. The hypotheses developed or derived from existing theories, however, contribute to the development of new theories and knowledge.

Research Questions

"In qualitative research, questions and problems for research most often come from real-world observations, dilemmas, and questions" (Marshall & Rossman, 1989, p. 28). Marshall and Rossman go on to suggest a number of questions with wide-ranging implications such as:

"Why is the program working well in this school but not in others? What is special about the people? The plan? The support? The context?" (p. 28)

"What are the various techniques used by lobbying groups as they try to influence education policy? Which are perceived to be the most effective?" (p. 28).

"How does play affect reading readiness? Through what cognitive and affective processes?" (p. 28).

"How do school-parent community relations of private and parochial schools differ from those of public schools? How are the differences connected with differences in educational philosophies and outcomes?" (p. 29).

"How do school superintendents gain control over school board members? What influence processes do they use?" (p. 29)

Other research questions that best could be answered with qualitative research methods include:

How do school principals spend their time?

What do teachers think the principal's role is and/or should be?

What actually takes place at school board meetings in a particular school district based on observations and school board minutes?

How do young children react to standardized testing situations?

How do state legislators view the state affiliates of the National Education Association and the American Federation of Teacher?

COLLECTION OF DATA

Research tools are administered on the sample subjects for collecting evidences or data. Most educational research will lead to the gathering of data by means of some standardized test or self-constructed research tools. It should provide objective data for interpretation of results achieved in the study. Administering questionnaires, testing, personal observations, interviews and many other techniques of collecting quantitative and qualitative evidence may obtain the data.

The researcher must know how much and what kind of data collection will take place and when. He must also be sure that the types of data obtainable from the selected instruments will be usable in whatever statistical model he wills latter use to bring out the significance of the study. The data collection is the accumulation of specific evidence that will enable the researcher to properly analyse the results of all activities by his research design and procedures. The main purpose of data collection is to verify the research hypotheses.

Need for Data Collection

The data are needed in a research work to serve the following purposes:

1. Collection of data is very essential in any educational research to provide a solid foundation for it.

2. It is something like the raw material that is used in the production of data. Quality of data determines the quality of research.

3. It provides a definite direction and definite answer to a research inquiry. Whatever inquiry has to give a definite answer to an investigation. Data are very essential for a scientific research,

4. The data are needed to substantiate the various arguments In research findings.

5. The main purpose of data collection is to verify the hypotheses.

6. Statistical data are used in two basic problems of any investigation

   (1) Estimation of population parameters, which helps in drawing generalization. '

   (2) The hypotheses of any investigation are tested by data collection procedure.

7. The qualitative data are used to find out the facts and quantitative data are employed to formulate new theory or principles.

8. Data are also employed to ascertain the effectiveness of new device for its practical utility. Data are necessary to provide the solution of the problem.

Meaning of Data

Data means observations or evidences. The scientific educational researches require the data by means of some standardized research tools or self-designed instrument. Data are both qualitative and quantitative in nature.

Score is the numerical description of an individual with regard to some characteristics or variables. Measurement process is employed to quantify a variable. Data are collected for both variables as well as attributes. These are gathered in terms of frequency and scores. It depends on the type of instrument employed for its measurement. Generally tests yield the data in the form of scores and questionnaires provide the data in the form of frequency. Data are things with which we think of.

Data and facts are used in educational research; therefore, it is essential to understand them clearly.

Difference Between Facts and Data

The facts and data have been distinguished in the following manner:

1 The facts are organized in their original form whereas data are organized in systematic order.

2. The facts do not have any coherence of system whereas data have an organic unity like body.

3. The facts are difficult to interpret. The interpretation of facts is usually subjective and employs the imagination of the researcher. Data can be interpreted easily and most objectively.

4. The facts are mysterious in nature we have to explore the facts but data have no mystery at all.

5. The facts are descriptive in nature whereas data are explanatory.

6. The facts are not amenable to objective statistical treatments whereas data can be easily *subjected to* in objective statistical treatment.

7. The facts may not be directly the basis of findings or research conclusions, but data are directly linked with research conclusions.

8. The facts are usually too broad and are not linked and *a* purposive *way* whereas data are always collected with a sense of purpose.

9. The facts are collected in historical or survey research whereas data e gathered in a scientific and experimental research.

TYPES OF DATA

The data collected from various sources through the use of different tools and techniques generally comprise of numerical figures, ratings, descriptive narrations, responses to open-ended questions, field secretive narrations, responses to open-ended questions, quotations, field notes etc. In educational research, usually two types of data are recognised. They are quantitative data and qualitative data.

I. Quantitative Data

Applying various scales of measurement gets quantitative data. The experiences of people are fit into standardised responses to which numerical values are attached, these data are close-ended and hardly provide any depth and detail. The quantitative data are either parametric or non-parametric.

Parametric data are measured data on interval or ratio scales of measurement. Non-parametric data are obtained by applying nominal or ordinal scales of measurement. These data are either counted or ranked.

2. Qualitative Data

Qualitative data are verbal or other symbolic materials. The detailed descriptions of observed behaviours, people, situations and events, are some examples of qualitative data. The responses to open-ended questions of a questionnaire or a schedule, first hand information from people about their experiences. Ideas, beliefs, etc., and selected content or excerpts from documents, case histories, personal diaries and letters are other examples of qualitative data.

CHARACTERISTICS OF A GOOD TOOL

There are many kinds of devices used by the researchers for collecting the data. Among them the most used ones are the psychological tests of various kinds. This section is devoted to the discussion of characteristics of a good psychological tool.

What makes a psychological device a good tool of assessment concerns both the researchers and the teachers in the field of education. It is one of the most basic questions confronting those who construct and use tests. Some of the factors that need to be considered in judging the quality of a test are

1. Relevance.
2. Balance
3. Efficiency
4. Objectivity
5. Specificity

Difficulty

)iscrimination

'ability

'y

'ty

1. Relevance-Relevance is one of the aspects of quality in a test. It emphasizes that the test must consist of items, which are relevant for the purpose to be fulfilled by the test. Hence. It requires a clear statement of the need-characteristics of the items. Relevance of psychological tool is determined by the extent to which the items in it possess the desired characteristics, i.e., relevance for the purpose in the particular set of circumstances. The items included in the test must provide tasks appropriate to the purpose of the test. For example, a test prepared for survey of intelligence in a large group may not be relevant for a few highly intelligent persons. Similarly, a test of creativity may not be relevant for measuring teaching aptitude items measuring interest in a particular job-field may not be relevant for measuring job satisfaction. Items measuring general achievement in a language test may not be relevant for measurement of creative art expression.

Relevance has nothing to do with such things, as item difficulty, possible ambiguity, grammatical flaws, semantic weaknesses, etc. which affect the discrimination power of the items, nor, it is intended to guarantee high quality items. It is intended only to answer the question "Does it serve the purpose ?

2. **Balance**-This refers to the desired proportions of items that measure each aspect of the trait. For example, if a test of academic alienation is based on measuring three dimensions such as mean meaninglessness, normlessness, powerlessness and if one dimension has 10 items, another 20 items, still another 15 items this cannot be considered a balanced test unless such differential weights are empirically justified.The quality of balance emphasizes that the test-items must sample representatively all the important aspects of the trait to be measured. For example, an aptitude test for teaching must specify in a balanced manner the number and types of items measuring different abilities that make for success in teaching profession. In case of an achievement test, similarly, a two-way grid called "blueprint" may be used to ensure balance by specifying the number of items and weight age given to various types of content and objectives of teaching.

3. Efficiency-A test that yields a large number of independent scorable responses per unit of time is the efficient test. An efficient test is one that consists of efficient items, efficient administration and scoring procedures. An item is efficient if it can be objectively scored in shortest possible time. An essay test is not efficient for that reason. T.A.T. and Rorschach tests too are not efficient if viewed in this context. Items involving difficult words and long sentences are less efficient. Objective *type* and machine scorable items are more efficient than sentence completion and fill-up the blank type items.

An efficient test makes the best use of the 'instructor's and students' time. In order to be efficient a test should not be too long. EPPS personality test cannot be considered an efficient test from this point of view. Although the longer test is said to be more reliable a test taking more than three hours time is considered impractical.

4. Objectivity-A test item is considered objective if all the experts choose the same alternative among several suggested ones as correct or give essentially the same free response answer. Essay type of tests is the *least objective from this point of view. An objective type of item, too,* does not automatically, produce objectivity in it. Objectivity is, however, an unavoidable quality to be looked into while constructing or selecting a psychological tool. Objectivity is reduced if the supposed truth, principle or theory on which a test-item is based is open to question, or if it is not stated explicitly. Items based on opinions or hypotheses cannot be expected to have sufficient objectivity. Most tests of personality seem to be weak from this point of view. Items based on factual information have high degree of objectivity. Items based on generalizations, interpretations, evaluation, and recommended action etc. increase the room for differences of opinions even among experts.. Though, such types of items are considered significant as they are said to be measuring higher levels of understanding and ability, they are less reliable.

5. Specificity-It is the complement of objectivity. A test shows specificity if a test wise novice in the field covered by the test receives a *near chance score. If an examinee's scores on a test depends to a* considerable degree on his general problem-solving or test-taking ability *rather than on his specific ability or knowledge required for performance* on the said test, this implies the test's specify. Items designed to test interpretation; evaluative judgement and recommended action are less specific, less efficient and less reliable.

Specificity is the most-important quality of a test, particularly of an Achievement test. It can be gauged by administering the test to several intelligent and testwise novices. The lower the score of these novices, the better. It should always be less than 20% of the difference between chance and perfect scores above the chance score. (R.L. Ebel, 1966, p. 298).

6. Difficulty-Ebel (p.298) says a test (in case of an achievement test) in which the average score is somewhat more than half of the maximum possible score is appropriate in difficulty. Roughly, this may be true in case of other tests also. Ebel also says that if the average score on a test is very much higher or very much lower than the midpoint of the range between highest possible and expected chance scores the test may be inefficient. In this case students may be wasting their time trying to answer questions, which nobody can answer, or reading and answering questions, which almost everyone can answer correctly. Expected chance score equals the number of items divided by number or alternative choices, e.g., in case of 50 item five-choices test it would be 10.

7. Discrimination-Good discrimination power of the test-items is another essential characteristic of a good test. It is indicated by the difference between good and poor or high and low groups of students on test. The more items classified as highly or moderately diascrimating the better the test. If the test items discriminate clearly between good and poor students the test scores will vary widely and the total test scores will also discriminate clearly between students at different levels of ability.

Score variability is measured by the standard deviation of the scores. The larger it is the better the test. A standard deviation of 1 /6 of the range between highest and the expected change score is said to be quite satisfactory. One-fourth S.D. of the range makes a poor test. If a test is too hard, too easy or composed of too many poorly discriminating items it will yield scores having a small standard deviation. Size of S.D. is an important factor of test reliability. Larger the S.D. higher the reliability.

8. Reliability-Reliability is, often, considered the most important statistical measure of the quality of a psychological test. It depends on several factors such as (i) number of items, (ii) item discrimination, (iii) item objectivity and (vi) difference among students on the trait measured. It is important because it determines test's validity also.

9. Validity-An appraisal instrument that measures what it claims to measure is valid. No test possesses "all-purpose" validity. A test may be highly valid for use in one situation, but invalid if used in another situation. APA. in 1966 defined the types of validity which should he used in assessing the usefulness of tests for a particular purpose. These are : (i) content validity, (ii) criterion-related validity, and (iii) construct validity The content validity is of great importance in case of achievement while criterion-related validity and construct validity are more important in case of tests of personality, intelligence, attitudes, aptitudes, values, etc. Construct validity is more difficult to assess and more difficult to understand. It is established by making inferences about things, which cannot be observed directly, e.g., intelligence, motivation, values, etc. In case of these tests face validity is also considered very important.

10. Suitability-Van Dalen and Meyer (1966) mention that when selecting a test, scale or inventory one must determine whether the instrument is suitable for the purpose. It is almost the same as relevance of the test. He must ask the questions: will it obtain the type of data that are needed? Will it produce measurement that is sufficiently precise for his purpose? Will it be suitable for the age and grade, subjects, time, locality in which he intends to use it. If two tests are equally reliable and valid, the test that is cheaper, more quickly and easily scored. Available in alternative forms and accompanied by norms and the manual should be selected.

INQUIRY FORMS

Inquiry forms are a set of data-gathering research tools, which make use of properly designed proformas for inquiring into, and securing information about certain phenomena schedule, checklist to ratings scale, score card and gory are questionnaire or attitude scale.

Questionnaire

A questionnaire is a device consisting of a series of questions dealing with some psychological, social, educational, etc; topic(s) sent or given to an- individual or a group of individuals, with the object of obtaining data with regard to some problems under investigation. Goode and Hatt (1952, p. 33) state that in general the word `questionnaire' refers to a device for securing answers to a series of questions by using a form which the respondent fills in himself. Barr *et al.* (1953, p. 65) define questionnaire as a systematic compilation of questions that are administered to a sample of population from which information is desired.

Questionnaire is a popular means of collecting all kinds of data in research. It is widely used in educational research to obtain information about certain conditions and practices, and to inquire into opinions and attitudes of an individual or a group. A questionnaire is either administered personally to a group of individuals or it is mailed to them to save a great deal of time and money in travel. In the former situation, the person administering the tools has an opportunity to establish rapport with the respondents, to explain the purpose of the study to the respondents, and to explain the meaning of questions to the respondents that may not be clear to them. In the latter situation, the mailed questionnaire is probably both the most used and most abused data-gathering research tool. It is mostly used when the individuals from whom we desire information cannot always be contacted personally without the expenditure of great deal of time and money in travel. The range of administration of a mailed questionnaire may be national or international. A mailed questionnaire is mostly criticized, because of an unfavourable reaction it generates among the respondents, to answer questions from strangers on subjects they are least interested in. Best (1977, p. 157) calls it "as the lazy man's way of gaining information". He. is of the opinion that the unfavourable reaction among the respondents is intensified when the questionnaire is long, the subject trivial in importance, the question items vaguely worded, and the form poorly organized. As a result of this, a small proportion of mailed questionnaires are returned, and therefore, the data obtained are of low validity. Best (1977, p. 167) cautions that a mailed questionnaire may be used with a group of respondents who have a genuine interest in the problem under investigation, who know the sender, or who have some common bond of loyalty to a sponsoring institution or organization.

Classification of Questionnaires

The questionnaires can be classified in terms of the nature of the questions, which are used. Questions may be asked in a closed or an open *form.* The researcher may use one type exclusively or both in combination. Questionnaires that call for short or check responses are known as closed form or restricted type. They include a set of questions to which respondents can reply in a limited number of ways. The respondent is invariably permitted to reply only with `yes' or `no', or 'no-opinion', or is requested to select an answer from a short list of possible responses. He is asked to place a tick (✓)mark in a space provided on the answer sheet or he may be requested to underline a response. Sometimes he is asked to insert brief answers of his own. For certain type of information, the closed type of questionnaire is useful, because it is easy to respond, takes little time to fill out, is relatively objective and is fairly easy to tabulate and analyse. While using closed-type of question items, it is advisable to provide for unanticipated responses by allowing an `open' category of response with a request, 'please specify' or `kindly mention' which enables the researcher to properly tabulate and classify such responses. The following example illustrates such type of question items:

Please tick mark (✓) the reasons given below for not introducing the `Grade system of Marking' by your school.

(a) Non-availability of administrative guidance and support ( )

(b) Non-availability of academic guidance and support ( )

(c) It is time-consuming ( )

(d) It is not effective in overcoming the defects of Numerical Marking ( )

(e) It cannot be changed and adopted according to the local/institutional needs. ( )

(f) Any other, please mention. ( )

... ...

... ...

... ...

... ...

... ...

The open-form or unrestricted type of questionnaire calls for a free response in the respondent's own words. The form of the questions is unstructured and no clues are provided to the respondent. The open form of questions provides for-greater depth of response and the greatest advantage of this type of questions is freedom that is given to the respondent to reveal his opinion and to clarify his responses. However, the responses to such type of questions are sometimes difficult to tabulate, organize and interpret. The following example illustrates this type of question:

State the reasons for not introducing the 'Grade-System of Marking' in your school.

Construction of Questionnaire

Constructing a good questionnaire requires both ability and perseverance on the part of the researcher. He should not use a `shotgun approach' by attempting to cover his field of investigation broadly in the hope that some of the responses will provide answers for which he is searching blindly. There are some hints, which a researcher may consider, useful while constructing, administering and analysing a questionnaire.

1. Purposes of the questionnaire. A good questionnaire must serve two major purposes. First, it must translate the objectives of an investigation into specific questions, the answers to which will provide the data necessary to test the hypotheses and explore the area defined by the objectives. For this, each question must convey to the respondent the meaning of each objective so that the responses thus obtained can be analysed and interpreted properly in the light of the research objectives. 'The statement of the research objectives and the specification of the data required to meet those objectives must precede questionnaire construction. Secondly, the questionnaire must motivate the respondents to communicate the required information. It is essential to include a courteous and carefully constructed covering letter to explain the purpose of the study. The covering letter should assure the respondent that delicate information will be held in strict confidence. The respondents will feel favourably disposed towards the inquiry if the purpose and nature of the study are stated in the covering letter.

2. Language. In the construction of a questionnaire, the primary criterion for the choice of language is that the vocabulary and syntax should offer maximum opportunity for complete and accurate communication of ideas between the researcher and the respondent. Since the researcher has to depend on written language alone to get the required information, he has to be careful while phrasing the questions. There are some principles that might be employed to make the Questions more precise. According to Best and Kahn *(1992, pp 184-185)* following are the principles of making the questions more precise:

(a) Define or qualify terms that could easily be misinterpreted. Such common words like `how much', `new', `curriculum', `democracy', 'progressive· education', `cooperation', and `integration' are all liable to misinterpretation. To the question, "What work are you engaged in now?" the respondent may be tempted to answer, "Filling, out your foolish questionnaire."

(b) Be careful in using descriptive adjectives and adverbs that have no agreed upon meaning. This fault is frequently found in rating scales as well as in questionnaire, `Frequently', `occasionally', and `rarely' do not have the same meanings to different persons. One respondent's 'occasion ally' may be another's `rarely'.

(c) Beware of double negative. For example, the use of double negative in "The State Government should *not* provide aid to the educational institutions in which education is *not* equal, regardless of race, creed, or caste" is misleading.

(d) Be careful of inadequate alternatives. In the question: "Are you married? Yes-No-" the alternatives Yes/No are inadequate. Does this question refer to present or former marital status? How would the person answer who is widowed, separated, or divorced?

(e) Avoid the double-barreled questions. "iv e them into two questions. Do you believe that gifted children should be placed in separate groups for instructional purposes and assigned to special schools?

In this question, one might agree on the advisability of separate groups for instructional purposes, but be very much opposed to the assignment of gifted students to special schools.

(f) Underline a word if you wish to indicate special emphasis. For example, "Should all schools offer modern foreign language?" will get the desired responses more easily than if the word modern was not emphasized by underlining.

(g) When asking for rating or comparisons, a point of reference is necessary. For example, "How would you rate this student teacher's classroom teaching? Superior-Average-Below Average" is vague until the respondent is

told with whom is the student teacher to be compared-an experienced teacher, other student teachers, former student teachers-or should the criterion be what a student teacher is expected to be able to do ?

(h) Avoid unwarranted assumptions. For example, to the question, "Are you satisfied with the salary rise that you received last year?" a `no' answer might mean that the respondent did not get any rise, or that he is not satisfied wilt the rise that he got.

(i) Phrase questions so that they are appropriate for all respondents. For example, "How many days per week do you send your student-teachers for practice teaching?" may not suit all respondents as some training colleges have continuous, some block, and some a combination of block and continuous teaching practice.

(j) Design questions that will give a complete response. The question would not reveal much information about the reading habits of the respondent. An additional item should follow it.

(k) Provide for the systematic quantification of responses. To ask respondents to rank, in order of preference, a specific number of responses from a given list of items permit a convenient way of tabulation by inverse weightings:

1st Choice	5 points
2nd Choice	4 points
3rd Choice	3 points
4th Choice	2 points
5th Choice	1 point.

The total weighted scores would be the score for the particular item.

(l) Consider the possibility of classifying the responses yourself rather than having the respondent choose categories. For example, if a respondent is asked to classify his occupation in the following categories, the result might be quite unsatisfactory.

(i) Skilled labour ____________

(ii) Unskilled labour ____________

(iii) Clerical work ____________

(iv) Managerial work ____________

(v) Profession ____________

(vi) Proprietorship ____________

It is likely that by asking the respondent one or two short questions about his work, it could be classified more accurately. .

(i) At what place do you work ?

(ii) What kind of work do you perform?

3. Information level of the respondents. The assumptions about the expertness of the respondent in a particular field or the amount of information he possesses should not be unrealistic. The information elicited by the questionnaire must lie within the respondent's present level of information.

The questions above the information level of respondents may result in resentment and embarrassment among the respondents. This problem is sometimes referred to as `expert error', that is, the error of ascribing to the respondent a degree of expertness in a particular field, which he does not possess.

4. *Social acceptance of responses.* The questions must provide the respondent a range *of* responses, which meets his criteria of social acceptability. A question constitutes a threat to the respondent's ego if he is, required to give an answer, which he feels, is socially unacceptable. The respondent should not be confronted with the necessity of giving a socially unacceptable response to a question. The annoying or embarrassing questions must be avoided.

If the information desired from the respondents is of intimate or delicate nature, consider the possibility of providing for anonymous responses to get objective and reliable information. Even if the respondent's name is necessary for the purposes of classification, it is essential to assure the respondent that his responses will be kept strictly confidential.

5. Leading questions. The questions should be objective with no leading suggestions as to the most appropriate response. For example, in a question "Would you say that you are in favour of co-education in secondary schools?", it is easier for the respondent to answer `yes' than 'no'. In answering `yes' he is merely agreeing with the language of the question. It is more difficult to respond, "no", since this response seems to contradict, or at least goes counter to the ideas of the person who worded the question. There are some words which involve respondents emotionally, either favourably or unfavourably, in a particular culture. It is advisable not to make use of such emotionally `loaded' words while phrasing questions of a questionnaire.

6. Sequence of questions. First, the questions should be limited to a single idea or to a single reference. Secondly, the questionnaire maker needs to give thought to the arrangement of the questions in a questionnaire. The questions should be so arranged that they permit the ideas of the respondents to flow logically. The sequence of questions must facilitate the easy progress of the respondent from, item to item and it should lead the respondent to anticipate the next question. Questions should be presented in a good psychological order by adopting the `funnel approach'. This is a procedure of asking the most general or the most unrestricted questions first and following it with successively more specific and restricted questions. This order helps the respondent to organize his own thinking and motivates him to respond logically and objectively. The following sequence. of questions on the `introduction of the innovation of internal assessment', illustrates the funnel approach:

(i) Is the innovation introduced by your school Yes/No

(ii) If yes, please mention the year from which it was introduced ....

(iii) Is the innovation still continuing in your school ? Yes/No

(iv) If yes, please tick mark (✓) how far the innovation has been useful in overcoming the defects of purely `External Public Examination'

(a) Greatly useful ( )

(b) Considerably useful ( )

(c) Somewhat useful ( )

(d) Little useful ( )

(e) Not useful ( )

(f) Not known ( )

(v) If no, please mention the year from which the innovation was discontinued

(vi) Please tick mark (√) the reasons given below for discontinuing, or not introducing the innovation :

(a) There is persistent over-assessment of the candidates by the teachers for extra-academic consideration such as personal like and dislikes, caste and community, payment of money for private tuition or through other forms of subterfuge.

(b) The innovation lowers the standard of education ( )

(c) The innovation makes the standard different from school to school. ( )

(d) The innovation is time-consuming ( )

(e) The innovation is highly expensive and requires large expenditure ( )

(f) Any other, please mention ( )

....

....

....

(vii) On the basis of your experience and scholarship you may wish to provide any additional information about the innovation which is not covered above. If so, please mention.

....

....

....

7. The form or type of questions. Another important consideration that weighs in the matter of constructing a questionnaire is that of 'form or type' of questions. As discussed earlier, the questionnaire may contain closed or open type of questions. Each type of these questions has its merits and limitations and the questionnaire framer must decide which type is more likely to supply the information required. Kahn and Cannell *(1957)* are of the opinion that the closed type of questions are well adapted to situations in which (1) there is only one frame of reference from which the respondent can answer the question; (2) within this single frame of reference, there is a known range of possible responses; and (3) within this range, there are clearly defined choice points which accurately represent the position of each respondent. In the open type of questions, the respondent is encouraged to structure his answer as he wishes and it permits the respondent to state his own frame of reference when this is desirable. In some research situations, it is useful to include both the open and the closed type of questions in combination.

8. Length of the questionnaire. A questionnaire should not be any longer than is necessary. The total number of questions must not be so many as to tire or bore the respondents. If too many questions are asked and the respondent becomes tired, the questions at the end of the series may not be well answered. If it is necessary to include a larger number of questions, it is advisable to have two separate questionnaires.

9. Experts' opinion. It is advisable to get all the help from experts for planning and constructing a questionnaire. Questions should be submitted to the experts for criticism and modified accordingly.

10. Preliminary tryout of the questionnaire. No matter how careful the questionnaire maker has been in phrasing his questions and designing his questionnaire, he needs to try them out with a few representative samples of the respondents before launching into the actual investigation. The first purpose of the pre-test is to examine the questionnaire from the research point of view. It is suggested that interviews with respondents should be conducted to see whether the responses fulfil the objectives of the investigation. Sometimes the tryout calls for major revision of the questionnaire and several tryouts are required until a workable questionnaire is developed. The second purpose of the tryout is to determine the extent to which the questionnaire fulfils the following two criteria:

(i) Does the questionnaire promote a congenial and appropriate relationship with respondents?

(ii) Do respondents understand the questions without having to be explained or reworded?'

11. Validation of a questionnaire. The validation of a questionnaire utilizes the same principles and procedures as the validation of any tool of measurement. Each question of the questionnaire must be related obviously to the topic under investigation.' In some situations, the questionnaire is validated against the actual overt behaviour, which acts as the external criterion. Relating question responses with the actual behaviour does this. Follow-up observations of respondent behaviour at a particular time or at some time in the future are also used to estimate the predictive validity of some types of questionnaires.

12. Reliability of a questionnaire. The test-retest method is the feasible approach to the working out of the reliability of questionnaires. The comparison of responses of an alternate form with the original form of questionnaire is also made to estimate the reliability. Besides, consistency of the question responses, the accuracy of responses and the comparison of the accuracy of the question responses to the interview may also be taken note of while talking of the reliability of questionnaire.

13. Administration of a questionnaire. The questionnaire can call for written or oral responses. Some questionnaires are designed with the intention that they should be answered in writing; others are designed in a way, which require an oral response. Questionnaires, which require written replies, are administered either by post or in a group situation such as a group of students in a class. It is always advisable to send a self-addressed stamped envelope along with the questionnaire to exert a moral pressure for return of duly filled questionnaire administered by post. In case of delay, one or two reminders may be helpful. In some situations, *it* may be appropriate to send another copy of the questionnaire with the follow-up letter. Questionnaires, which call for oral replies, are usually presented to one subject at a time in an interview.

The percentage return of questionnaires affects the degree of confidence a researcher may place in the data collected. If the percentage of response is greater, the researcher may have greater confidence in the collected data. A response rate of 50 per cent has been considered adequate whereas 60 per cent as good.

14. Analysing and interpreting questionnaire responses. Quantification of data obtained by the questionnaire is generally achieved through tabulation and counting. The totals are converted into proportions or percentages. Calculation of contingency coefficients of correlation is often made in order to suggest probability of relationship among data. Computation of Chi-square statistics is also advisable.

Limitation of a Questionnaire

1. The questionnaire cannot be used with children and illiterates.
2. The return of the mailed questionnaire is often as low as *40* per cent to 50 per cent. As a result of this poor response, the data obtained are often of limited validity. The respondents who return the questionnaires may not be representative of the' entire group. It will make the sample a biased one and thus vitiate the findings.
3. Sometimes respondents may not like to respond in writing to the questions of intimate and confidential nature or to the question involving certain controversial issues.
4. It is sometimes difficult to formulate and phrase questions on certain complex, delineate and intricate problems.
5. There is no check on a respondent who misinterprets a question or gives incomplete or indefinite responses.
6. Sometimes the respondent may modify his earlier original responses to the questions when he fords that his responses to latter questions are contradicting the previous ones.

OBSERVATION

Observation is the process in which one or more persons observe what is occurring in some real-life situation, and they classify and record pertinent happenings according to some planned scheme. It is used to evaluate the overt behaviour of individuals in controlled and uncontrolled situations. Observational methods have occupied an important place in descriptive educational research.

As a good research too, observation needs proper planning, expert execution, and adequate recording and interpretation.

Planning for Observation

Observation as a research technique must always be expert and directed for a specific purpose. It is neither haphazard nor unplanned. The planning for observation includes definition of specific activities or units of behaviour to be observed, the nature of the groups of the subjects to be observed, the scope of observation-individual or group, determination of the length of each observation period, deciding about the tools to be used in making the observation and recording, etc.

According to Good (1966, pp. 244-245) planning for observation includes the following factors:

1. 1 . An appropriate group *of* subjects to observe.
2. Selection and arrangement *of* any special condition for the group.
3. Length *of* each observation period, interval between periods, and number *of* periods.
4. Physical 'position *of* the observer and possible effect on the subject or subjects.
5. Definition *of* specific activities or units *of* behaviour to be observed.
6. Entry *of* frequencies or tallies in the record, as a total for the entire observation period or by sub-division *of* time within the observation period.
7. *Scope of* observation. whether for an individual child *or* for a group.
8. Form *of* recording, including consideration *of* mechanical technique and such quantitative factors as number, time, distance, and spatial relationship.
9. Training *of* the observer in terms *of* expertness.
10. Interpretating *of* observations.

Execution of Observation

An expert execution of observation includes:

1. Proper arrangement of specific conditions for the subject or subjects to be observed.

2. Assuming the proper role or physical positions for observing.

3. Focusing attention on the specific activities, of unit', of behaviour under observation.

4. Handling well the recording instruments to be used

5. Utilizing the training and experience fairly well in term of making the observation and recording the facts.

Observation may be either participant or non-participant. In the participant observation, the observer becomes more or less one of the groups under observation. In such situations, the observer will be in sight of the person being observed and may actually take pare in some activity %% 1tlr tin observed individual or group. The observer may play any one of 't % rill roles in observation, with varying degrees of participation, as a visiting stranger, an attentive listener, an eager learner; or a more complete role as participant observer.

In the non-participant observation, observer takes a position where his presence is not disturbing to the group. He may follow in the detail the behaviour of one individual or may describe one or two behaviour characteristics of a dozen or more individuals. In this type of observation, a one-way vision screen that permits the observer to see the subject but prevents the subject from seeing the observer is useful.

Observation may also be classified as unstructured and structured., Unstructured observation is mainly associated with participant observation and it is often an exploratory technique. The structured observations are much too formal and they are designed to provide systematic description to test casual hypotheses. Structured observations are executed in controlled situations like classroom or laboratory settings. Interaction analysis of the classroom verbal behaviour of a teacher is an example of structured observation. Structured observations start with relatively specific formulations. There is much less choice with respect to the content of observation. The observer sets up in advance categories of behaviour in terms of which he wishes to analyse the problem, and keeps in mind the time limit under which he has to make the observation. In the unstructured observations, it may not be possible to categorize behaviour in advance of observation. Instead of using predetermined categories, the observer considers aspects of behaviour in terms of their context or the situations of which they are part.

Recording and Interpreting the Observation

The recording of the observation data may either be simultaneous or soon after the observation. In the former case, the observer goes on recording his observation data simultaneously with the occurrence of the phenomena observed. In the latter case, the observer undertakes to record his observations not simultaneously with his actual observation process, but immediately after he has observed for a unit of time while the details is still fresh in his mind.

In viewing, classifying and recording behaviour, the observer must take utmost care to minimize the influence of his biases, attitudes and values on the observation report. The observer should know what he is looking for in a given situation and should carefully and objectively record relevant data. The subjectivity on the part of an observer is partly due to his emotional involvement, his selective perceptions and his different powers of recall. In order to overcome the biases introduced by the human observer, various mechanical instruments are used to obtain a more accurate record of events. The use of cameras, tape-recorders, stop-watch, binoculars, audiometer, stethoscope, light meter, thermometers, one-way vision screen or mirror, etc. allows behaviour to be measured to a degree of accuracy which could not be achieved by the human observer. It is advisable to develop an observation form while making observations. The specific behaviours to be observed and recorded should be listed on this form. The observation form should be simple and the behaviours listed on it may be clearly specified and examples given where necessary.

Observation is done either directly, as when the observer plays a passive role and observes without intervening in any way; or in an interview, where the observer plays a more active role, by asking a series of questions or administering a test, and where he observes the behaviour of the interviewee as well as recording his responses.

In addition to rating scales and checklists, the direct observation makes use of: anecdotes, time sampling method, incident-sampling method, and controlled diary method.

1. Anecdotes. The anecdote has been the most widely used method for describing naturalistic behaviour. It is a word description of a behaviour episode. There is no set pattern for anecdotal writing, and various styles have been used. Brandt (1972) has given the following suggestions for improving the scientific quality of anecdotes:

1. Write an anecdote soon after viewing the incident. if some time lag is necessitated by the situation, jot down a key word *or* two to aid your memory during the more complete writing.
2. Include the basic action or statements of the chief person in the episode, that is, what he did or said. Include enough setting details to indicate where and when the behaviour occurred, under what conditions, and who were involved.
5. Responses or actions of others to the chief person's behaviour should be included.
6. Use direct quotations wherever possible in order to preserve the flavour of how things were stated.
7. Anecdotes should preserve the sequence of actions and responses of the original behaviour incident.
8. Anecdotes should be objective, accurate, and complete as far as important details are concerned. Good literary style, correct grammar and spelling, and even complete sentences are inconsequential. Words chosen should be precise and unambiguous, nouns and verbs primarily. Subjective terminology exemplified by most adjectives and adverbs should be used sparingly.

9. If research resources are sufficient, use of tape recorder and typist to transcribe anecdotes into written form generally increases the amount of detail that can be included over simple stenographic or handwritten recording.

Anecdote descriptions have served as useful tools in behavioural research. Such descriptions have been extensively used in examining classroom practices: in analysing community influences on development: in assessing change in interpersonal behaviour of hyper aggressive children undergoing residential treatment.

2. The time sampling method. It is not usually possible to observe behaviour continuously for long periods because of the expenses and dynamic nature of behaviour. By 'time-sampling' method, behaviour can be studied for a number of short periods of time, which are systematically spaced over the total period of study. For example, a child's behaviour may be studied for the whole school day by means of a series of observations, each of ten minutes duration. It is worthwhile to study children over long periods of time by this technique to get a fair picture of their behaviour.

3. The incident sampling method. The incident sampling method concerns the observation of the behaviour of an individual in selected incidents or situations in which he becomes involved. It involves the observation of certain instances of selected behaviour. After a series of such observations of selected behaviour, an observer may have sufficient data to draw inferences about the typical pattern of behaviour of the individual.

4. The controlled diary method. Himmelweit and his associates first used the 'controlled diary' method in 1958 to study the television-viewing behaviour of children and more recently by Wragg in 1968 to investigate the leisure activities of boys and girls. In this method, the observer keeps a diary in which he records certain aspects of the behaviour of a subject. The information gathered by controlled diary method is supplemented by the observation data gathered by other means.

Reliability and Validity of Observational Measurement

In observational measurement, Brandt (1972) mentions about three kinds of reliability. First is revealed by the amount of inter-observer agreement in records of the same behaviour. Lack of agreement may indicate insufficient training of the observers, ambiguous identification of characteristics to be rated or described, indistinguishable or overlapping categories, or observations made at somewhat different moments in time.

A second kind of reliability has to do with the inconsistencies of a single observer from one time to another. Asking an observer to view and rate or code at different times exactly the same behaviour can make estimates of the degree of this kind of reliability.

A third kind of reliability is concerned with the estimate of the variability of the trait itself. There are significant variations in human behaviour from one time to the next, one situation to another. The estimates of the degree of such variations can be made by collecting a considerable amount of observational data of the same traits and calculate the, degree of similarity-dissimilarity over varying types of settings and time periods. Resulting correlation coefficients are often referred to as `stability coefficients'.

An observational measurement can be valid only to the extent that recorded differences in score represent actual differences in behaviour rather than differences in the impressions made on different observers. A number of extraneous variables, such as maturation of subjects during the course of observation, reactive effects of subjects, change in observers or *scales. etc.* may produce variations in the obtained measures of observation. To overcome the variations due to the reactive effects, it is necessary not to make the subjects feel that they are being observed. An observation should take place in as natural settings as possible and not influenced by the presence of the observer or by his measuring or recording tools.

Best (1977, p. 178) is of the opinion that both reliability and validity of observational measurement are improved when observations are made at frequent intervals by the same observer, or when several observers record their observations independently.

Advantages and Limitations of Observation

If properly used, observation method has the following advantages:

1. It provides a direct procedure for studying various aspects of human behaviour, which may be the only effective way to gather data in a particular situation.

2. It enables the observer to code and record behaviour at the time of its occurrence.

The following are some of the limitations in the use of observation method:

1. A subject may intentionally attempt to exhibit an artificial behaviour when he knows that he is being observed.

2. Observation method is time consuming and sometimes too costly.

Projective Techniques

Projective techniques employ the word `Projection' which means to project one's own unconscious desires on some external objects. One of the major defects in the subjective and objective techniques is that they do not clearly study the unconscious mind of the individual. They merely concern with the conscious part of the personality or mind, which is only 1/10th of individual's mind.

Projective techniques deal with the conscious as well as unconscious mind. The unconscious mind is 9/10th part of the individual's mind and has much to do with personality. The inner urges, wishes, emotions etc. are not visible to an outsider and to the individual himself. Thus the evaluation of personality through projective technique will give the whole circumference of personality. Hence, they are the best tools of personality measurement.

These techniques are based on the mechanism of projection. Here, unstructured test material is presented. The whole situation is vague, undefined and unstructured. The subject is asked to project his wishes to the vague test situations. The way in which this projection takes place in an individual, gives an understanding of the personality of that individual.

Rorschach Ink Blot test

This test is named after *Hermann Rorschach.* It' was developed in the year 1921. In this test there are 10 Inkblots printed on white cards. First five cards contain black and white, thr4 contains, red, black and white, and last two cards are multi-coloured. These cards are given to the individual one by one.

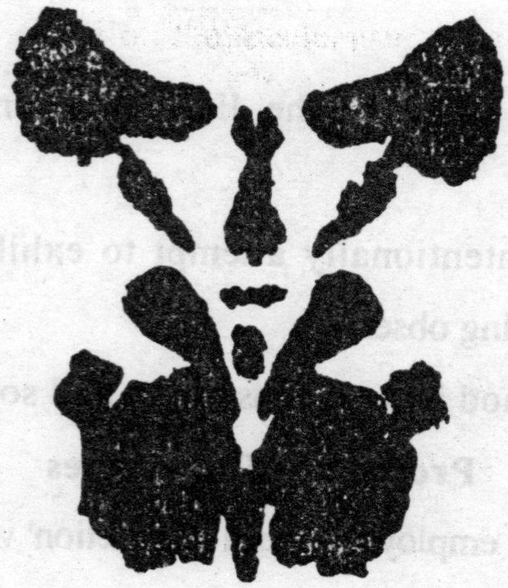

Figure -An Inkblot of Rorschach Test

Administration: The test is , }ministered under conditions usually necessary for psychological testing, quiet room, rapport etc. The cards are presented one after another, and all of them are placed in the same position before the subject. The subject is simply asked *"What this might be"* or *"what could that be"?* The subject is allowed to turn a card as he pleases but is not allowed to keep the card at an unusual distance greater than his arms' length. All the responses are taken down vervatism. If the subject is unresponsive, an encouragement is given by using words like, *"but most people see something"* or *"most people see more than one thing".* It is always better to get more than one response from the subject. Usually, there *is no time limit for the test* but some psychologists note down the reaction time for each card and make use of that in the final interpretation. After completion of the test, *doubtful points are clarified* with the help of the subject through what is called *Inquiry.*

Interpretation: In the test, the psychologist tries to understand (1) the degree and mode of intellectual control of the subject, (2) the responsiveness of his emotional energies, (3) his mental approach to problems and situations, (4) his creative and imaginative capacities and the use he makes of them; (5) a general estimate of the degree of security and anxiety, and (6) the degree of maturity in the total development of personality. The responses of the subject are recorded and studied from three aspects (1) location, (2) determinants, and (3) contents.

Location: Location refers to the *particular part of a blot to which a single response refers.* Some of the common symbols used in this connection are: W = whole blot area; D = large common detail; d = small common detail; s = white space; Dd = unusual detail; other details regarding the size; actual location, such as inside edge, etc. are also marked with different symbols.

Determinants: By a determinant *is meant the particular aspect of the blot, which directs the perceptual activity.* The common determinants are: M = movement; F = Form; C = Colour; T = Texture (shading). There is also a separate symbol for gray and black. The symbol `K8 is used for the surface appearance.

Content : Content refers to *the actual meaning of the word.* The common symbols are H=Human figure; A=Animal figures; Hd=Human details; Ad=Animal details; Obj=Man made objects; Pl= plants; At = anatomical details. *Intellectual activity is* mostly indicated by F, W, D etc. Mostly C or combinations like CF The internalized emotional life is indicated mostly by M indicate the externalized emotions.

Recent Modification of Rorschach

The following four methods for the use of the test in groups have been advanced:

1. In this method the Rorschach plates are projected on a screen for *a controlled time and written responses are received from the group.* This method is called group Rorschach. This-has made Rorschach a group technique.

2. The multiple choice Rorschach : In this method a series *of responses are projected on-the screen* and the individuals are required to choose responses according to their will.

3. In this method series of *ready-made responses are projected on the screen and the subjects, rank these responses.* It gives better results than multiple choices. Dr. Eysenck proposed this method.

4. The fourth method is called the Self-administering Rorschach. In this *the individuals select certain inkblots and develop stories about them. Munroe developed this test.* In its present form it needs a lot of improvement.

5. Recently advanced method of Rorschach called the *inspection method,* provides a method for rapid evaluation of records. Munroe, its originator has reported its success in the prediction of college success.

Rorschach technique is now a days being used for *guidance, selection, prediction, diagnostic and research purposes.* It is used to diagnose and understand the *normal and abnormal personalities.* However, it needs an *expert service, rich experience of clinical psychology and a thorough understanding of depth psychology.* It is of course dangerous to put this important toot in the hands of a fresh psychologist.

The Thematic Apperception Test (T. A.T.)

The tool of the personality measurement was developed *byMorgan and Murry* in 1935. It is at par with Rorschach technique in quality.

Actual Test-T A.T is fundamentally based upon the mechanism of projection. The test material *is standard and published.* The standard *test contains 30 pictures. Ten pictures are for men alone, 10 for women alone and 10 mixed ones for both men and women.* All the pictures are more or *less vague.*

Administration -Necessary instructions are given before hand to the subject. These instructions may vary in number with the situation and the subject but their content is a standard one. All *the pictures are numbered.* The degree of *ambiguity increases with the increasing numbers.* The subject is *seated at ease under normal* *environmental conditions.* The pictures are shown to him *one by one and he is asked to make up a story about each picture.* He is asked to weave the story pointing out some of such things as *what events have led up to the present occurrence; what the character in the pictures; thinking and feeling, and what the outcome will be.* Murry recommends that the important factors like *age, se, vocation, family etc. should also be recorded.*

Interpretation -According to Murry the list should take one hour at the most for 'its administration. He recommends two sessions for the test. The test should follow *a short interview in which -the doubtful points should be clarified.* After finishing the test and interview, all the stories are studied and analysed under the points: *(1) the hero, (2) the needs of the hero, (3) the presses of the hero, (4) the theme-and (5) the outcome.* The interpretation of the stories is made in the light of these five points to evaluate a given personality. It is generally accepted that the subject identifies himself with one of the characters in the picture that will usually be the hero of the story. Hence, the functioning of the hero in the story is taken to give clues to the understanding of the subjects, own personality. Also, one's inner needs and the various ways in which his social environment, in general and the family n particular press upon him or stimulate him are brought out in the stories.

Direct Modifications of the T. A. T.

1. **Shortening the numbers of S-pictures**-According to this, modification certain pictures *are eliminated from the test. Thus* the test is shortened. The pictures are eliminated in the light of *the nature of the subject and the experience the expert.* It saves time.

2. **Combining with other pictures**-The second modification is to use the TAX pictures with combination of some other pictures. Here some pictures, which seem *to cause some harm to the patient are rejected out and few other pictures, which the tester thinks proper to reveal out the personality, are included from outside.* The additional pictures may be ready made or drawn.

3. **Administration under frustrating conditions** -A group of experimenters at the *Worcester State Hospital,* developed a modification of the TA.T., including 5

of the Murray's cards and 6 new ones. Thus, it becomes a new test of 11 cards which, when used under frustrating conditions, gives a good assessment of personality. *Poorly adjusted persons show emotional states where* as well adjusted ones show integrity of personality.

4. Selection of pictures - In this modification the subject is required to select any number of pictures from the whole test and develop stories about them. In this, the effect of the examiner's personality is reduced to the minimum and the testee expresses his needs and presses quite well.

5. Administration under Group situations-In this modification, the pictures are projected on the screen and the group of individuals is required to write down the various stories. These stories are interpreted individually to evaluate personality. This has extended the use of TAX to groups.

6. Children's Apperception Test (CAT)-A more important modification of the test is-the one by the Bellaks devised for use with children of 3 to 11 years. This test is known as ***the children's apperception Test*** (CAT). **In** this set, *the figures are mostly of children and of animals.*

The set consists of *10 pictures depicting situations* of family relationships, toilet training, feeding habits etc. This test is very useful with children.

T A. T is widely used for various purposes. It is used for *selection, guidance, classification, promotion, and evaluation and for diagnosis in mental hospitals etc.* Its use for the groups is becoming popular *day by* day. However, the test requires an expert service and its interpretation mostly depends on the experience and skill of the psychologist.

Word Association Test (W.A.T.)-One of the oldest projective techniques for studying personality is the word-association test (Galton, 1879). This test consists in presenting a word to a subject and asking him to answer as quickly as possible with the first word, that comes to his mind. Later psychologists, particularly after Jung's use of the test, have employed this test for detecting `complexes' or areas of emotional conflicts. The interpretation rests on two factors, (1) the responses ward and (2) the reaction time. Inability to make any response or mere repetition of the stimulus word is also significant in understanding one's emotional blockings. Though, today this test does not have the importance of projective tests like the TAT or the Rorschach, it is still very useful in certain situations.

The Sentence Completion Test-The sentence completion test requires the subject to complete a sentence, of which the first word or words are given in the test itself. Originally, Ebbinghaus as a test of intellectual ability devised this test. (Particularly verbal). As a method of assessing personality, it is traced to the works of Payne and Tendler during the third decade of this century. This test is really based on the same principles as the word association test. Here also, when the subject is asked to complete the sentence, without giving time to deliberate on it, his unconscious processes will direct the response. Suppose, one of the items is, "I feel happy when :" If the subject is not deliberate about it, invariably the completed sentence will give some idea of his desires, hopes and annoyances. Investigations have been made to find out the best form for presenting the incomplete sentences. Sentences beginning in the third person have been found to be more useful. Just like the word association test, this is useful in detecting one's inner emotional conflicts, attitudes aversions etc. with reference to specific persons or situations. Now a days, LS.B.S. (Incomplete sentence Blanks) are gaining more and more popularity in the area of personality measurement.

Drawing and Painting Projective Technique

Spontaneous drawing and paintings are used for measuring the mental ability and personality of the individual. Generally drawings are used to know the specific ability in Arts, but here we employ their diagnostic value as they measure the personality etc. In drawings, we observe more on (1) colour pattern, (2) movement in the figure, (3) size of the figure, (4) form of the figure and (5) lines of the figure. On the basis of these and such other criteria we use to evaluate.

(A) Draw a Person Test-Here the child is asked to draw a person's figure. After the drawing is over, he should ask the following questions -Why have you drawn such a figure? Write some story on this figure. More questions regarding the character and environment may be asked to the subjects. The main theory behind this test is that child draws `self' or reflections. of self, his needs, wishes, urges etc. This test is evaluated on the following dimensions

(1) Structured feature (size of figure)

(2) Background

(3) Details

(4) Symmetry

(5) Proportion

(6) Shading ,

(7) Content

(8) Clothing

(9) Accessories

(10)Facial expression

(11) Postures etc.

Analysis and interpretation of this test is not so reliable as TA.T etc.

(B) House, Tree, Person Test – In this test the child is asked to draw house, tree and person. The child may project his own feelings about their family members etc. through the drawing house. The figure of 'tree' reflects the kind of role-playing in their life and ability to draw satisfaction from his environment. The third figure 'Person' represents his general and specific inter-personal relationships.

Play Technique

Play is a natural tendency. The children should be given opportunity to play. Plays of children give ideas about the expression of feelings, imagination, thinking, attitudes etc. Thus, the children may be diagnosed on the basis of diagnostic value of the play. Play has got therapeutic value also. This value indicates how person is helped to care his emotional tensions, e.g. suppose a child is jealous of his younger brother but not allowed to give threatening to him by family members. He may express this feeling by having rough handling of some particular toy (instead of younger brother) in a way he wants. Thus, his personality may be described through the observation of the play.

There are some tests, prepared by psychologists on the basis of play theory and its relation to personality e.g. *Lewenfield's World Test.*

Buhhler revised it. This test contains 300 pieces of different forms e.g. people, houses, animals, bridges, trees, cars and fans etc. Children are asked to make use of this material and allow making the world of his own.

Psychodrama or Role playing

We usually say that man has to play several roles in his life. It is believed that role play can be a good technique to understand the personality of children. Here, in this technique we ask children to do something and we observe while they are doing the things or playing their roles. We ask them to act as their father, mother, sister, brother etc. This task of playing the roles is much unstructured and he has to use words, reveals habits etc. of the parents with whom he is more impressed or annoyed. Thus, by psychodrama we provide some outlets also to release his tensions and emotions. This has got both diagnostic as well as therapeutic values.

Generally, the themes are related to family, love, death, economics, problems, security, and status etc. By psychodrama we can diagnose the child's social relationship with others and also his manners of dealing with others.

The advantage of Psychodrama method

(1) We may find some sort of reactions of children.

(2) We may know what the children. want to do in future.

(3) We may know about family situations, adjustment and vocational interests etc.

(4) We may understand and help him in facing interviews etc.

(5) It may also used as a teaching device for formation of better attitude etc.

(6) We may help in raising discussion power.

(7) 'It is easy, economic and simple.

(8) Here observation is always in creative situation.

(9) Role play creates and helps in developing confidence among the children.

Superiority of the Projective Techniques

1. The whole test situation is vague and the examine cannot guess.

2. The whole situation is ambiguous and the testee cannot know the correct answer.

3. The whole test material is published.

4. The instructions are standard and they do not vary from subject to subject.

5. These techniques reveal out the conscious as well as the unconscious personality. These techniques are the only techniques, which read out the unconscious personality. The subject tells things about himself, which are ever unknown to his own self.

6. The interference of the examiner is minimized in them.

7. They are equally applicable for the normal and abnormal individuals.

8. They have high reliability and validity.

9. They are objective in scoring and interpretation.

10. Above all, these techniques do not measure a part of personality but they give an X-Ray picture of the total personality. Indeed, they are the best tools of personality assessment.

Limitations of the Projective Techniques

1. These techniques require an expert service for the administration, scoring and interpretation. Ordinary teachers and the persons with a meager knowledge of psychology cannot use them.

2. They require sufficient experience and skill for their administration, scoring and interpretation. A fresh psychologist finds it difficult to use them.

3. They are chiefly concerned with the unconscious aspect of personality. Many psychologists are of the opinion that they under-estimate the conscious aspect of personality. Personality is both conscious and unconscious.

4. They consume a lot of time. The examinees feel fatigue and boredom.

5. They are more applicable for the abnormal persons.

6. It is difficult to establish their reliability and validity.

7. Above all, they are subjective because the scoring and interpretation depend upon the experience, skill and personal education ofthe psychologist.

List of some Important Foreign Tests of Personality

1. Woodworth : Personality data sheet.
2. Woodworth : Psycho-Neurotic inventory.
3. Pressy : X-O Test.
4. Freyd & Hcidbreder : Intro-extra test.
5. Allport & Allport : Ascendance & submission Test.
6. Thurstone : Personality schedule.
7. Jashper : Depression-elation test.
8. Thorpe, Clark & Tigs : California test of personality.
9. Hathaway & M.C.Kinley : Minnesota multi-phoric personality
10. Darley & M.C.Namara : Minnesota personality scale.
11. Cornell index.
12. Shipley, Gray & Newby : Personality inventory.
13. Jurgensen : Classification inventory.
14. Guilford & Zimmerman : Temperamental survey.
15. Thurstone : Temperamental schedule.
16. Remmers : S R A Youth inventory.
17. Maslow : Security insecurity inventory.
18. Berdie & Layton : Minnesota counselling inventory.
19. Gorden : Personality inventory.

20. Masculinity and feminity test.
21. Bernnith : Self-sufficiency test.
22. Wilson : Stability instability scale.
23. Goush : California psychological inventory.
24. California Personality inventory.
25. Neymann & Cohlstedt : Extrov.-Introversion Test.
26. R.B. Cattel : Contact Personality Factor Test.
27. R.B. Cattel : 16 PE Questionnaire Form A, B, E.
28. R.B. Cattel : Jrs. Sr. High School Personality Questionnaire.
29. R.B. Cattel : Eary School Personality Questionnaire.
30. Porter & Cattel : Children Personality Questionnaire.
31. R.B. Cattel : Humour Test of Personality.
32. Edwards : Personal Preference Schedule.
33. Eysenck : Personality Inventory.
34. Eysenck : Maudsley Personality Inventory.
35. California Personality inventory.
36. Bell's Adjustment Inventory.
37. Word Association test by Jung.
38. Kent & Rosannoff -Free Association test.
39. Rosenweig-P F Study.
40. Rotters Sentence 'Completion test.
41. Rorschach test.
42. TA.T
43. C. A. T
44. Lowenfield -Mosaic test.

Some Important Indian Personality Test

1. S. L. Das -Motion picture group test of personality.
2. Rabindra Nath-Rigidity picture test.
3. Murti & Singh-Rigidity and flexibility test.

4. Pati -Inventory for Insecurity inferiority & aggression.
5. E.G.George-Personality inventory.
6. Mazumdar-'Personality inventory.
7. S. K. Mitra-Sentence Completion test.
8. S. K. Mitra-Word Association test.
9. J. V P Sinha -Dependence Pronness scale.
10. G. L. Julka-Fear, aggression and anxiety scale.
11. Usha Sidhana-Fear check list.
12. Kundu & Sen-Introversion and Extroversion test.
13. S. P Kulshrestha- Introversion and Extroversion test.
14. P F Aziz etc. -Introversion and Extroversion test.
15. Singh & Singh-.Introversion and Extroversion test.
16. Shantamani & Hafeez-Introversion & Extroversion test
17. Mutheya.-Motivation Personality Inventory.
18. Mutheya-Personality humour test.
19. Mutheya-Picture frustration test.
20. Mohsin -Emotional Maturity test.
21. Quadary-Emotional Maturity test.
22. Ram Murti-Emotional Maturity test.
23. Yashbir Singh-Emotional Maturityy test.
24. Sinha & Verma-Moral Judgement test.
25. Virendra Sinha-Self-disclosure inventory.
26. J. G. Tripathi-Ego-strength-test.
27. Sherry & Sinha-Family relation inventory.
28. Kulshrestha & Kothiyal ISPT Personality test.
29. S. D. Kapur -Adaptation of 16 PF
30. Jalota & Kapur- Adaptation of MMPI.
31. A"sthana-Adjustment inventory.
32. Pramod Kumar -Adjustment inventory.
33. Saxena- Personality Adjustment inventory.

34. Mittal-Adjustment inventory.
35. Bengali-Youth Adjustment analyzer.
36. Sinha & Singh -Adjustment inventory for college students.
37. Sinha & Singh-Adjustment inventory for school students.
38. H. M. Singh-Marital Adjustment inventory.
39. Kulshrestha ISPT Adjustment Inventory for blind students.
40. Kapur -Adaptation of Cattell's test of Anxiety Questionnaire.
41. D'. N. Sinha-WA. Anxiety scale.
42. Sinha & Sinha -Comprehensive Anxiety Scale.
43. Kundu-Neorotic Personality inventory.
44. Indian Adaptation of T A. T
45. Indian Adaptation of C. A. T
46. Udai Pareekh -Adaptation of PF test.
47. Sharma & Chatterjee- Mosaic test.

SOCIOMETRIC TECHNIQUES

The term *Sociometry* is defined as the measurement of the social relationships that exists among the members of a group. Sociometric techniques attempt to describ4 attractions or repulsions between group members by asking them to indicate whom they would select or reject in various situations. Such techniques are used in various educational situations to study social adjustment, group dynamics, learning motivation, discipline, and other problem areas that involve social relations.

Numerous sociometric techniques are used to measure social interaction within groups, but Sociogram, Sociometric Matrices. Guess-Who Technique and social Distance Scale are most frequently used in educational research.

Sociogram

The classroom teacher, counsellor, or psychologist to study the interpersonal relationships of groups often uses the sociogram. In the research situations, it is used to study the problems of learning, motivation, discipline, and group dynamics.

To construct a sociogram, the researcher generally begins with the question such as "With whom would you most like to work on a small group project? Give your first, second and third choice." Each member of the group is provided with a form on which he can write the names of the members he has chosen. The group members are assured that the information given by them will be held in strict confidence. If there are boys and girls in the group, then the boys may be represented by triangles and girls by circles. A choice may be represented by a single pointed arrow (→), a mutual choice by an arrow pointing in opposite direction (↔). Rejections may be represented by dotted lines (....). The members who are chosen most often are referred to as 'stars', those not chosen by others as 'isolates'. Small groups made of members who choose one another are cliques'.

The next step in the construction of a sociogram is the tabulation of the choices made by the group members. For the sake of illustration, the data giving the name and corresponding number of each member of the group are presented in the following data sheet (Table 5.4). In the first three columns, the students own choices are recorded. In the next three columns, the number of times that each student is chosen by others, and in the last column, the total choices are recorded. The data are based on the choices, which are taken from the form on which students have listed their preferences.

Table 5.4 Sociometric Data Sheet

Sr. No.	*Student*	*Student choice 1st*	*2nd*	*3rd*	*Times chosen 1st*	*2nd*	*3rd*	*Total choices*
1	Shyam	2	4	15	0	1	0	1
2	Ali	4	1	3	1	0	1	2
3	Bagat	5	7	2	0	1	3	4
4	Krishana	10	7	3	1	1	1	3
5	Gopal	7	9	10	2	3	1	6
6	Rekha	8	3	5	1	0	1	2
7	Bansi	11	5	3	2	3	0	5
8	Vijay	6	5	9	1	0	0	1
9	Anjani	10	5	6	0	1	2	3
10	Daleep	13	7	12	3	2	1	6
11	Akbar	7	10	4	2	2	0	4
12	Rakesh	5	10	13	0	0	1	1
13	Anand	17	11	19	2	1	3	6
14	Suresh	10	11	13	0	2	1	3
15	Harish	11	16	14	1	0	1	2
16	Abbas	15	14	19	1	1	1	3
17	Satish	19	13	16	1	1	0	2
18	Basant	13	17	9	0	0	0	0
19	Roop	16	14	13	1	0	2	3

The first student on the data sheet is Shyam. In the "students' "choice" column, this student has selected student number 2 (Ali) as his fist choice student number 4 (Krishana) as his second choice and student number 15 (Harish) as his third choice. The column headed "Times chosen" shows that Shyam is listed as a second choice by one student, but is not listed as a first or third choice by any student. The total number of times he has been chosen by other students, therefore, is one and this is recorded in the "Total choices" column. Similarly, the data for other members of the group can be interpreted.

From the "Total choices" column, it is seen that three students, Gopal, Daleep and Anand, have been chosen six times and one student, Bansi, has been chosen five times. These students are referred to as "Stars". Moreover, one student Basant has not been chosen at all by other group members. Such a student is called an "isolate". Shyam, Vijay and Rakesh have been seldom chosen, and they are called as "neglectees".

The next step is to construct a sociogram. A sociogram provides a diagrammatic picture of the group's relationships. The following procedure is used in constructing the sociogram:

1. Place the names of the stars in the centre of the sociogram, using triangles to denote boys, and circles to denote the girls.

2. Place the names of those receiving the next highest scores (in circles and triangles) near the names in the centre but far enough to permit the drawing of lines connecting triangles and circles.

3. Place the isolates (who receive no scores) and the seldom chosen individuals around the outer area of sociogram.

4. Use lines to indicate choices and arrowheads to show direction of choice. A solid line might be used for a first choice, a broken line for second choice, and a dot-dash line for third choice. Sometimes different colours are also used for first, second and third choices.

Interpretation of the Sociogram

The sociogram is interpreted by noting its general shape and palters If the lines indicating choices show that a few individuals have chosen each other but seldom any one else, a clique is indicated. These cliques indicate lack of cooperation. When a segment of the group is completely cut off from the rest of the group, there is evidence of a cleavage or social splint in the group. Long lines with much over-lapping of choice and many individuals choosing each other indicate a well-integrated group. It means that the group has good leadership, co-operation and group spirit.

The following sociogram, as shown in the Figure 5.3, representing the social relationships of 19 students indicate that there are several stars, a few neglectees and only one isolate. There is no evidence of cliques or cleavages, and the group appears to be well integrated socially.

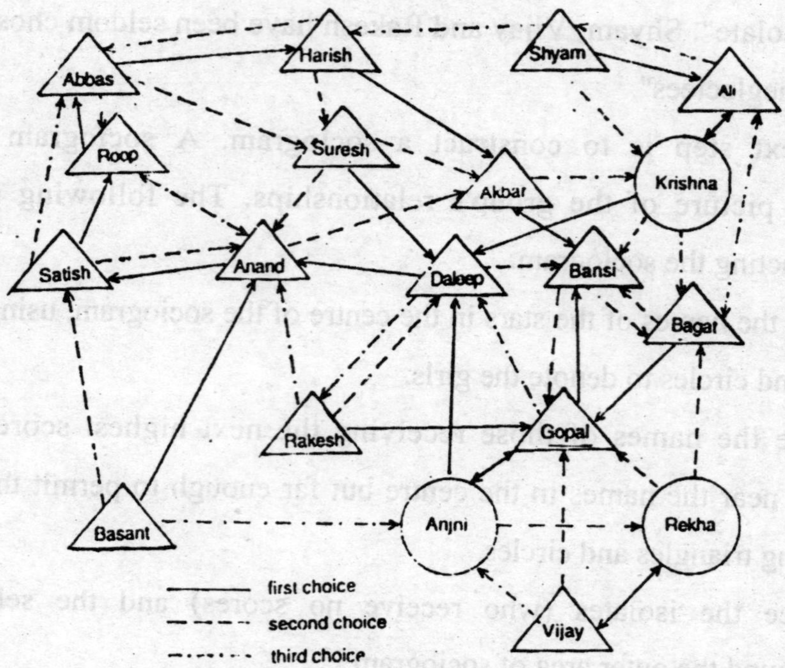

FIG. 5.3 A Sociogram for a group of 19 students

Sociometric Matrices

A sociometric matrix is a rectangular arrangement of number of indicating the choices made by the members of a group. An example of 4x4 matrix (four rows and four columns) is shown in the following Table 5.5.

Table 5.5 A Sociometric Matrix of four Member Group for a Two Choice Question

Student	*Rakesh*	*Kamal*	*Moti*	*Prakash*
Rakesh	0	1	1	0
Kamal.	1	1	0	0
Moti	1	0	1	0
Prakash	0	1	0	0
Total	2	3	2	0

In this example the question asked was, "With whom would you like 'to work on a group project? Choose two mates". In the matrix shown in Table 5.5, the numeral 1 is used to indicate a choice, while 0 is used to indicate no choice. It is seen from the matrix that Rakesh has chosen Kamal and Moti. These choices can be shown by Rakesh -Kamal and Rakesh -Moti. It is also seen that Moti has chosen Rakesh and so the choice is reciprocal. It can be shown as Rakesh ↔ Moti.

By adding the choices in each column, it is easy to find the extent to which any group member is chosen by others in the group. In this example, Kamal has been chosen three times and so he is most popular (star). Prakash has not been chosen at all and is termed an `isolate'.

Various sociometric Indices are computed from the sociometric data. The choice status is the measure of the extent to which a member is chosen by his group. The index is calculated by the following formula:

$$CS_j = \frac{\sum c_j}{N-1}$$

In which

CS_j = the choice of status of the individual j

$\sum c_j$ = the sum of the choices in the subject column A, B, C, D, etc.

N = the number of individuals in the group.

In the above example, the choice of status of Kamal *is 3/3* = 1, of Moti is 2/3=0.66, and of Prakash is 0/3=0

'Social Expansiveness' is another measure. It indicates the extent to which the group members tend to choose others. The formula for computing this index is:

In which

$$E = \frac{\sum c_{ij}}{N}$$

E = index of expansiveness

ΣC_{ij} = the sum of all choices made by all group members

N = the number of individuals in the group.

Guess-Who Techniques

The Guess-Who technique was developed by Hartshorne and Mav (1929), for use particularly with child raters. In this technique, a student is asked to read each descriptive statement presented to him and then to write down the name of the student who best fits that description. The student may use more than one name for each statement, and lie is also allowed to use his own name. Examples of statements that might be used in this kind of technique are:

1. There is a person who is always doing little things to make others happy.

2. There is a person who is disliked by others and has lots of enemies.

The scores for each student is the sum of the number of times he is chosen for each descriptive statement. If the positive statement indicates socially desirable qualities and the negative statement indicates undesirable ones, the total. score will be the algebraic sum. For example, if a student is mentioned positively 9 times and negatively 3 times, his total score will be + 9 + (-3) = + 6. If there are several positive and negative statements for a number of behavioural attributes, it is possible to get a score for each attribute for each student of the group. These scores are useful in the study of individual roles and serve as measure of his reputation.

Social-distance Scale

Social-distance scale is another technique used in the description and measurement of social relationships. E.S. Bogardus 1933 developed this technique. It attempts to assess to what degree an individual, or a group of individuals, is accepted or rejected by another individual or group. Various scaled situations, with score values ranging from acceptance to rejection, are established, and the individual checks his position by choosing one of the points on the scale.

Reliability and Validity of Sociometric Techniques

The concept of reliability and validity may not apply directly to sociometric techniques, but most of the reported studies dealing with the relation of the results obtained by the use, of Sociometry to actual behaviour show moderately high correlations.

Advantages and Limitations of Sociometric Techniques

Sociometric Techniques are easy to administer and interpret. They arc less expensive and less time consuming.

These techniques have certain limitations also. First, information provided is limited by the nature of the sociometric questions and the number of choices used. Secondly, the individuals do not reveal the raisons why they chose or reject some members of the groups. Thirdly, the sociometric data and results do not suggest how the sociometric status *of* individual of the social structure of a group can be changed. Finally, the techniques air specific rather than general in their application.

SAMPLING

The Meaning and Importance of Sampling

Statistical methods, like much of scientific methods, consist of mainly organized commonsense. So is with sampling, H.J. Butcher of the University of Manchester explains the meaning and importance of sampling as : "When we turn over the top layer of apples on a barrow or outside a green grocer's, when we dig a spadeful of soil to see if it is heavy or light, when we set an examination paper to test the progress of a class... in all these cases we are practicing a rudimentary kind of sampling and drawing conclusions about a population from information provided by a sample."

Scientific research aims at generalizations, and generalization where it is not dependent or pure deductive logic as in mathematics is usually based on samples. No botanist or zoologist has examined every plant or animal of a particular species, nor has any child psychologist examined every human child. Even the most scholarly historian cannot examine every relevant document. Yet generalizations are made, and all these subjects have progressed by the examination and analysis of sample data.

Bloomers and Lindquist have stated the importance of sampling in these words, "A large majority of the research studies in Education and Psychology or for that matter, in many other fields, are of a type known as sampling studies. In such studies, measurements or observations are made of a limited number of sample of individuals or objects in order that generalizations or inferences may be drawn about still larger groups or populations of the individuals or objects that these samples are supposed to represent."

Imagine the difficulty of conducting a reading experiment with all Indian fifth grade children as subjects. The study of population of this size would require the services of lakhs of research workers, the expenditure of crores of rupees and hundreds of thousands of class hours.

Fortunately, the process of sampling makes it possible to draw valid inferences or generalisations on the basis of careful observation of variables within a relatively small proportion of the population.

By studying the samples of a defined population, educational research aims at making generalizations, which can be applied, to the population. Borg outlines the importance of research design as, "Perhaps the most important factor in determining the generalizability of research results is the selection of the sample used in collecting the research data." There will be wastage of time, money and energy if the research data are not generalizable to some degree beyond the sample used in the research.

Sampling Theory : In the words of W.G. Cochran, "Sampling theory attempts to develop methods of sample selection and of estimation that provide at the lowest possible cost estimates that are enough for the purpose." Sampling theory is the underlying factor of all types of sampling methods and techniques. The theory enables prediction of the characteristics of population.

Bases of Sampling

The choice of the sample as representative of the whole group is based upon the following assumptions:

1. Homogenity amids complexity: Fundamentally speaking, the students are similar in many respects so that a study of some of them will throw significant light upon the whole group. Beneath the diversity and complexity of the nature of students, there is an underlying similarity and homogeneity.

2. Possibility of representative selection: It has been observed that if a certain number of units are selected from a population or universe on purely random basis, each unit has an equal opportunity of being included in the sample as the representative of the whole group.

3. Cent per cent accuracy not essential: In large scale studies, the research workers have to depend upon averages and estimates which are considered as fairly significant in an enquiry. The results of sampling studies turn out to be fairly accurate to permit valid generalizations.

Characteristics of a Good Sample

1. A good sample reproduces the characteristics of the population with the greatest possible accuracy, of course within restrictions imposed by its size.

2. A sample should be free from error due to bias or due to deliberate selection of the unit of sample.

3. A good sample should be free from random sampling error.

4. It should be selected by a procedure where there is no cónnection between the method of selection and the characteristics under consideration.

5. It should be free from incomplete coverage of the units selected for study, i.e., if should not ignore the failures in the sample in responding to the study.

6. Properly selected small samples may be relatively much more reliable than large samples poorly selected.

7. A good sample is adequate in size so that it can become really reliable.

8. Only such units should be included in the sample, which, as far as possible, are independent.

9. In the selection of a good sample, measurable or known probability sample techniques are used.

Uses of Sampling

1. A large population can be satisfactorily covered through sampling.

2. Sampling saves a lot of energy, money and time.

3. When the data are unlimited, this method becomes very handy.

4. Sampling technique is very useful when the units are relatively homogeneous.

5. The use of this method becomes inevitable when cent percent accuracy is not required.

6. Sampling makes intensive study possible when the number of individuals to be studied is manageable.

Steps in Sampling Procedure

W.C. Cochran has suggested the following principal steps in the sampling procedure

1. Formulation of the clear statement of the objectives of the study.
2. Clear demarcation and definition of the population to be sampled.
3. Use of appropriate tools and devices of measurement.
4. No overlapping in the choice of a sampling unit.
5. Selection of adequate size of the samples.
6. Supervision of the work.
7. Collection of samples.
8. Tabulation and analysis of samples.
9. Dissemination of the information obtained.

Advantages of Sampling

1. Reduced cost : Sample is a fraction of the population. Hence it is economical. If the data are collected from the entire population, costs will be very high.

2. Greater speed : Sampling is less time-consuming than the census.

3. Greater scope : Sampling simplifies matters relating to collection, and tabulation etc. of data.

4. Greater accuracy: Since sampling reduces the volume of work and careful analysis of fieldwork is possible.

5. Convenient organisation: On account of small numbers, it does not require elaborate facilities and paraphernalia.

6. Exhaustive and intensive data : Since the number is limited, it is possible to collect exhaustive and intensive data.

7. Suitable in limited resources : This method enables the research worker to work even with limited resources.

8. Better rapport : In a manageable sample, it is possible for the investigator to establish meaningful rapport with the respondents.

9. Easy scrutiny : Data can be scrutinized easily.

Disadvantages of Sampling

1. Biased Selection : Sampling may involve biased selection of respondents on the part of the research worker.

2. Difficulty in selection : Selection of a truly representative sample is very difficult. A large number of factors stand in the way of selecting good samples.

3. Specialised knowledge needed : Sampling method needs a specialised knowledge and in its absence, the investigator may commit serious mistakes.

4. Problem of cooperation : The subjects of the sample may be widely dispersed. Some of them may even refuse to cooperate with the researcher.

5. Less accuracy: Sampling is not suitable where a higher standard of accuracy is expected.

6. Limited nature : Sometimes, the universe is so small or so heterogeneous that it is not possible to derive a representative sample. In such a situation census study is the only alternative.

IMPORTANT CONCEPTS RELATING TO SAMPLING

Population : By population in a research project means the aggregate or totality of objects, subjects or individuals regarding which inferences are to be made. A population is any group of individuals that have one or more characteristics in common that are of interest to the researcher.

The notion of a population implies a wider group from which the sample is drawn. Statisticians usually refer to this wider group as the 'population' (occasionally as the 'universe'). The statistical concept of population, is therefore, more general than the common usage. In ordinary speech we talk of the population of a country or of a town but more rarely of the population of a school.

Sample : A sample is a small proportion of a population selected for observation and analysis. By observing and analysing the sample, a research worker makes certain inferences about the characteristics of the population from which it is drawn.

Statistics : A measured value based upon sample data is statistics.

Parameter : A population value inferred from a statistics is a parameter.

Sampling error : It is simply the difference between the value of a parameter and that of corresponding statistics or the difference between population value and sample value.

Sampling distribution : By sampling distribution we mean the relative frequency distribution of an infinity of determinations of the value of this statistics. Each determination is based on a separate sample of the same size and selected independently by the same presented procedure from the same population.

Sampling bias : If the mean of the sampling distribution of a statistics coincides with or equals that of the corresponding parameter it (the statistics) is said to be unbiased. On the other hand if the mean of its sampling distribution does not coincide with the parameter it is said to be biased.

Standard error : The standard error of any statistics is the standards deviation of its sampling distribution

Size of Sample

According to Parten-"An optimum sample in survey is one which fulfils the requirement of efficiency, representativeness, reliability and flexibility. The sample should be small enough to avoid unnecessary expenses and large enough to avoid intolerable sampling error."

Large or Small Samples

Large samples these are desirable and often essential under these conditions:

1. Presence of many uncontrolled variables: When it is not possible for the research worker to control some of the important variables that could have an effect upon the research findings, it is advisable to employ large random samples. This would develop more confidence in the research worker and his findings become more reliable.

2. Possibility of small differences : In many educational groups, research problems where only small differences on the dependent variables are expected, it is desirable to use large samples.

3. When groups must be broken into sub-groups : When groups are analysed on the basis of rural or urban area, boys and girls, income status of the family, etc., a large number of cases should be selected.

4. When the population is not homogeneous on the variables being studied : If every person in the population was exactly alike in the variable studied, a sample of one would be adequate. As the population becomes highly heterogeneous, large sample must be used.

Small Samples

Small samples are more appropriate in the following types of cases :

(a) Role-playing studies.

(b) Depth interviews.

(c) Projective measures.

Sampling problems

Lindquist has pointed out some of the difficulties in obtaining a truly representative sample which indicate the need for serious consideration in determining the sample:

"Because the individuals comprising any of these populations differ from one another, and because chance or uncontrolled influences always play some part in determining which of these differing individuals are to constitute the sample used, any single fact obtained from a sample (such as a mean, median, percentile, standard deviation, etc.) is almost certain to differ by some amount from the corresponding fact for the whole population. Such 'obtained' facts, therefore, may never be accepted at their face value as exactly descriptive of the population involved, but must always be considered only as approximations to, or as only estimates of, the corresponding 'true' facts. In order that any such obtained fact may be properly interpreted, then, we need to know how 'good' an estimate it is of the corresponding fact for the whole population, that is we need to have some description of the dependability or reliability of the estimate and must qualify accordingly and generalization based upon it. Such descriptions are extremely important since without them we might attribute real significance to facts that are of only accidental origin."

Important Considerations in Drawing Samples

1. Is the population from which the sample is to be drawn carefully defined?

2. Are the methods of sampling fully desirable?

3. Is the sample size large enough for the purposes investigation?

4. Is there any possibility of bias in the sampling methods adopted.

5. Has the likely effect been discussed if the sample is nonrandom?

Types of Sampling Designs or Methods of Sampling : Several methods have been devised to select representative samples. In general two types of techniques of sampling are as follows

1. Probability Sampling : Method of sampling which gives the probability that our sample is representative of population is known as probability sampling.

2. G.C. Halmstadter : A Probability sample is one that has been selected in such a way that every element chosen has a known probability of being included. Generally probability sampling is used in Fundamental Research (F.R.) since in F.R. our purpose is to generalize the results.

There are two laws of probability sampling :

(1) Law of Statistical Regularity, and

(2) Law of Inertia of Large Sample.

(1) Law of Statistical Regularity: This law involves the probability principle. A small sample may be good representative of the population, if the subjects of sample are selected at random. The conclusions drawn from the sample may be generalized for the population. The sample 'statistics' are the estimates of the population parameters. The parametric test of significance can be used for this purpose.

(2) Law of Inertia of the Large Sample : It is the corollary of the first law. A large sample is more stable or good representative as compared with small sample. The sample error is inversely in proportion to the size of sample. It can be shown with the help of the following formula:

$$SE_M = \frac{\sigma}{\sqrt{N}}$$

If N size of the sample increases the sampling error or standard error the mean decrease. If it tends to infinity, the sampling error will be zero.

$$SE_M = \frac{\sigma}{\sqrt{N}}$$

Therefore, parametric tests are used for inferential purpose.

(2) Non-probability Sampling : If there is no such idea of probability then the method of sampling is known as *non- probability sampling.* Non-probability sampling is generally used in Action Research (A.R.), since in A.R. we study a class without any generalization purpose.

Characteristics of Probability Sampling : The following are the main characteristics of probability sampling:

(1) In probability sampling we refer from the sample as well as the population.

(2) In probability sampling every individual of the population has equal probability to be taken into the sample. Probability sample may be representative of the population. The observations (data) of the probability sample are used for the inferential purpose.

(3) Probability sample has not from distribution for any variable.

(4) Inferential or parametric statistics are used for probability sample.

(5) There is a risk for drawing conclusions from probability sample.

(6) The probability is comprehensive. Representative ness refers to characteristic. Comprehensiveness refers to size and area.

Characteristics of Non-probability Sampling : The following are the main characteristics of non-probability sample:

(1) There is no idea of population in non-probability sampling.

(2) There is no probability of selecting any individual.

(3) Non-probability sample has free distribution.

(4) The observations of non-probability sample are not used for generalization purpose.

(5) Non-parametric or non-inferential statistics are used in non probability sample.

(6) There is no risk for drawing conclusions from non-probability sample.

1. Types or Techniques Probability Sampling : There are a number of techniques of taking probability sample. But here only six important techniques have been discussed as follows :

(1) Simple random sampling.

(2) Systematic sampling.

(3) Stratified sampling.

(4) Multiple or Double sampling.

(5) Multi-stage sampling, and

(6) Cluster sampling.

2. Types of Non-probability Sample: There are the following four types of non-probability sample

(1) Incidental or accidental sample.

(2) Purposive sample.

(3) Quota sample.

(4) Judgement sample.

1. PROBABILITY SAMPLING

(1) Simple Random Sampling

A simple random sample is one in which each element of the population has an equal and independent chance of being included in the sample *i.e.* a sample selected by randomization method is known as simple-random sample and this technique is simple random-sampling. Randomization is a method and is done by using a number of techniques as:

(a) Tossing a coin.

(b) Throwing a dice.

(c) Lottery method.

(d) Blind folded method.

(e) By using random table or 'Tippett's Table'.

Advantages

(a) It requires a minimum knowledge of population.

(b) It is free from subjectivity and free from personal error.

(c) It provides appropriate data for our purpose.

(d) The observations of the sample can be used for inferential purpose.

Disadvantages

(a) The representativeness of a sample cannot be ensured by this method.

(b) This method does not use the knowledge about the population.

(c) The inferential accuracy of the finding depends upon the size of the sample.

(2) Systematic Sampling

Systematic sampling is an improvement over the simple random sampling. This method requires the complete information about the population. There should be a list of informations of all the individuals of the population in any systematic way. Now we decide the size of the sample.

Let sample size = n

and population size = N

Now we select each $\frac{N}{n}$ the individual from the list and thus we have the desired size of sample, which is known as systematic sample. Thus for this technique of sampling population should be arranged in any systematic way.

Advantages

(a) This is a simple method of selecting a sample.

(b) It reduces the field cost.

(c) Inferential statistics may be used.

(d) Sample may be comprehensive and representative of population.

(e) Observations of the sample may be used for drawing conclusions and generalizations.

Disadvantages

(a) This is not free from error, since there is subjectivity due to different ways of systematic list by different individuals.

(b) Knowledge of population is essential.

(c) Information of each individual is essential.

(d) This method can't ensure the representativeness.

(e) There is a risk in drawing conclusions from the observations of the sample.

(3) Stratified Sampling

It is an improvement over the earlier method. When employing this technique, the researcher divides his population in strata on the basis of some characteristics and from each of these smaller homogeneous groups (strata) draws at random a predetermined number of units. Researcher should choose that characteristic or criterion which seems to be more relevant in his research work.

Stratified sampling may be of three types

(1) Disproportionate stratified sampling.

(2) Proportionate stratified sampling.

(3) Optimum allocation stratified sampling.

(1) Disproportionate sampling means that the size of the sample ir, each unit is not proportionate to the size of the unit but depends upon considerations involving personal judgement and convenience. This method of sampling is more effective for comparing strata, which have different error possibilities. It is less efficient for determining population characteristics.

(2) Proportionate sampling refers to the selection from each sampling unit of a sample that is proportionate to the size of the unit. Advantages of this procedure include representativeness with respect to variables used as the basis of classifying categories and increased chances of being able to make comparisons between strata. Lack of information on proportion of the population in each category and faulty classification may be listed as disadvantages of this method.

(3) Optimum allocation stratified sampling is representative as well as comprehensive than other stratified samples. It refers to selecting unis from each stratum should be in proportion to the corresponding stratum the population. Thus sample obtained is known as optimum allocation stratified sample.

These three types are clear from the table as given below :

Level	Disproportionate str. Sampling	Proportionate str. Sampling	optimum allocation stratified Sampling	
			Population	Sample
H. G.	35	25	250	25
A. G.	43	50	400	40
L. G.	22	25	350	35
Sample	100	100	1000	100

Advantages

(a) It is (more precisely third way) a good representative of the population.

(b) It is an improvement over the earlier.

(c) It is an objective method of sampling.

(d) Observations can be used for inferential purpose.

Disadvantages

(a) Serious disadvantage of this method is that it is difficult for the researcher to decide the relevant criterion for stratification.

(b) Only one criterion can be used for stratification, but it generally seems more than one criterion relevant for stratification.

(c) It is costly and time-consuming method.

(d) Selected sample may be representative with reference to the used criterion but not for the other.

(e) There is a risk in generalization.

(4) Multiple or Double or Repeative Sampling

Generally this is not a new method but only a new application of the samplings we discussed above. This is most frequently used for establishing the reliability of a sample. When employing a' mailed questionnaire, double sampling is sometimes used to obtain a more representative sample. This is done because some randomly selected subjects who are sent questionnaires may not return them. Obviously, the missing data will bias the result of the study, if the people who fail to reply the-query differ in some fundamental way from the others in respect to the phenomena being studied. To eliminate this bias, a second sample may be drawn at random from the non-respondents and the people interviewed to obtain the desired information. Thus this technique is also known as repeated or multiple sampling. This double sampling technique enables one to check on the reliability of the information obtained from the first sample. Thus, double sampling, wherein one sample is analysed, and information obtained is used to draw the next sample to examine the problem further.

Advantages

(a) This sampling procedure leads to the inferences of free determine precision based on a number of observations.

(b) This technique of sampling reduces the error.

(c) This method maintains the procedure of the finding evaluate the reliability of the sample.

Disadvantages

(a) This technique of sampling cannot be used for a large sample. It is applicable only for small sample.

(b) This technique is time consuming, costly, and requires more competition.

(c) Its planning and administration is more complicated.

(5) Multi-Stage Sampling

This sample is more comprehensive and representative of the population. In this type of sampling primary sample units are Inclusive groups and secondary units are sub-groups within these ultimate units to be selected, which belong to one and only one group. Stages of a population are usually available within a group or population, whenever the researcher does stratification. The individuals are selected from different stages for constituting the multi-stage sampling.

Advantages

(a) It is a good represernative of the population.

(b) Multi-stage sampling is an improvement over the earlier methods.

(c) It is an objective procedure of sampling.

(d) The observations from multi-stage sample may be used for inferential purpose.

Disadvantages

(a) It is a difficult and complex method of sampling.

(b) It involves errors when we consider the primary and secondary stages.

(c) It is again a subjective phenomenon.

(6) Cluster Sampling

To select the intact group as a whole is known as a Cluster sampling. In Cluster sampling the sample units contain groups of elements (clusters) Instead of individual members or items in the population. Rather than listing all elementary school children in a given city and randomly selecting 15 per cent of these students for the sample, a researcher lists all of the elementary schools in the city, selects at random 15 per cent of these clusters of units, and uses all of the children in the selected schools as the sample.

Advantages

(a) It may be a good representative of the population.

(b) It is an easy method.

(c) It is an economical method.

(d) It is practicable and highly applicable in education.

(e) Observations can be used for inferential purpose.

Disadvantages

(a) Cluster sampling is not free from error.

(b) It is not comprehensive.

All these above are techniques of probability sampling.

(2) Non-probability Sampling Techniques

Non-probability is also known as non-parametric sampling which are used for certain purpose.

(1) Incidental or Accidental Assignment

The term incidental or accidental applied to those samples that are taken because they are most frequently available, i.e. this refers to groups which are used as samples of a population because they are readily available or because the researcher is unable to employ more acceptable sampling methods.

Advantages

(a) It is very easy method of sampling.

(b) It is frequently used in behavioural sciences.

(c) It reduces the time, money and energy, i.e., it is an economical method.

Disadvantages

(a) It is not a representative of the population.

(b) It is not free from error.

(c) Parametric statistics cannot be used.

(2) Judgement Sampling

This involves the selection of a group from the population on the basis of available information thought it is to be representative of the total population. Or the selection of a group by intuition on the basis of criterion deemed to be self evident. Generally investigator should take the judgement sample so this sampling is highly risky.

Advantages

(a) Knowledge of the investigator can be best used in this technique of sampling.

(b) This technique of sampling is also economical.

Disadvantages

(a) This technique is objective.

(b) It is not free from error.

(c) It includes uncontrolled variation.

(d) Inferential statistics cannot be used for the observations of this sampling, so generalization is not possible.

(3) Purposive Sampling

The purposive sampling is selected by some arbitrary method because it is known to be representative of the total population, or it is known that it will produce well-matched groups. The idea is to pick out the sample in relation to some criterion, which are considered important for the particular study. This method is appropriate when the study Places special emphasis upon the control of certain specific variables.

Advantages

(a) Use of the best available knowledge concerning the sample subjects.

(b) Better control of significant variables.

(c) Sample groups data can be easily matched.

(d) Homogeneity of subjects used in the sample.

Disadvantages

(a) Reliability of the criterion Is questionable.

(b) Knowledge of population is essential.

(c) Errors in classifying sampling subjects.

(d) Inability to utilise the inferential parametric statistics.

(e) Inability to make generalization concerning total population.

(4) Quota Sampling

This combined both judgement sampling and probability sampling. The population Is classified Into several categories: on the basis of judgement or assumption or the previous knowledge, the proportion of population falling Into each category is decided. Thereafter a quota of cases to be drawn is fixed and the observer is allowed to sample, as he likes. Quota sampling is very arbitrary and likely to figure in Municipal surveys.

Advantages

(a) It is an improvement over the judgement sampling.

(b) It is an easy sampling technique.

(c) It is most frequently used in social surveys.

Disadvantages

(a) It is not a representative sample.

(b) It is not free from error.

(c) It has the influence of regional geographical and social factors.

Since research *design is* a plan by which research samples may be selected from a population and under which experimental treatments are administered and controlled so that their effect upon the sample may be measured. Therefore, a second step in the establishment of an experimental design is to select the treatments that will be used to control sources of learning change in the sample subjects.

Characteristics of A Good Sample

The following are the main characteristics of a good sample:

1. A good sample is the *true representative* of the population, corresponding to its properties. The population is known an aggregate of certain properties and sample is called sub-aggregate of the universe.

2. A good sample is *free from* bias, the sample does not permit prejudices, the learning and pre-conception, imaginations of the Investigator to Influence its choice.

3. A good sample is an *objective* one; it refers objectivity In selecting procedure or absence of subjective elements from the situation.

4. A good sample maintains accuracy. It yields an accurate estimates or statistics and does not involve errors.

5. A good sample is *comprehensive* in nature. This feature of a sample is closely linked with true-representativeness. Comprehensiveness is a quality of a sample, which is controlled by specific purpose of the investigation. A sample may be comprehensive in traits but may not be a good representative of the population.

6. A good sample is also *economical* from energy, time and money point of view.

7. The subjects of good sample are easily *approachable*. The research tools can be administered on them and data can be collected easily.

8. The size of good sample is such that it yields accurate results. The probability of error can be estimated.

9. A good sample makes the research work more feasible.

10. A good sample has the practicability for research situation.

Advantages of Sampling Technique according to R.A. Fisher

Fisher has enumerated the following four advantages of sampling technique.

1. It has a greater *adaptability*.
2. It is an *economical* technique.
3. It has high *speed* for generalization.
4. It has a greater *precision* and accuracy in the observation.

Advantages, of Sampling Technique according to W.G. Cocharan

He has given the following four advantages of sampling technique:

1. This technique has *great accuracy*.
2. It has a greater *speed* in conducting a research work.
3. It has a greater *scope* in the field of research.
4. It *reduces the cost* of observation or data collection.

ERRORS IN SAMPLING

The samples of behavioural research are not representative and suffer from two types of errors

(1) Random error, and (2) Systematic error.

These errors can be classified further as

(a) Sampling errors, and (b) Error of Measurement.

Thus, it provides a four-ways classification and has been shown in following manner

	Random	Constant
Sampling	A	B
Measurement	C	D

Cell A refers to the unavoidable errors that occur whenever sampling is done. The sample selected at random may be high, low or average with regard to the trait measured. Selecting a large sample can minimize this error.

Cell B refers to errors of bias in sampling, *i.e.* sampling errors, which do not cancel out, but rather lean systematically in one or the other direction of the population value. This error is due to any decision of researcher for selecting subjects for the sample. The systematic error exists; the data are of limited use as the basis for generalizing to the population. Thus, *Cells A* and *B* refer to the errors and sampling.

Cells C and D refer to errors in the process of measurement, rather than to errors in sampling. The errors in *Cell C, which occur from the simple fact measurement derived from any instrument of less than complete reliability,* are inevitable in some degree of error. The error of measurement is cancelled out by selecting a large sample. Sum of errors of measurement is always zero.

Cell D concerns with another bias-that is due to systematic errors of measurement. If, in the testing of subjects for intelligence, the test administrator allows an extra three minutes for the test, there will be probably be systematic tendency for the sample statistics to be higher than the population parameters.

The systematic errors are the bad errors in both in sampling and in measurement. The magnitude of random sampling errors as they affect the sample statistics as given below

$$SE_M = \frac{\sigma}{\sqrt{N}}$$

If greater accuracy is re[illegible]n be obtained by increasing the 'size of sample or the homogeneity of the variable under investigation or by using adequate sampling design.

If the results obtained are systematically higher or lower than the 1 corresponding true value, the sample is biased and the discrepancy is called an *error of* bias.

Size of Sample

One of the first questions that the researcher typically asks, concerns with the number of subjects that need to be included in his sample. Technically, the size of the sample depends upon the precision the researcher desires in estimating the population parameter at a particular confidence level. There is no single rule that can be used to determine sample size.

The best answer to the question of size is to use as large a sample as possible. A larger sample is much more likely to be representative of the population. Furthermore, with a large sample the data are likely to be more accurate and precise. It was pointed out in that the larger the sample, the smaller the standard error. In general, the standard error of a sample mean is inversely proportional to the square root of n. Thus, in order to double the precision of one's estimation, the sample size would need to be quadrupled.

It is often suggested that one should include at least 30 subjects in a sample since this number permits the use of large sample statistics. Statistically speaking, a sample n = 30 is considered large, since with this n, the t-distribution and the normal curve are practically the same for hypothesis testing purposes. In experimental research, one should select a sample that will permit at least 30 in each group. Descriptive research typically uses larger samples; it is sometimes suggested that one should select 10-20 per cent of the accessible population for the sample.

Determine the Size of Sample- It is the crucial problem for the research scholars to determine the size of sample. In an experimental study, it is essential to equate the control and experimental groups, but in survey study sample should be representative of population. Therefore, size of sample is an important aspect for the representativeness. Mouly has suggested a statistical criterion for determining the size of the sample.

Other things being equal, the larger the sample, the greater the precision and accuracy of the data it provides. It is a common belief that the precision of data is determined primarily by the size of the sample, rather than by the percentage of the population represented in the sample. The term 'large sample' is vague, it varies with nature of study. The exact procedure by which to determine the sample size required varies with the nature of the variable and its sampling distribution, but the basic procedure can be illustrated in connection with the mean of random samples based on normal probability distribution. The chances are 95 to 5 that a sample in separated sampling will fall within the interval $M \pm 1.96\ SE_M$.

The next question is the degree of accuracy required. Generally 95 to 99 per cent confidence intervals are acceptable i.e. 5 to 1 per cent error. If the variable of the study is the intelligence and the sampling errors were kept within 5 per cent at the 95 per cent confidence level. The investigator can use the formula for the standard error of the mean to provide the required size of sample.

$$1.96\ SE_M = 5, \qquad 1.96 \cdot \frac{\sigma}{\sqrt{n}} = 5$$

Where σ = S. D. of the population

n = Size of the sample

5 is percent of sampling error

In this illustration I. Q. distribution σ = 16

$$\sqrt{n} = 1.96 \times \frac{16}{5} = 9.30$$

$$n = 96$$

If the investigator wants more precise, the sampling error is kept within 1 per cent at the 99 per cent confidence level. The following formula is used for determining the size of sample : $\frac{\sigma}{n}$

$$2.58\, SE_M = 1\ ; \quad \sqrt{2.58} \quad = 1$$

$$2.58 \times 16 = \sqrt{n} \qquad \sqrt{n} = 41.28$$

$$n = 1681.$$

Thus, he would need a sample of 96 case in order to meet the conditions of 5 per cent error at 95 per cent confidence level. He would require a sample 1681 case for 1 per cent error at the 99 per cent confidence level.

Generally in behavioural research more than one variable are taken into a study. In such situation he should consider standard deviations of the distributions of the variables. The highest S.D. is to be considered for calculating the size of the sample. In this way a researcher can determine the exact size of sample indicating the sampling error in per cent. He should not use an arbitrary criterion for determining the size of his sample.

UNIT-3

LEARNING OBJECTIVE

Major Approaches to Research -Descriptive Research-Ex-post facto Research-Laboratory Experiments-Field studies-Historical Research-Research Designs

MAJOR APPROACHES & RESEARCH

DESCRIPTIVE RESEARCH IN EDUCATION

Research is basic to every field of knowledge. It is a tool of tremendous importance for verifying, testing and validating current and old knowledge and also a potent means of creating new knowledge. It has, during the past two-three decades, moved to the centre of the behavioural sciences. Most of the textbooks in behavioural sciences may, now, be found to be research-based. Apart from the quantity, its quality, particularly its methodology, has registered a great improvement. Now, we find more genuine problems being identified for research in every field, more relevant and meaningful structural plans being used, more sophisticated statistical techniques of analyzing data being applied. The investigators are seen equipped with much better research skills all over the world. Yet, side by side, there seems to be a still greater scope for improvement of methodology of research in behavioural sciences. A major approach to research in behavioural sciences discussed in this chapter is descriptive research.

DESCRIPTIVE RESEARCH

This is the most popular type of research in the field of behavioural sciences. Every third study may, perhaps, be classified under this category. The salient features of this type of research are discussed as follows

1. Meaning and Nature

Literally, descriptive research means an investigation, which focuses on just describing the phenomenon telling, as an outcome of research, what it is. In the past the tradition of this type of research was making reliable and valid assessment of existing conditions, determining the nature of dynamic processes, describing the systems, groups and people. But recently descriptive research has brought within its purview even the investigations of relationships among variables and various kinds of phenomena.

Like other types of research, descriptive research also follows such steps as (1) identifying and defining the problem, (2) stating objectives and hypotheses, (3) collecting relevant data, both qualitative and quantitative, (4) analysis of data, (5) drawing inferences and conclusions. In order to delimit the scope, it also defines population and specifies the way the sample has to be selected. It uses all those methods of sampling, which are used in case of other types of research.

2. Types of Descriptive Research

Van Dalen (p. 206) has included three types of studies under descriptive research. The same line of thinking is presented in this Chapter also. These three types of studies are:

(A) SURVEY TYPE OF RESEARCH

1. Meaning and Nature of Survey Research

The purpose of survey type research, according to Kerlinger (p. 410) is to discover the relative incidence, distribution, and inter-relations of sociological and psychological variables. Survey type studies, by and large, describe the **current status** of a phenomenon, some group of people, an institution, some existing practice, policy or event. Sometimes, they **compare** the status with some available standards and make suggestions for **improving** the status. Survey research as being used in social sciences is, however, different from the status survey and is considered enough scientific if looked from methodology point of view.

In most researches of survey type small samples are studied and on the basis of that, inferences are drawn about the whole or at least larger populations. They emphasize that if this is the purpose, the sample should be drawn randomly. These are generally, called sample surveys.

2. Types of Survey Research

A lot of things have been studied through survey research. It is very difficult to classify them into clear-cut types. However, they can be categorized as (1) institutional surveys, (2) Job surveys, (3) population surveys, (4) documentary surveys, (5) public opinion surveys, (6) community surveys, (7) sociological and psychological surveys. Documentary surveys are also known as "content analysis", or "activity analysis" or "informational analysis" which are quite akin to historical research. Sociological surveys focus on sociological facts, opinions, attitudes, social habits, social customs, etc. Psychological surveys describe the status and distribution of psychological variables like intelligence in the group or larger population.

3. Methodology of Survey Research

The methodology of survey research emphasizes using rigorous sampling methods and sampling designs, design of the study including specification of objectives, hypotheses and plan of collecting information. The methodology of this type of research uses various kinds of tools such as questionnaires, interviews, personal visits, inspection of records, use of standardized psychological tests. The methodology very specifically stresses the preparation of some sort of flow chart which tells the researcher (1) what are objectives, (2) to achieve them what kind of information is needed to be collected, (3) from whom or where this information has to be collected, (4) how this information or data has to be tabulated and analysed.

In no way survey type of research should be considered inferior to any other research.

4. Steps of Survey Research

The researcher to begin with must decide and describe.

1. What is the purpose of the study ? Descriptive ? Explanatory ?
2. Is a survey appropriate for this question ?
3. What is the question or hypothesis to be tested ?
4. What is the population of interest ?
5. What method of data collection is appropriate given the purpose question, and population ?
6. What method of data analysis is intended and is appropriate, given the purpose, population, question, and data ?

Sampling phase

The researcher must decide and describe.

1. What is the intended size of sample ?
2. What is the type of sample ? Cross-sectional". Longitudinal ?
3. What is the intended universe, that is, what does the sample purport to represent ?
4. What types of sampling procedure is appropriate, given the sample size, type, and intended representativeness?

Data Collection

The researcher must decide and describe.

1. What is the basic mode of data collection ? Interview (personal, telephone) ? Questionnaire (individual, group) .
2. Flow can questions be asked or concepts of interest be accurately measured, given this mode of data collection and this population ?
3. How long is the interview, questionnaire, or phone call ?
4. Flow will scales be constructed ?
5. What checks are there on the validity and reliability of the data collected?

Data Analysis

The researcher must decide and describe.

1. Flow will data be made ready for computer processing Transcriptive data entry ? Automatic data entry.?
2. How will data be edited and cleaned ?
3. How will it be possible to show that a given explanation is tenable ? Are there ways to test competing alternative hypotheses ?
4. What data analysis procedures will be used ? Are they consistent with the purpose of survey and the quality of the data ?
5. What procedures will be used for documenting data files and data procedures?

Survey Designs

Surveys are primarily conducted to answer "what" of the research question. When a researcher is interested to know what has happened, he uses the survey research design. For example, you may be interested to know how many children are enrolled in a primary school at the block/district level, what is the dropout rate, what is student/teacher ratio in a district, what is the level of achievement of students of a specific grade in a specific subject, what is the impact of a training programme, what is the level of participation of students in school activities, and so on. Thus, survey method is used to obtain descriptive and evaluative information in education. Using this method almost every area of education can be surveyed.

In survey design, information is collected through various techniques. While use of questionnaire and its derivatives (such as questionnaire, checklist, rating scales, tests, etc.) are more commonly used, the information is also collected through structured interviews, and observation schedules. It is perfectly possible to collect qualitative data within a survey. Even physiological measures (heart beat, blood pressure, breathing rate, cholesterol level, etc.) can be collected using survey approaches, of course with different instruments.

Surveys are of different types such as cross-sectional and longitudinal surveys. These types have been discussed in greater detail under developmental studies.

(B) INTER-RELATIONSHIP STUDIES

These are studies, which aim at going a step further instead of stopping at just describing the phenomenon like the survey type studies. Three types of such studies have been described by Van Dalen (p. 218). These are : (1) case studies, (2) causal-comparative studies, (3) correlational studies. Each of these is described below:

(a) Case Study

This type of research is a **comprehensive** and an intensive probing into a phenomenon. A single unit, institution, person, group of people, community or family is studied to bring out the processes and dynamics of its functioning. Depending upon the objectives to be achieved, it collects information about various aspects of the unit or the individual from various sources. The information, thus collected, is analyzed and inferences are drawn as to why and how the existing problems, status, functioning, etc. have come to be as they are. All the facts collected are sorted out, rearranged and woven afresh around key questions emanating from the objectives. Case studies may be of numerous types. Anything that is studied in depth makes a case study. Basic steps involved in a case study, generally, include : (1) establishing the problem or the case or deciding about the objectives to be achieved, (2) diagnosis of the problem, i.e., collecting all kinds of information hypothesized to be leading to the existing problem, (3) analysing and organizing information so as to reach some conclusions regarding its relationship to the problem, (4) deriving inferences, conclusions, generalizations.

Case studies are quite popular in the fields of guidance and counseling, social work, economics, industries, psychology and sociology. In the field of guidance and counseling the counselors make case studies of problem children to find out an answer to the question; why and how the behaviour problem has developed ? Similar is the work of the social workers that try to find out how a social problem is caused. Case studies in the field of economics and industries aim at finding out the dynamic processes that cause the failure of an industry or that underlie the inadequate functioning of an economic policy.

When compared to survey research, a case study may be seen operating Vertically, while the survey research operates horizontally. A case study goes in depth, while the survey covers a broad area for investigation. The case study confines, at a time, to the study of just one single individual or organization, while the survey may involve a large number of units to be studied simultaneously.

The purpose of the case study is mainly therapeutic while the purpose of survey research is to just describe the present status. The case study focuses on causal relationships among various factors while the survey is interested mainly in collecting, arranging, tabulating information for generalization. An individual or an institution about the cause of the problem faces generalization in case of a case study, while in case of the survey research generalization is done for the larger population?

The case study research is very useful in certain situations such as understanding of a problem child or understanding the cause of malfunctioning of an organization. In fact, in such situations no other type of research can serve the purpose. However, there are a few serious limitations of these kinds of studies. One of these is that the case study bas **no external validity as** the results obtained can not be generalized to any other unit beyond the single unit studied. Secondly, it has a high degree of subjectivity. Whatever the results are drawn from a case-study may be just the figment of imagination of the person who conducts the study. However, all these shortcomings of case-study approach may be made less serious if the researcher tries to control his subjectivity and sticks to more objective thinking by reporting facts precisely and making judgements on the basis of adequate evidence. A carefully and objectively conducted case study, no doubt, may yield valuable results.

(b) Causal-Comparative Studies

This is another types of research which has been categorized under inter-relationship studies which are of descriptive nature.

1. Meaning and Nature

Basically, the purpose of these studies is to find out whether there is any causal relationship between a phenomenon and certain other factors or conditions hypothesized to be related to it. That is why they are called causal studies. They are called comparative also for the reason that in most cases, the causal relationship is established on the basis of **comparisons** of similarities and differences among phenomena. From the point of view of purpose to be achieved causal-comparative studies are very close to experimental studies as in both it is the **causal** relationship which is aimed to be established. But, from methods point of view they are much different from one another. In case of an experimental study the researcher manipulates the independent variable and, then, observes its effect on the dependent variable, while in case of the causal-comparative study the researcher gets the dependent variable as a **naturally** occurring phenomenon; and from this point he proceeds on to identifying the various antecedents which may have been related to its occurrence. For example, the researcher comes across a group of children with negative attitudes towards teachers. He meets the phenomenon of negative attitudes of children as it has already occurred naturally. This is his dependent variable. Now, he proceeds to find out what those factors are that are related to children's negative attitudes. This he does by comparing various personal, social and environmental characteristics of these children with those of the children who do not have negative attitudes. On the basis of this kind of comparison, he describes why the said group of children had developed negative attitudes towards teachers. This method has emerged from Mill's method, which says, "If two or more instances of the phenomenon under investigation have only one circumstance in common, the circumstance in which alone all the instances agree is the cause (or effect) of the given phenomenon" (Mill, 1846, p. 244).

2. Importance

The importance of these studies lies in the fact that the true experimental method of identifying causal relationship is not applicable in actual situations of life,. In actual situations of life, it is not possible to manipulate the independent variable and study its effects. For example, it is not possible in actual situations of life to create conditions, which can deliberately develop less negative and more negative attitudes in children. Hence, in these situations only such methods as causal comparative studies can be applied. And a very large number of situations are of this kind. This makes these kinds of studies important.. These types of studies are more practical, feasible and meaningful for this reason. All the investigations in which differences between groups are studied are of this kind and are considered important.

3. Disadvantages

Though very useful, causal comparative studies have their own limitations. Lack of control of variables and lack of possibility of its manipulation of independent variable render them of limited value, as their resume cannot be generalized to any larger population. Nor, the results obtained can be considered to be very reliable. The precision of these studies is always poor. In fact, though titled as causal, it is not possible for these studies to establish which is the cause and which is the effect. They cannot have high internal validity.

(c) Correlational Studies

The purpose of these studies also, like the causal-comparative studies, is to find out relationship between variables. But, while the other methods tell only about the fact of relationship, the relationship exists or not, correlational studies go a step further and also tell how much is the relationship. In case of these studies, it is possible to find out the magnitude of relationship in the form of a mathematical quantity known as the coefficient of correlation. They also tell whether the relationship is positive or negative. The magnitude of relationship varies between + 1.0. The coefficient of correlation of +1.0 indicates perfect relationship in the positive direction and that of -1.0 indicates perfect correlation in the negative direction. In between these there are high and low relationships on the continuum.

Correlation studies use statistical methods of finding out coefficients of correlation. These are used for studying more complex relationships such as studies of predictive nature and multivariate analysis.

One great disadvantage of correlational studies is that they do not tell which is the cause and which is the effect. In the kind of relationship that is discovered between the variables, causal relationship can not be established on their basis. This makes correlational studies different from experimental studies.

(C) DEVELOPMENTAL STUDIES

This is another type of descriptive studs. This type of study aims at describing the change that takes place in the growth and development of an organism or an institution or some social process over a determined period of time. It also describes what factors and conditions in what manner brought about the change. Van Dalen (p. 228) discusses two types of this kind of research-***Growth Studies and Trend Studies.***

(a) Growth Studies

Growth studies can be made in any field. But, most common are the studies of human growth and development. They describe how the human organism develops, what characteristics develop at what stage of life, which forces and factors are responsible for these developments. These studies have been of two types- **longitudinal and cross-sectional.**

In case of longitudinal studies the same child or the same group of children is measured on several variables at different age levels with the result that the study stretches over a number of years bringingmost critical changes taking place at critical age levels. For example, a group child is measured on intelligence, social habits, emotional stability, self concepts, interests and other personality characteristics at the age-level 5, 6, 7, 8, 9, 10 and I1 years. By comparing these measures, the researcher is in a position to describe the developmental change-taking place.

The cross-sectional research measures several different groups of children of different ages simultaneously on certain variables of interest and compares the groups among themselves to find out how they differ and what dominant characteristics are shown at different age-levels. Such studies are completed within a short duration of time. For example, simultaneously at one point of time, a researcher administers his tools for measuring a few variables mean on five, six, seven, eight and nine year old children compares them`, On the scores on each variable for all the age-groups basis of this comparison, he describes which traits are dominant at which age level, or which dominant characteristics define a particular age-group.

It is difficult to say whether longitudinal or cross-sectional approach is better. Both have their advantages and disadvantages. The longitudinal method is considered more appropriate a technique of studying human development. It has several advantages. But, at the same time it has certain weaknesses also. It gives, no doubt, more accurate assessment of the developmental change. But that may not be true about all individuals as the group of children that is studied. may not be representative of any larger population. Another weakness is that it is difficult to keep all the subjects within the study over a low-, pod of time. Several of them may be lost to the investigation for several reasons. Also, it is very time consuming. It is difficult to wait for the results for such a long time.

The cross-sectional study on the other hand is considered to be handy and adequately manageable. Hence, they are more popular. They have the advantage of being completed within a short duration. They reveal the status of the children of different age groups on several variables simultaneously. Yet, they, too, have several weaknesses. One of these is that the groups that are compared are not, many a time, comparable.

Both the types of studies are, however, considered quite useful if the purpose is to understand growth and development.

Children grow very fast. They also learn very quickly. If one observes a child admitted in grade I for some time, one finds many changes in the child's behaviour. The researchers who want to know change in behaviour over time can apply cross-sectional or longitudinal designs for their study.

Suppose, a researcher is interested to know the change in height and weight of the child after every six months for a period of three years. Another researcher may be interested to know how many words children can recognize when they are 4 years old, 4% years old. 5 years old, and 6 years old. In these types of studies one can either employ a cross-sectional design or a longitudinal design.

A cross-sectional design is relatively simpler. It involves collection of information from different groups of pupils (varying in age) at a single time. For example, you want to know the number of words children can recognize. You select four groups of children: 4 years old, 4/2 years old, 5 years old and 6 years old. In other words, in this design, the researcher attempts to study the impact of age on behaviour or learning. The design is simple and consumes less time, money, etc. But it fails to explain the processes involved in learning. Also persons born at different time periods cannot be considered equal in terms of their cultural and historical experiences.

Longitudinal design, in contrast, involves study of same group of children over a number of times. For example, in the above example, children, who are 4 years old will be tested on the first occasion. Thereafter, the researcher will wait for 6 months and only after the children attain the age of 4% years they will be subjected to testing. The same group of children will be tested when they are 5 and 6 years old. It is evident that this method is more time-consuming and costly. It is also characterized by the problem of attrition. Considering the current high dropout rate, by the time you go for second testing many children might have dropped out. So you get lesser number of pupils. The same group of children is tested on several occasions, which enhances the possibility of carryover of learnt material from one occasion to another. The advantage is that it helps in understanding the processes involved in learning.

(b) Trend Studies

Trend studies also constitute a sort of developmental type of research as they also observe and assess what characteristics prominently and consistently emerge at different times. But, they do not stop only at this point describing only these consistently dominating characteristics. They are future-oriented also in the sense that on the basis of these consistently dominant characteristics or trends they also predict what will be the future status of these trends, how will they affect the institution, the people, the environment, the output and other various aspects. For example, the study of the rates of enrolment at primary level of education for the past ten years may enable the researcher to predict what will be the situation in the next live or ten years, how many schools will have to be opened, how much financial allocation will be required per year, and so on.

This kind of research uses methods and techniques of various other research strategies such as historical research, survey techniques and content analysis, etc. Studies of school enrolment, population changes, employment opportunities, specific social changes, etc. may he considered belonging to this category research. For certain purposes, they may be considered very useful.

Ex-Post Facto Research : The Variant of Experiment Research

Every research has a plan which tells the researcher to move into certain specific directions at certain specific stages. It constitutes a detailed guideline for carrying out the research work. The basic elements of a research design are identification of the objectives of research, formulating hypotheses for achieving these objectives, specifying the population and sampling procedures, specification of tools to be used for measuring variables, describing procedures of collection of data, specification of analysis of data and discussion of results. It is a kind of "blue-print" which describes "what", "why" and "how" of the research to be conducted. Kerlinger (1973, p.300) says that a research design is the plan, structure and strategy of investigation so as to obtain answers to research questions. It is to him the overall scheme or programme of the research.

The research designs of all types of researches are not alike, though basic elements, by and large, remain the same. The designs of historical research, survey type research and experimental research differ from one another in several ways. The steps that are involved in each one of them basically remain the same as enumerated above. But, what has got to be done at what stage and how remain no more the same. For example, hypotheses have to be formulated in case of every one of them. But, how these hypotheses have to be tested will differ from one type of research to another. A detailed description of all these elements or steps prior to conducting that research constitutes what a research design is. All experimental researches are not designed and conducted in the same way. Depending upon their unique ways of designing there are different kinds of experimental research. Mainly they are classified as follows:

1. The laboratory experiment or True experimental Research.
2. Ex-post Facto Research.

3. Field Experiment
4. Field Studies
5. Experimental Simulation

LABORATORY EXPERIMENTS

Laboratory experiment is classified as the true experiment which is defined as the highly controlled behaviour setting of research. This type of research is different from other kinds of researches in that (1) this is conducted in the laboratory instead of the field, and (2) also that this is conducted in a setting in which most of the relevant factors can be controlled through manipulation of the independent variable and randomization of subjects to treatment groups alongwith randomization of treatment conditions to subjects. One very great quality of the true or laboratory experiment is that in this it is possible to arrange observations and conditions in such a way that the result obtained is considered to have only one interpretation such as x is the cause of *y*. If some other explanation is also possible, to that extent it will not be considered valid. This, of course, is the ideal. But, all experimental studies are only approximations to it. In fact, experimentation consists in the modification of the conditions determining an event and in the observation and interpretation of the resulting changes in the event itself. In order to achieve this, the researcher creates the setting in which behaviour needs to be observed and analyzed. This is the contrived setting of the experiment which distinguishes it from other types of researches. As described by Kerlinger (p. 400-401) there are three purposes of laboratory experiments : (I) to discover functional relationship between phenomena under "pure and uncontaminated conditions", (2) testing of predictions which are derived from theory and other researches, and (3) to define theories and hypotheses, to formulate other hypotheses and to build theoretical systems, Hence, experimental research should be considered, largely, theory- oriented. It is a very useful tool in the hands of the researcher to create valid new knowledge. However, this is true only when the experiment is conducted under the circumstances and conditions, which are ideally, controlled which every time is not possible. Depending upon the degree of ideal conditions provided for rigorous control, the experimental designs vary in the degree of precision that can be obtained.

A few variants of the laboratory experiment have been discussed as follows:

EX-POST FACTO RESEARCH

The purpose of this research is to identify functional relationship among phenomena by relating their occurrence to hypothesized factors or conditions. Ex-post-facto research also aims at finding out most answers to problems, Efforts are made, in this, on establishing of some consequence. In this sense it is an experimental research'.

l. Meaning and Nature

Ex-post-facto research is an empirical enquiry in which attempts are made to find out the possible cause of some phenomenon of interest. Discovery of causal relationship between the phenomenon in question and some antecedent is its essential objective. From this point of view this should be considered an experiment. But, it is not considered an experiment for several reasons. Mouly (p. 335) calls this an 'experiment in reverse" which simply means that' the sequence of dependent and independent variables as found in the experiment is reversed in case of the ex-post-facto research. In the experiment it is the independent variable which comes first for consideration. It is manipulated by the researcher. The researcher varies it in certain well thought out ways and, then, imposes these conditions or treatments on the groups in a predetermined manner. Having allowed the independent variable to operate on the groups for some time, he measures its effect on the dependent variable's scores of the two or more groups and, then, compares them. The dependent variable, thus, comes after the independent variable as a function of the operation of the independent variable. Thus, the experiment proceeds from the independent variable towards the dependent variable. But, in case of the ex-post-facto research, the researcher proceeds from dependent variables towards the independent variable. It begins with existing groups that are different and attempts to find out the causes of these differences. For example, there may be a study on "the determinants of low achievement motivation in 11-year old children of a city". In this study what the researcher does, is that he selects two groups of 11-year old children, one having low achievement motivation and another having high achievement motivation, Thus, he proceeds with the dependent variable "achievement motivation". He selects two differing soups on this. After this he moves to find out the factors and conditions, which may be responsible for this difference, (i.e., he considers independent variable).

Ex-post-facto, literally, means "starting after the fact". This means that the study begins after the phenomenon has occurred. For example, the fact of low achievement motivation occurs; only after that the researcher goes to find out its causes (the independent variables). It is very much like the causal comparative studies generally discussed under descriptive studies.

An ex-post-facto study is different from a true laboratory experiment in the following ways:

(a) In the experiment the independent variable is manipulated and its effect on dependent variable is observed and studied. In the ex-post-facto research the dependent variable is measured first; and after that the independent variable or variables are studied.

(b) In the experiment, rigorous control of extraneous variables is introduced through randomization, matching, etc. with the result that the treatment effects are believed to have been caused by the independent variable under study. In case of ex-post-facto research the investigator cannot have this much rigorous control and, hence, its results are much less dependable. In case of ex-post-facto research direct control of variables (independent and extraneous) is not possible. Neither experimental manipulation nor random assignment of subjects is possible in case of expost-facto research.

(c) In the experimental and the ex-post-facto study both the kinds of researches it is possible to draw subjects at random. But, in case of expost-facto research it is not possible to assign the subjects to treatment groups randomly which is possible in case of an experiment. In case of expost-facto research subjects "assign themselves' to groups. They "select themselves" into groups on the basis of characteristics of the dependent variable. As Kerlinger (p. 381) puts it, "The subjects and the treatments come as it were already signed to the groups".

(d) Mouly (p. 335) says that ex-post-facto research can provide support for any number of different and-sometimes contradictory hypotheses for the reason that it collects highly uncontrolled data, which may generate a number of alternative hypotheses. For that reason, he suggests, that ex-postfacto research should better be considered as surveys useful in the derivation of hypotheses, which are tested through experimental approaches.

2. Critical Appraisal

Though ex-post-facto research suffers from many shortcomings, it will not be wisdom to say that it is merely "correlational" and useless. It has certain weaknesses no doubt; but at the same time, there are situations in which no design other than the ex-p6st-facto design is applicable or feasible. A critical appraisal of ex-post-facto research is presented in the following pages

There are three main weaknesses of ex-post-facto research which have already been discussed : (1) impossibility of manipulation of independent variable, (2) impossibility of randomization of subjects, and (3) poor internal validity due to lack of control of extraneous variables. All these inadequacies of this type of research, ultimately, result into one consequence: inadequate and less valid explanation of the relationship between dependent and independent variable. For example, if the study has come out with the finding that "children's anxiety-riddenness is due to parental inadequate relationship with children" by using low anxiety-ridden and high anxiety ridden children groups and comparing them on parent child relationship, it may not be very meaningful and valid because the difference between, these groups may also be due to some genetic factor, some environmental condition, or socio-economic status of the home. This, no doubt, is a weakness of this kind of research. But, this can be improved by testing all such possible alternatives or "control" hypotheses. And if some condition or conditions are found to be related and they also appear to be reasonable, plausible in° view of certain theories, preconceptions and past research they may be accepted. There will be less risk in that. On the other hand, if parent-child relationship is found to be related to children's anxiety through a highly controlled experiment, this may have high internal validity, but may not have high applicability as such controlled situations are hardly found anywhere in the homes and the society. Greater the control in experimentation, particularly in case of human beings, less will be the applicability of findings for this reason.

In spite of these weaknesses, ex-post-facto research has its importance in the field of psychology; sociology and education because most situations in these fields are such as conditions of true experiment cannot be met. There are a large number of variables in these fields, which cannot be manipulated. For example, variables such as intelligence, anxiety, motivation, and for that reason all the organism variables cannot be manipulated. Similarly, social pressures, social attitudes, socio-economic status of people, castes, social mobility etc. are factors, which cannot be manipulated. In education institutional climate, teachers' motivation, teachers' effectiveness, etc. are the variables that cannot be manipulated. In fact, such factors are too many in these fields, and manipulable variables are too few. Looking from this point of view the importance of ex-post-facto research emerges more vividly in spite of its weaknesses. The purpose of making this statement is not to undermine the importance of the experiment, but only to emphasize that each type of research has its advantages and disadvantages, which must be known to every researcher in order to enable him to make the best judgement in the actual situation of research. A thorough understanding of all types of researches, their weaknesses as well as advantages and the care with which each one of them should be used, open-mindedness and demands of the situation are sonic of the things that should be used in a particular case of research.

FIELD STUDIES

This is another approach to research in behavioural sciences much different from field experiment and laboratory experiment.

Meaning and Nature

As described by Kerlinger (p.405) **field studies** are ex-post-facto scientific enquiries aimed at discovering the relations and interactions among sociological, psychological, and educational variables in real social structures. It is obvious from this description that field studies are (1) ex-post-facto studies and (2) they are conducted in real life situations i.e. actual behaviour settings such as schools, homes, communities, etc. The behaviour setting is not, at all, disturbed and the behaviour observed is true and natural, not the behaviour influenced by the research process.

Barker (1956) considers this kind of a study as one in which the researcher is only a "transducer". One very important characteristic of a field study is that it observes, analyzes and investigates into the behaviour "as it is". The researcher observes only what is naturally there without disturbing it. In these studies, as has been observed by Kerlinger (p. 405) the researcher "ordinarily manipulates no independent variables".

There are two types of field studies as described by Katz (pp. 75-83) : (1) exploratory and (2) hypothesis-testing. The exploratory type studies seek what is rather than **predict relations.** The purposes of the exploratory type field studies are : (1) to find out critical variables, (2) to identify relations among variables, (3) to form the basis for further rigorous testing of hypotheses. The purpose of hypothesis testing type of field studies is to discover relationships among variables. For example, studies of correlates of academic achievement, correlates of delinquent behaviour, correlates of memory loss, etc. may be considered of this kind.

Critical Appraisal

Kerlinger (p. 406) strongly feels that field studies are "strong in realism, significance, strength of variables, theory orientation and heuristic quality". Since the studies are made in the actual situations of life, their results must be considered realistic in the sense that they can be applied to other similar situations also. The studies have significance because they yield a lot of information about phenomena in the field and this information may be used in carrying out more rigorous experiments. In case of these studies the variables show themselves more vividly as there are no surrounding conditions, unlike the laboratory experiment, which can suppress them. For example, achievement motivation of children measured in a school will have much greater variance as compared to children's achievement motivation measured in the laboratory. Field studies are not only factual; they lead to theory building also. The relations that are revealed by them may be built up into some plausible theory to be tested through more rigorous experimentation at a later stage. By being heuristic in nature means that they raise during the course of one study many more questions that may be answered through further research. For example, if it is found in one study that children's negative self-concepts are related to their home environment, it raises questions like: is it parent-child relationship, is it socio-economic status of the home, is it the sibling relationship, is it tire absence of father in the home which causes negative self-concept? These may be answered by further research.

In spite of these qualities, the field study research has several weaknesses. It has all those weaknesses, which have been described in connection with ex-post-facto studies. The relationships between variables discovered in the field studies are always less valid as compared to the laboratory and field experiments. This is due to the complexity of field situation. Because the investigator does not make any intervention and observes only what is naturally there without disturbing it, the field study is reduced to the level of a correlational study or to a trends study.

GENERAL REMARKS

In this write-up six strategies of experimental and non- experimental research have been discussed. Each one of them has its own advantages and disadvantages. One should not think that this is the best and that is the worst approach. Depending upon the objectives, feasibility of manipulation and control permitted by the situation each one of them may be found useful. The reality of research in behavioural sciences is such that the investigator is always required to be ready to make compromise between "realism" and "precision" i.e. accuracy, between internal validity and external validity, between control and natural settings, Judged from this point of view the field studies or expost-facto research ' maximize realism and concreteness of the behaviour system. The field experiments go a little away from this in the direction of intrusiveness, i.e. control and manipulation of variables. The laboratory experiment entirely discards the concrete, naturally occurring behaviour system and, thus, moves away from realism.

One thing that has got to be remembered by the investigator is that "realism", "precision" and "generality" are all very much desirable in every research, but they **can not** be maximized at the same time. The laboratory experiment has the highest degree of **precision, control, manipulation** and **measurement** of variable. Sequentially, then, field experiment, and expost-facto study respectively give up control and manipulation in the interest of realism and concreteness of the behavioural system under study. The three most desired qualities of research present before the researcher a three-horned dilemma. All are most wanted, rather essential. Yet, all of them cannot be maximally achieved in any single study. Choosing a strategy to increase one automatically will decrease another one. The trick is, therefore, not to search for the "right" strategy but to pick up the strategy that is best for your purposes and circumstances; and then to use all the strengths of that strategy and do whatever can be done to limit or offset its inherent weaknesses. This seems to be the best and most realistic approach to the consideration of these strategies of research.

Historical Research In Education

Usually, genuine research is begun because someone has asked a question, and set out to discover the answer. The question may relate to something in the past, present or future. If the question pertains to something some phenomenon, some event, some process, some development in the past and its answer is systematically and scientifically attempted to be discovered it is designated in the literature historical research. Historical research is critical search for truth about the past. Historical research in education is an inquiry about educational phenomena as they emerged, existed and developed. Historical research in education employs historical method of study. It aims to ascertain the nature, causes and reliability of educational happenings of the past with a view to contribute to better understanding and interpretation of the present and the future. Historical research in education involves activities that are common to all other investigations, but the nature of its subject matter presents some peculiar problems that require application of some special standards and techniques. Reliance on dependable sources of information about educational phenomenon, authentication of sources and the validation of evidence through an elaborate system of internal criticism with humanly possible objectivity are the basic tools of historical research in education.

There are three basic purposes of historical research

1. To understand and interpret the present problems and events of education in the light of the past occurrences is one purpose of historical research in education. The present, in fact, is nothing but a change emerging from the past. An understanding of the historical past of educational matters, policies, developments and their impacts may save education from repeating old-time mistakes and may also support some current desirable orientations. For example, the critical study of the role of discipline and values in the life of the individual and the society as part of ancient Indian education may strengthen the current Indian policy

of emphasizing value education. Such historical researches in education may support some of the present educational changes and control policy making.

2. To satisfy scholarly curiosity and desire of the educators and the educationists may be another purpose of historical research in education Curiosity and exploration is the basic instincts of the humans. Many people in and outside the field of education are curious to know and some naturally want to explore 'what was about it in the past, in the ancient India, in the mediaeval period ? For example, the curiosity to know 'what was taught to children in the schools in 16th century', 'how the system of training of teachers originated in India, 'what were the standards of education during the British period in India', 'how education was financed in pre- independence India', etc. is basic to human nature. Historical research in education satisfies this instinct of curiosity at least of those scientists who have a strong desire to arrive at an accurate account of the past of educational events and practices.

3. To link the past to the present and to the future may also be considered a desirable purpose of historical research in education. Preservation of cultural heritage and history of nations onward march are valuable and essentially desirable. This need is felt by every society in all spheres of human life. In the field of education this need is intended to be satisfied by its historical research.

Steps of Historical Research in Education

Following are the steps involved in the historical research in education:

1 . Formulation of the problem.

2. Collecting the data, i.e., the source material

3. Criticism of the source material, i.e. establishing the validity of the data. It includes (a) authenticity of the source, and (b) validity of its contents.

4. Formulating hypotheses to explain educational events and phenomena.

5. Interpreting and reporting the findings.

Collecting Data

Having identified the problem, the researcher moves on to collecting the data, i.e., the source matter or historical evidence. Sources of historical data are categorized as (1) primary source, (2) secondary source.

Primary sources are the basic material of historical research. Without these historical research loses its meaning and significance. Primary source includes original (provided by an actual eyewitness) documents and relics such as (1) official records (minutes of meetings, committee reports, legal documents etc.), (ii) institutional records, (iii) memoirs, biographies, diaries, personal letters, books, etc. These are studied along with changes, modifications, agreements-disagreements that might have taken place in course of time. **Secondary** Sources include information provided by a person who did not himself observe the phenomenon; for example reports appearing in newspapers, periodicals, encyclopedias, etc. Both of these sources are important. But, primary sources are most important.

Locating the source material is an arduous process. The researcher has to spend several hundred hours sitting in a library, museum, offices of educational institutions and organizations, talking to the old-timers, going to the bookshops, visiting school sites, examining correspondence, scrutinizing lecture notes and files of retired people etc.

Whether primary or secondary source the researcher does not assume that it is genuine. He considers it most important to establish its authenticity by subjecting it to rigorous tests. The methods used for this purpose are (a) external criticism, and (b) internal criticism, or validity of its content.

External Criticism

External criticism is the tool the researcher in case of historical research uses for checking the genuineness i.e. the validity of the source, which may be a document or a relic or a record. He tries to establish whether it is the original one, which was actually produced by the person, or persons who are said to claim it. He has to take a hard decision whether the source is admissible as evidence. He has to answer many questions about it such as who produced it, when and why to establish whether it is original, actual and real. He is required to establish authorship of historical data beyond doubt. He must ensure that the source document or record is not a fraud, a fictitious or tampered record. In case of written document he may face the problem of plagiarism and copying which he solves by examining the language, style, spelling, handwriting, printing of the document, as they may be typical of some person. He also tries to find out whether the events, things and places that a man of that period could have known, whether anyone altered the manuscript, whether the name of the author, date and place are there, whether the contents hint upon its being original. In some situations he may require the help of philologist, anthropologist, chemist, artist, literatiers, etc.

Internal Criticism (Establishing Validity of data)

External criticism is concerned with establishing the time, place and authorship of the document and establishing that its language and form, etc. are original as employed by the authors i.e., establishing that it is original and has not been tampered with. Internal criticism, on the other hand, requires to verify and ensure that the contents of the document, the information and other details, i.e., the data given in the document are valid and trustworthy. The researcher is required to verify what exactly author meant by what he wrote, whether all that the author wrote is credible, under what conditions and circumstances the author wrote all that, whether the arguments underlying the author's write-up are valid. The researcher, then, tries to make as correct interpretation of data as possible. This is what Van Dalen (p. 185) considers "reading a document through the author's eyes". The point is that faithful and errorless analysis and interpretation of the author's meaning is of great importance.

An appraisal of author's reputation, integrity and competence, motives, circumstances under which the document was written, etc. goes a long way in establishing the validity of the data given in the document.

Formulating Hypothesis:

Van Dalan suggests that on the basis of the data or evidence, thus collected, the researcher formulates tentative hypotheses that explain the occurrence of events and conditions. By this he means identifying underlying hidden meanings, connections, patterns or general principles on the basis of which the phenomenon under study can be systematically and scientifically explained. After constructing the hypothesis attempts are made on searching for evidence that will confirm or disconfirm the hypothesis. Mouly, however, does not bring in this stage in the process. F-te talks of only four steps (i) the problem, (i), Data. (ii) Analysis, and (iv) interpretation of the data. Van dalen (p. 195) however emphasizes that the hypothesis helps the historian determine what is relevant or irrelevant to a study and provides a framework for stating the conclusions of the study in a meaningful manner.

Interpretation and Reporting Findings

At this stage the researcher has to weave all the facts along with their interpretation around the hypotheses and make a sound generalization saving what is what, Van Dalen *(p.195)* says, "Weaving raw data into a cohesive, well-proportioned colourful exposition requires painstaking labour." Mouly *(p. 214)* points out that having established the authenticity and validity of the data the historian must address himself to the tasks of interpreting the facts in the light of the problem. He cautions that a historian should use analogy as a source of hypothesis or a frame of reference very carefully as historical parallels can be oriented in a number of directions depending on the historian's view. In the interpretation of facts and data impersonality is extremely important. The researcher is required to determine trends, which the data suggest by synthesizing and interpreting rather than by merely enumerating and summating the facts. The report to be presented must be sufficiently systematic interlinking the facts and leaving no gaps between them. The report must have an attracting style of writing and show that it makes a contribution in terms of newly discarded data or new interpretations reflecting scholarliness.

RESEARCH DESIGN AND SAMPLING

The third step of any scientific research is to prepare a research design. Research design is a mapping strategy, which is based on sampling technique. It essentially includes objectives, sampling, research strategy, tools and techniques for collecting the evidences, analysing the data and reporting the findings. Thus, research design is the statement *of* the object of the inquiry and how a satisfactory culmination to be effected. A research design is the work before getting the project underway.

Meaning of Research Design

Research design is a choice of an investigator about the components of his project and development of certain components of the design. A design of research does not consist of an ordered sequential step-by-step procedure. It is a planning stage of research, which is usually made logically visualizing its practicability. The selection *of* research components is done keeping in view of the objectives *of* the research. Research hypotheses also provide the basis for designing a research work. A research design includes the following components:

(a) Research method or research strategy.

(b) Sampling design.

(c) Choice of research tools, and

(d) Choice of statistical techniques.

A design of research is good or not, it is judged by standards such as the degree of accuracy attainable on the level of relevant evidence sought. A distinction should be drawn between statistical significance and substantive significance and appropriately applied. Above all, a good research design must be practical.

The review of the literature and related research reports are set as an important component of design. Also the classification and development of the classes of inquiry and their models are offered as major aspects *of* research design. Designing of research may be described as a mapping, because the research design components tend to fit into three distinct but interrelated parts; it is convenient to discuss the design components within these three components.

Kerlinger asserts that research design has two basic purposes *(1)* to provide answers to research questions, and (2) to control the variance.

A research design, components and proposals should give an adequate attention to each appropriate and applicable design component.

Definition of Research Design

Reduced to the simplest of terms, "research design is a mapping strategy. It is essentially a statement of the object of the inquiry and the strategies for collecting the evidences, analysing the evidences and reporting the findings."

It should be made clear that the design components are in part mandatory and in part choices made by the researcher. Just as the object of the inquiry often determines the class of inquiry or model to be utilised, so too, does the model or class of inquiry determine the consideration and development of certain of the design components. In fact, it is essentially the variation in some of the design-components that differentiates among the classes of inquiry.

Design Format for a Research Proposal

Title:

I. Problem Statement and its clarifying components.

(A) Statement of the problem.

(B) Clarification of the problem statement:

1. Definitions.
2. Delimitation.
3. Assumptions, and
4. Theory base.

II. Group Components for Operation -

(A) Hypothesis/Question design.

(B) Sample population - sample or group at hand design

1. Population defined, delimited and defined.
2. Sample delineated, delimited and defined.

3. Group at hand delineated, delimited and defined.

(C) Observation Design

1. Data (evidences) Collection

2. Instrumentation

(a) Questionnaire.

(b) Schedule.

(c) Sources

(d) Standard measures.

(D) Statistical Designs

1. Descriptive statistical design

2. Inferential statistics for generalization design.

3. Statistical randomization procedures for control design.

4. Computer assistance design.

(E) Organizational Design.

III. Significance and Review Sections

(A) Significance of the objectives of the Inquiry.

(B) Review of the Related Literature and Research Reports.

The object is to test the relationships indicated in the hypotheses in such a manner that the researcher will be able to either accept or reject the hypotheses. To accomplish this, a basic design must be established which will (1) allow the researcher to control the different variables and (2) ensure that the controlled treatments are comparable.

Characteristics of Good Research Design

In a general sense we could answer the question (what makes for good research design) ? With such statements as the design should be appropriate for the *hypotheses* or the design should be *feasible* within the limits of available *resource*. The following are the specific characteristics of a good research design :

1. It should be free from bias or learning's.
2. It should be free from confounding effect. A good research design eliminates confounding of variables or kept it to a minimum so the results can be interpreted separately.

3. There should be a statistical precision. Employing most appropriate statistical technique can test the hypotheses.
4. There should be enough scope to impose the control over the situation. There are basically four ways by which control can be enhanced:
   (a) Through the method of Randomization
   (b) Holding conditions or factors constant.
   (c) Building conditions or factors into the design as independent variable.
   (d) Statistical adjustment.

Potential Problems in Research Design

There are several difficulties, which make poor research design:

1. Inadequately stating and testing hypotheses.
2. Missing or unusable data.
3. Bias in sampling.
4. Inadequate measurement.
5. Lack of precision in statistical technique or inappropriate statistical devices.

Research Methodology : Research methodology involves the systematic procedures by which the researcher starts from the initial identification of the problem to its final conclusions. The role of the methodology is to carry on the research work in a scientific, and valid manner. The method of research provides the tools and techniques by which the research problem is attacked. The methodology consists of procedures and techniques for conducting a study. Research procedures are of little value unless they are used properly. The tools and techniques will not get the work done. The researcher must learn the proper use of research method.

Research methodology involves such general activities as identifying problems, review of the literature, formulating hypotheses, procedure for testing hypotheses, measurement, data collection analysis of data, interpreting results and drawing conclusions. Thus, research methodology consists of all general and specific activities of research Mastery of the research methodology invariably enhance understanding of the research activities. Thus, it seems that research design and methodology have the same meaning i.e. mapping strategy of research.

Suitability in Shaping Methodology of Educational Research

Webster has defined methodology as "the science of method or arrangement" which is not a particularly useful definition. Method is defined as orderliness and regularly or habitual practice of them in action." By placing stress on 'arrangement', orderliness, regularity and habitual practice, the methodologies derive their substance essentially from the classically ideal controlled experiment, which permeates rightly or otherwise, in the literature of educational research. The methodology means with reference to research that it is a type of inquiry.

Suitability as a criterion for consideration of a type of inquiry is much like that of utility but suitability of educational research methodology requires two conditions:

- Internal validity (control), and
- External validity (sampling).

Kish referred to internal validity as control and to external validity as representation of sample. Thus, internal validity (control) is the condition, which permits blaming the independent information variable for the findings or being certain that the observation was produced by the information variable. External validity (sampling or representation) is a condition permitting the generalization or inference for the findings to the population from which the sample was drawn.

The Crucial Issue of Educational Design : It is difficult to design a research project that meets both of these conditions. The classical ideal controlled experiment is endowed with both of these attributes. However, in education the controlled experiment will tend to be strong on internal validity and less strong on representation (external validity). There is virtually no claim to external validity in more control observation.

At this risk of over simplification, the investigation may be described as possessing less control concern than does the study and even less of a claim to external validity. The choice of this type of inquiry depends, in part, on the attainability of control and/or representation with a given research project and in part, on the relative need for control and/or representativeness.

The other type of inquiry is 'action research'. Control or internal validity and representativeness or external validity are desirable conditions. However, 'action research' is an adhoc methodology and he conditions of control and/or representativeness are special applications. Thus, they are discussed as they are individually applied.

Internal Validity

The world we know is composed of variables. A *variable* is described as a thing subject to change or fluctuation. *Research is a* process by which knowledge is either increased or clarified and progress is stimulated towards man's need for problem solving. But problem solving and understanding derive from control or knowing the effect of a particular variable on other variables.

Internal Validity derives from the control of variables. Control variable or constant is frequently added to the set or substitution for the development variable. A most common set of variables consists of dependent, independent and intervening variables. The use of independent variable to describe the variable to be manipulated and dependent variable to describe the other part of the relationship is frequently erroneously applied to a given research inquiry.

Information variables : All the independent variables are information variables. An information variable is the treatment applied to a group of subjects to discern the effect it has on the group characteristic.

The information variable is the treatment applied to a group of subjects to discern the effect it has on the group under the conditions imposed. The experimental variable and control variable are information variables.

Confounding Variable: The intervening variables are confounding variables. A confounding variable is one which, if not controlled or held constant between groups, will cloud the certainly about the effect the information variable has on the group characteristics- the dependent variables identified as relevant confounding variables having to be controlled in the given inquiry. The dependent variable is the constant.

Relevant confounding variables may also lay the subjects. Sometimes these variables are overlooked because they are not apparent.

Internal validity is accomplished to some extent by selection or control of the relevant confounding variables. It is essentially a procedure of matching the subjects on the basis of the confounding variables.

Randomization is another procedure in the attempt to attain satisfactory or acceptable internal validity. It should be noted that statistical randomization does neither eliminate nor control the confounding variables.

External Validity

External Validity (sampling for representation) is the condition permitting the generalization or inference of the sample findings to the population from which the sample was selected.

Representation is a desirable condition in the experiment and especially demanding condition in the *survey* research.

As the likelihood of representation (external validity) increases through sampling procedures, the certainty of internal validity (control) decreases. Because findings derived from samples are subject to error, procedures such as sampling-error statistics are used for estimating the accuracy of the sampling-findings. A sampling error is the difference between the true measure of the population (parameters) and an estimate of that parameter which is the sample-finding or observed measure. The degree of external validity is reported as level of confidence at .01, .0., level of significance.

The .01 level means that if other samples were drawn from the sample population, the like hood of obtaining a comparable sample-finding is 99 in 100 samples.

UNIT-4

LEARNING OBJECTIVE

Qualititative Research- Ethnographic-Developmental- documentary analysis-Validity and limitations of findings- factors influencing Validity of research findings-Research Report -Developing a research proposal (synopsis)- Writing research report and evaluation of research report.

QUALITATIVE RESEARCH

In qualitative research the data are not of numerical nature. It is more in descriptive narration form. The main focus under qualitative research is on an individual or a site covering elaborate and comprehensive details. Case study, ethnographic study and action research study are sonic examples of qualitative research.

Qualitative research is almost opposite to the well-structured quantitative research. It is carried out more in a naturalistic manner with a holistic approach. The credibility of qualitative research totally depends on the capabilities and experience of the qualitative researcher. He has to think reflectively, historically and biographically in order to make connections among live experience in a given social and cultural context. He has to have his own strategies of data-gathering approach. Observation, unstructured questionnaire interview schedule, available written records are some of' them. The dynamic and holistic approach provides a comprehensive insight into the phenomena.

Qualitative research cannot be considered as generalisable as the quantitative research by its very nature and approach. The credibility of such research depends more upon the capabilities and experience of qualitative researcher. A qualitative research is valid if it represents accurately those features of the phenomena, which it intends to describe. The approach is holistic and dynamic in nature. as against the pre-decided set of parameters in quantitative research, and provides comprehensive patterns emerging from detailed and unstructured elicitation of information.

In qualitative method the researcher goes to the field without being constrained by predetermined categories. Thus the researcher is open to any response that he may get in (lie field. This allows the researcher to stud\ the selected issues in depth and in detail. For instance, in qualitative method you don't essentially cam· with you a questionnaire or a test to the school being studied. Rather your observation and the interviewee's responses give various dimensions of the study. In qualitative inquiry the researcher is the instrument. Validity of observation therefore- to a great extent depends upon the skill competence and rigour of the person doing the fieldwork Flexibility, insight and ability to build on tacit knowledge are the strengths of the researcher. Systematic and rigorous observation, skillful interviewing (which is snore than just asking questions) and content analysis arc the characteristics of qualitative data.

The qualitative methods consist of three kinds of data collection (a) in-depth open ended interviews (b) observations- and (c) anal\sis of written documents. Data from interview consists of direct quotations from people about their experiences, opinions feelings and knowledge. The observation data consists of detailed description of people's activities, behaviours, actions; interpersonal interactions and organizational processes. Document analysis yields excerpts, quotations, correspondences, publications and reports, personal diaries and open-ended written responses to questionnaires. You should note that skills of interviewing and observation are fully integrated in a qualitative research. The skilled interviewer is also a skilled observer able to read non-verbal messages, sensitive to how interview setting can affect what is said, and attuned to the nuances of the interviewer interviewee interaction and relationship, Similarly, skills of interviewing are also essential for an observer because during field work lie will need and want to talk to people. A participant observer gathers a great deal of information through informal, naturally occurring conversations.

The data for qualitative analysis typically conies from f field work.. The researcher makes first hand observations of activities and interactions, sometimes engaged personally in those activities as a *"Participant Observer", as* a member of the group. The qualitative researcher talks to the people about their experiences and perceptions. More formal individual or group interviews are conducted. Sometimes symbols (i.e.. language, appearance and gesture) that are part of interaction between people are also noted. Extensive *field/ notes* are collected. *The investigator records critical events.* Critical events need not be spectacular.

They are simply things that seem to the observer to be of more interest than other events occurring at the same time and are, therefore, worth documenting in greater detail. These critical events are small but communicate messages. The voluminous raw data in these field notes are organized into readable narrative description with major themes, categories, and illustrative -case examples extracted through content analysis.

Qualitative methods focus on the processes, i.e. how something happens. -To the qualitative researcher what one does is less important than how he does it. Identification and explanation of the process requires detailed description. The experience of the process typically varies for different people_ and participants perceptions are a key process consideration," For this reason qualitative research is often charged with subjectivity. '

Qualitat1ve research adopts a holistic perspective in which units of analysis arc particular kinds of events, occurrences incidents, institutions and so on. Conclusions arc drawn about sonic events on the whole in which group comparisons have no meaning as is done in quantitative research.

Qualitative inquiry typically focuses in depth on relatively small samples-even single cases (may be one child, one institution or one event) which arc selected purposefully. These cases are *information rich cases* from which one can learn a great deal about Issues of central importance. The variety meaningfulness, insights, generated Gone qualitative inquiry depends more on the information richness of the cases selected and the observational and analytical capabilities of the researcher than with the sample size, etc. as is the case with the quantitative research.

OTHER SPECIFIC CHARACTERISTICS OF QUALITATIVE RESEARCH

A few specific issues and themes related to qualitative research are described as follows:

(a) Naturalistic Inquiry

Qualitative designs are naturalistic. Such an. inquiry is conducted "in situation", in the natural setting where behaviour/or event takes place. For example. If you want to study the teaching methods adopted in a particular school, you go to the school and observe the teaching methods of teachers in their natural context. The research setting is a natural occurring event, programme, and relationships, and interactions. The researcher makes no attempt to adulterate for example; the way students interact with the teacher and amongst themselves the way teacher interact with the students. The researcher's job is to observe and take note of what happens in a naturally occurring situation.

(b) Inductive Analysis

Qualitative methods aim at exploration, discovery and inductive (specific to general) logic. The researcher attempts to make sense of the situation Without Imposing pre-existing expectations or categories on the phenomenon. Categories or dimensions of analysis emerge from open-ended observations and interviews as the researcher comes to understand the situation.

(c) Direct Personal Contact : Going to the field

One of the important attributes of qualitative inquiry is that the researcher makes direct and personal contacts with people under study. Thus contact is made in two ways. First, the researcher remains physically present With the people for a period of time. Second, he develops closeness by sharing their experiences and earning their confidence. In other words, the researcher becomes a part of the group, both physically and socially, by participating in their social functions and sharing their experiences ideas and values. This helps the researcher in describing and understanding both the externally observable behaviours and internal states (such as worldview, opinions, values, attitudes, symbolic constructs, and so on). Thus, field work involves getting one's hand dirty, participating in actual group or societal activities, and getting to know the members of the society on a personal level.

(d) Holistic Perspective

Qualitative researchers strive to understand the phenomenon as a whole. For example, if you are studying the functioning of a primacy school you do not break it in terns of teachers students headmasters, building; de. Rather, you study, the school as a unit and attempt to establish linkages between its different constituents. Remember, whole is considered a complex system that is greater than suns of its parts.

(e) Unique Case Orientation

You have heard about case studies. What is a case ? A case nothing but a specific person (be it a student or a teacher), institution (sell events or process which is different from rest of the masses and in which researcher is interested. It is an information rich source. By employing methods of naturalistic observation, qualitative inquiry, and document analysis, one presents detailed portrayals of the case. Good case studs provide more valid portrayals, better basis of personal understanding of what is going on, and solid ground for considering action.

(f) Design Flexibility

The design of a naturalistic inquiry cannot be specified in advance. It must emerge, develop and unfold as the study progresses. Only focus of the study plans 'for observations and interviews, and primary questions to be explored can be decided- by the researcher in advance. Qualitative inquiry requires high tolerance for ambiguity and uncertainty trust in the ultimate value of what inductive analysis will yield.

It should be noted that there is no *ideal* condition for conducting a qualitative inquiry. It can be conducted an where and in any context. It is important to understand the connections between strategic ideals and required practical tactics in the real world. Real world situations seldom resemble the theoretical ideals taught in the classroom.

IMPROVING THE QUALITY OF QUALITATIVE RESEARCH THE TRIANGULATION WAY

In order to improve the quality of qualitative research triangulation of various aspects and devices may be used. These may be.

Methodological Mixes : Triangulation

One important way to strengthen qualitative research is through *triangulation,* or using the combination of methodologies in the study of the same phenomenon. It is based on the logic that no single method ever adequately solves the problem because each method reveals different aspects of empirical reality. Therefore, multiple methods of observation must be employed. There arc four basic types of triangulation (a) Data triangulation.

It refers to the use of variety of sources of data in a study. For example, you cam compare observational data with interview data. compare what people say in public with what they say in private, compare what people say over time, compare what different categories of people (e.g. students, teachers. community_ members) say about a phenomenon.

(b) Investigator triangulation

You should not depend upon the observation of one investigator. Rather, more than one investigator should be collecting data. This reduces the personal biases of the investigators.

(c) Methodological triangulation

This refers to the use of multiple methods to study a single problem. It is also possible to combine qualitative and quantitative approaches. Thus you can combine the methodologies of participant observation, qualitative Interviewing and questionnaires or tests to collect the required information.

(d) Theory triangulation

You may use multiple perspectives to interpret a single set of data.

Ethnography: An Example of Qualitative Research

Ethnographic (ethno = culture, graphic = description) research focuses on the question: "what is the culture of this group of people." Participant observation is the principal method of ethnographers. This entails intensive fieldwork in which the investigator is immersed in the culture of the study. A researcher can conduct an ethnographic study of a school. He would be then exploring the culture of the school. The question that arises is what is this culture ? Culture is that collection of behaviour patterns and beliefs that constitute "standards for deciding what it is, standards for deciding what it call be, standards for deciding how one feels about it, standards for deciding what to do about it, and standards for 'deciding how to go about doing it".

MANDATES IN COLLECTING QUALITATIVE DATA

There are certain requirements for undertaking a qualitative inquiry. These are

i) The researcher must get· close enough to the people and situation, being studied to personally understand in depth and details of what goes on. That is, the researcher must participate, and become a part of the research,, setting..

ii) The researcher must aim at capturing what actually takes place and what actually people say : the perceived facts.

iii) The qualitative data must include a great deal of pure description of their activities; interactions and settings.

iv) Qualitative data must include direct quotations from people, both what they' speak and what they write down.

Thus, a qualitative inquiry is conducted in a natural setting, which requires a researcher to personally make contacts with the people under study. The qualitative research focuses on a holistic perspective. Adopting a neutral perspective, the researcher attempts to strengthen his findings adopting triangulation methods. The qualitative data descriptive in nature.

Ethnographical Research

Research in education can be classified in a number of ways different points of view. But from the point of view of focus methodology one very broad classification can be *experimental versus Descriptive Research.* In both of these the purpose and the methodology, quite different from one another. If the purpose is not to establish the cause effect relationship and the methodology is not that of the experiment, research can drays be classified as descriptive. Within the domain of the descriptive search there can be placed variously described researches as analytical research, evaluation research, historical research, l research, policy research and ethnographic research, depending upon focus around which their methodology and related activities revolve. Ethnographic research centers around the *analysis* and *description of* historical evolution and *current status of* the phenomena, emphasis qualitative- phenomenological perspective.

Meaning of Ethnography

Ethnography literally means that branch of anthropology that treats historically *of* the origin and filiations of races and-nations. It has more less the same connotation in the context of research in education. It j method of research used in anthropology of education. It is defined as a technique *of* describing and accounting for the behaviour of people analyzes hove people perceive the dynamics *of* their own acting sensibly in relation to others and also the procedures they use to do this. It is concerned with both (1) what is in the minds of the natives. i.e. the members *of* a group of community and also with their overt behaviour. In its most formal sense is called "ethno science" various aspects of which are presented in the bi *Culture and Cognition* by Spradlev. Driving the past 15-20 years do ethnography has become very popular in studies of schooling. By implication, it is comparative and cross-cultural.

Ethnographic Research : Basic Characteristics

Etlinography involves intensive data collection on many variables over an *extended period of time* in *a natural vetting.* It is also sometimes, called "naturalistic research or "field research". It may be considered a kind of qualitative research. Like qualitative research ethnographical research also uses participant observation as its methodology. Guba draws a distinction between naturalistic and rationalistic research. Ethnographical research lie considers naturalistic enquiry. By rationalistic enquiry he means controlled research, which is more likely to use quantitative methods such as random selection of subjects and use of psychological tests and statistical methods of analysis. But, the main difference between quantitative and ethnographical research lays not so much in methodologies as in the setting and the degree of control sought.

Ethnographical research is relatively a recent development in the field of education, which emerged as a reaction to dissatisfaction with the traditional methods of research for investigating certain kinds of educational problems.

In the field of education ethnographic research can be conducted in situations in which human behaviour constitutes one of the important variables. It may be human behaviour in the context of an organization such as the school, the college, the university the family the. Community, an office or any other educational system. Ethnographic studies describe the context, present as well as the past. They answer questions like why is it so how has it come to be so, What is actually happening, how do people think feel and act. But, it is not these pre existing research questions that make ethnographic research so distinct from other types of researches. Rather, it is its methodology that distinguishes it from other types of studies. A few important characteristics of the ethnographic research are:

1. Basically, it is *qualitative* and *descriptive* research. Its purpose is to describe a phenomenon or a situation; for example, education in a village, operating values in a school or the school system, organizational behaviour in the university or the university system, life in the classroom, and like that. It is qualitative in the sense that the data that are collected are only qualitative and analysis of the data is also done qualitatively using analytical method.

2. The unit of observation in an ethnographic study in education is a classroom or even a school. The ethnographer works more inductively by observing many aspects of the learning environment. He observes and identifies factors associated wi:h effective and ineffective environments.

3. The rationale underlying the ethnographical research is that behaviour occurs in a context and hence accurate understanding, of behaviour requires understanding of the context in which it occurs.

4. It is a kind of field research in which behaviour is studied in its natural context or setting. But, it is not a field study in the same sense in which it is understood in case of experimental research. Its method is different from that of the experimental research.

5. It assumes that to understand human behaviour it is necessary to know how people interpret their realities. For that reason it is necessary, as is assumed in it, that one should study the thoughts, feelings and actions of people. *Differential perceptions* should be focused at and interpreted in relation to the problem. It is the *latent meanings* of the context, which the ethnographer considers important and tries to uncover. In fact- the ethnographer studies the *total context* and takes a *It-holistic* view of the behaviour. Holistic approach to the study of the problem is also a basic consideration of ethnographic research.

6. Ethnographic research uses case 'stud\ design in which it is one Single unit, all individual or an Institution group or a conlInunlty which is studied in depth.

7. Ethnographic procedures can be used in basic applied and evaluation research. It pray is used to explore the given field of researcher to gain insight into the research problem and provide a basis for development of hypotheses. It may also he used to gather *supplementary material* that would help interpret findings obtained by other techniques.

8. Ethnographic research may involve participant and non-participant observation or both. But. by and large it is participant observation which is used.

9. In fact- ethnographic research is a "multi-instrument" research. It uses a variety of data- collection devices along with observation. It involves *verbal* and *non-*

verbal techniques of data collection. Verbal techniques include tools such as questionnaire, interviews, attitude scales and other psychological tests and tools. Non-verbal techniques include such strategies as the use of recording devices and examination of written records.

Method and Procedure

The ethnographical research studs have four major aspects of the framework in which it is conducted. These are:

1. **Specifying Objectives** or research questions or purposes of the study in a broad perspective. These are in the form of foreshadowed problems, not rigid preconceived ideas but flexible targets. Foreshadowed problems state the initial focus and conceptual framework. Other questions develop from the *site*. The selection of research questions for a particular study *actually occurs after data collection so* that they may reflect the reality of the field. The research problem begins with the relatively general research question.

2. **Specifying the Research Design** and methods of collecting data, kind of data, tools for data collection and method of analyzing data.

3. **Direct On - Site Observation** in the natural setting is the basic method or tool used for collection of data. Observation for an *extended time* is the most, elementary requirement for obtaining a valid database. The ethnographer *selects a research role* that Melds data valid for the purpose and the focus of the study is observing and recording field data from *multiple data source*. The data are *qualitative and descriptive* recorded in very minute detail, and gathered from words, records, written documents, talks with people, behavioural anecdotes, customs and ways of living, songs, dramas, photographs anything that throws light on any aspect of the problem or emerging questions. Its major technique of data collection is participant observation, meaning thereby that the researcher acts as a member' of the group being studied aiming at describing *both thinking* about behaviours and actual behaviours from the native's point of view. It also uses in some cases extensive formal and informal *unstructured interviews, clinical interviews, content analysis* and case-study approaches. These are tools of

qualitative research which ethnographic research also uses in order to find out how natives *categorize objects, conditions of being, behaviours, people etc.*.

Ethnographic research *has no fixed* or *rigid* research design, fixed hypotheses, fixed objectives. Everything is flexible and changeable at any,:' stage. It is designed and redesigned again and again, Same is the case with the data. They too are not predetermined. Once collected and reviewed conceptualized may be recollected as reconceptualized. *The cycle may on like this for a long time till a definite perspective emerges.*

Analysis of data triangulation in their case includes cross- checking different data sources from different time periods *using techniques of constant comparison and synthesizing multiple perceptions.* It also includes *descriptive narration, analytical interpretation* and *theoretical interpretations.*

The quality of the study is determined by the *logical relationship* among the purpose, methodology, findings and contribution to knowledge. This is done in the analytical framework. Psychological analysis is preferred to political analysis. Systematization emphasizing problem statement, conceptual or theoretical framework, review of literature, methodology statements, are not considered very important in case of anthropological research. It is conducted in a very unstructured situation.

To sum up, ethnographical research is field research which (i) synthesizes the perspectives of the participants, the latent meanings of the context and views of the observers, (ii) , asserts that for understanding human behaviour study of actions, thoughts, and feelings of people and the way they perceive their environment and realities is essential, (iii) consists of foreshadowed problems that constitute its initial focus and conceptual framework and guide the field work. (iv) is not limited to data collected and questions framed, but gives rise to other research questions, (v) Depends on actual on-site observations for sufficiently long time for obtaining relevant data, (vi) emphasizes total context or holistic view by observing and *recording* field notes from various sources, (vii) uses techniques of cross checking data, (viii) uses case study design, (ix) frames hypotheses or research questions after data collection, (x) describes the context at abstract level using descriptive narration. analytical interpretation or theoretical interpretation (xi) adopts procedures that can be used in basic, applied and evaluation research.

Critical Evaluation

Some experts in the field say that ethnographical research is unsystematic and haphazard. The criticism does not seem to be quite fair. Ethnographers plan their research studies as carefully as other researchers using other methods. It is true that its results are difficult to analyse and findings difficult to replicate. This is also u fact that it tends to be more costly than other kinds of researches. Proper use of ethnographical approach requires the accurate recording of large amount of data, over long periods of time. by persons who are thoroughly trained in observational methods.

DEVELOPMENTAL STUDIES

This is another type of descriptive studs. This type of study aims at describing the change that takes place in the growth and development of an organism or an institution or some social process over a determined period of time. It also describes what factors and conditions in what manner brought about the change. Van Dalen (p. 228) discusses two types of this kind of research-

Growth Studies and Trend Studies.

(a) Growth Studies

Growth studies can be made in any field. But, most common are the studies of human growth and development. They describe how the human organism develops, what characteristics develop at what stage of life, which forces and factors are responsible for these developments. These studies have been of two types- **longitudinal and cross-sectional.**

In case of longitudinal studies the same child or the same group of children is measured on several variables at different age levels with the result that the study stretches over a number of years bringingmost critical changes taking place at critical age levels. For example, a group child is measured on intelligence, social habits, emotional stability, self concepts, interests and other personality characteristics at the age-level 5, 6, 7, 8, 9, 10 and I1 years. By comparing these measures, the researcher is in a position to describe the developmental change-taking place.

The cross-sectional research measures several different groups of children of different ages simultaneously on certain variables of interest and compares the groups among themselves to find out how they differ and what dominant characteristics are shown at different age-levels. Such studies are completed within a short duration of time. For example, simultaneously at one point of time, a researcher administers his tools for measuring a few variables mean on five, six, seven, eight and nine year old children compares them`, On the scores on each variable for all the age-groups basis of this comparison, he describes which traits are dominant at which age level, or which dominant characteristics define a particular age-group.

It is difficult to say whether longitudinal or cross-sectional approach is better. Both have their advantages and disadvantages. The longitudinal method is considered more appropriate a technique of studying human development. It has several advantages. But, at the same time it has certain weaknesses also. It gives, no doubt, more accurate assessment of the developmental change. But that may not be true about all individuals as the group of children that is studied. may not be representative of any larger population. Another weakness is that it is difficult to keep all the subjects within the study over a low-, pod of time. Several of them may be lost to the investigation for several reasons. Also, it is very time consuming. It is difficult to wait for the results for such a long time.

The cross-sectional study on the other hand is considered to be handy and adequately manageable. Hence, they are more popular. They have the advantage of being completed within a short duration. They reveal the status of the children of different age groups on several variables simultaneously. Yet, they, too, have several weaknesses. One of these is that the groups that are compared are not, many a time, comparable.

Both the types of studies are, however, considered quite useful if the purpose is to understand growth and development.

Children grow very fast. They also learn very quickly. If one observes a child admitted in grade I for some time, one finds many changes in the child's behaviour. The researchers who want to know change in behaviour over time can apply cross-sectional or longitudinal designs for their study.

Suppose, a researcher is interested to know the change in height and weight of the child after every six months for a period of three years. Another researcher may be interested to know how many words children can recognize when they are 4 years old, 4% years old. 5 years old, and 6 years old. In these types of studies one can either employ a cross-sectional design or a longitudinal design.

A cross-sectional design is relatively simpler. It involves collection of information from different groups of pupils (varying in age) at a single time. For example, you want to know the number of words children can recognize. You select four groups of children: 4 years old, 4/2 years old, 5 years old and 6 years old. In other words, in this design, the researcher attempts to study the impact of age on behaviour or learning. The design is simple and consumes less time, money, etc. But it fails to explain the processes involved in learning. Also persons born at different time periods cannot be considered equal in terms of their cultural and historical experiences.

Longitudinal design, in contrast, involves study of same group of children over a number of times. For example, in the above example, children, who are 4 years old will be tested on the first occasion. Thereafter, the researcher will wait for 6 months and only after the children attain the age of 4% years they will be subjected to testing. The same group of children will be tested when they are 5 and 6 years old. It is evident that this method is more time-consuming and costly. It is also characterized by the problem of attrition. Considering the current high dropout rate, by the time you go for second testing many children might have dropped out. So you get lesser number of pupils. The same group of children is tested on several occasions, which enhances the possibility of carryover of learnt material from one occasion to another. The advantage is that it helps in understanding the processes involved in learning.

(b) Trend Studies

Trend studies also constitute a sort of developmental type of research as they also observe and assess what characteristics prominently and consistently emerge at different times. But, they do not stop only at this point describing only these consistently dominating characteristics. They are future-oriented also in the sense that on the basis of these consistently dominant characteristics or trends they also predict what will be the future status of these trends, how will they affect the institution, the people, the environment, the output and other various aspects. For example, the study of the rates of enrolment at primary level of education for the past ten years may enable the researcher to predict what will be the situation in the next live or ten years, how many schools will have to be opened, how much financial allocation will be required per year, and so on.

This kind of' research uses methods and techniques of various other research strategies such as historical research, survey techniques and content analysis, etc. Studies of' school enrolment, population changes, employment opportunities, specific social changes, etc. may he considered belonging to this category research. For certain purposes, they may be considered very useful.

Documentary Data Analysis

The nature of the data depends mostly upon the type of tool or technique used by researchers for collecting these data. Most of the information in behavioural sciences including social psychology and education is in the form of verbal and other symbolic behaviour. The verbal data gathered through questionnaires, observation or interview is mostly qualitative in nature. These data indicate what people have said in their own words about their experiences and interactions in natural settings, and after careful analysis, the data provide useful and depth answers to the research questions of decision makers and information users. Patton *(1982, p. 22)* emphasizes that:

> Qualitative data provide depth and detail. Depth and detail emerge through direct quotation and careful description. The extent *of* depth and detail *will* vary depending upon the nature and purpose *of* a particular study.

The responses to open-ended questions on a questionnaire are detailed and comprehensive. These responses are neither systematic nor standardized. However, they permit the researcher to understand situations as seen and felt by him. Since the responses to open-ended questions are longer and detailed, they help the researcher to understand in depth the points of view of other people, their level of emotion, their characteristics, their attitudes and values, and their experiences. Patton *(1982, p. 28)* is of the view that responses to open-ended questions in the form of direct quotations reveal level of emotions of respondents, the way in which they have organized their world, their thoughts and experiences about certain happenings, and their perceptions.

The data gathered through participant observation or an open-ended/ unstructured interview is also descriptive in nature. These strategies are most comprehensive for understanding fully the complexities of a particular situation. Participant observation provides first hand information to the researcher about some social event in depth and detail. Data gathered through participant observation generally include: (i) description of the setting of the social situation; (ii) activities that take place in the setting; and (iii) description about people who participated in the activities and their extrinsic behaviour during the activities. The descriptions may be in the form of field notes specifying some basic information pertaining to the place where the observation takes place, the persons present during the observation, nature of the settings, type and nature of various types of interactions and activities during the observation. The field notes taken during observation contain direct quotations of the people who participated in the observation as well as the observer's own feelings and reactions. Patton *(1982, p.10)* states that notes taken by the observer becomes the eyes, ears and perceptual senses for the researcher. These notes are of immense help to the researcher if they are factual, accurate and comprehensive.

It is not possible to find out what is in and on other individuals' mind while observing their extrinsic behaviour. Through participant observation, it is difficult for an observer to know the feelings, thoughts and intentions of others and also about the behaviours that took place in earlier situations. However, through open-ended/unstructured interview, it is possible to find out from people those things, which had happened earlier or could not be observed during the participant observation. It provides framework within which the researcher should be able to gather information from people conveniently and accurately. The information mostly pertains to a programme, the reaction of participants about the programme and the type of change the participants perceive in themselves after their involvement in the programme. The data are mostly in the form of responses to structured and unstructured questions put to the respondents by the researcher during an informal conversation. The responses are generally direct quotations from respondents in their own words and provide details about situations, events, people, experiences, behaviour, values, customs, etc. The information gathered during or after an interview includes notes taken by an interviewer along with his detailed comments about what people say about their experiences, what they think and feel about the phenomena under study, and what they know about the phenomena.

ORGANIZATION OF QUALITATIVE DATA

The qualitative data gathered using open-ended questionnaire, participant observation and in-depth interview are voluminous. They need to be organized and classified into specific patterns, categories, and descriptive units to avoid any chaos. However, before any such classifications, it is advisable to make some copies of all the data. Patton *(1982, p.298)* suggests to make four copies and store one complete copy in a safety deposit box as these data are priceless and unique. In case of loss of any data, it is impossible to recapture what was actually observed during a participant observation or what exact conversation took place during an open-ended in-depth interview. The second copy should be used for further treatment of the data throughout. It is essential to ensure that the field notes taken during participant observation or open-ended interview are complete. The third copy may be used to fill the missing gaps, if any, identified during their scrutiny by the researcher. Additional notes can also be recorded in this copy. The organization of qualitative data involves a lot of cutting and pasting for which fourth copy may be used.

Actual classification or organization can begin only after the copies are made. There are no formal or universal rules, which a researcher may follow in organizing the data in various units, patterns. or categories. It requires a creative approach and a lot of perseverance to give a meaningful look to the data. The researcher may read the contents of field notes about the interview or observation carefully and he may note down his comments in the margins or attach small pieces of paper with his written notes using staples or tags. The next step is to arrange the data in topics for which the researcher may use abbreviations. The abbreviated topics are written either in the margins of the relevant data or on a slip of paper which may be attached with the relevant page. However, it may be noted that the researcher should make several readings of the information or data before they arc completely indexed. The process of classifying or labeling various kinds of data and preparing a data index is the essential step in the organization of qualitative data. Sometimes there are large data and it is not possible to develop a simple classification system. In such situations, the data are organized with the help of computers. Computers help in developing systematic and comprehensive classification schemes using code numbers for different categories and sub-categories. The computerized classification system permits the use of organized data by severalt groups of people over a long period of time. It permits easy cross-classification and cross comparison of descriptive narrations for complex analysis. The elementary details about the nature and use of computer are discussed in chapter 7.

ANALYSIS AND INTERPRETATION ON QUALITATIVE DATA

Analysis of qualitative data means studying the organized material in order to discover inherent facts. These data are studied from as many angles as possible either to explore the new facts or to reinterpret already . known existing facts. The content analysis, inductive analysis and logical analysis are mostly used in analysis of qualitative material.

CONTENT ANALYSIS

Content analysis is concerned with the classification, organization and comparison of the content of document or communication. In the context of communication research, Berelson *(1952, p. 18)* remarks that:

Content analysis *is* a research technique *for* the objective. systematic, and quantitative description of the manifest content of communication.

Cartwright *(1970, p. 424)* uses the terms "content analysis" and "coding" interchangeably as both the processes involve objective, systematic, and quantitative description of any symbolic behaviour. Since content analysis is concerned with the classification, evaluation and comparison of the content of communication or document, it is sometimes referred to as "documentary activity" or "information analysis". The communication may be in the form of responses to open-ended questionnaire, conversation as a result of interview, or description of an observed activity. It may also be in the form of official records (census, birth, accident, crime, school, institutional and personal records), judicial decisions, laws, budget and financial records, cumulative records, courses of study, content of text books, reference works, newspapers, periodicals or journals, prospectus of various educational institutions or universities, etc., direct quotations, and notes of an interview.

Berelson *(1952)* has specified three broad approaches that a researcher may adopt in content analysis. These include: (i) characteristics of content: (ii) producers or causes of content; and (iii) audience or effects of content. In any singly study, he may or may not adopt more than one of these approaches.

(1) Characteristics of Content

In this approach, the researcher is interested primarily in the characteristics of the content itself. He may focus either on the *substantive nature* of the content or upon the *form* of content. Berelson *(1952)*. as quoted by Cartwright *(1970)*, has listed six uses which are concerned primarily with substantive characteristics of the content. In the first two of these, the researcher either tries to describe trends in communication content over periods of time by employing methods for sampling the total flow of communication at successive points in time and to use the same system of classification throughout or he attempts to trace the development of scholarship in the publication of reputed scientific journals. For example, a researcher may study and record trends in articles on *concept of adult education* in the Indian context appearing in Surveys of Research in Education (Buch, *1973, 1979, 1987 & 1991). A* scrutiny of the topics of research in *distance education* over a period from *1980* to *1995* appearing in various scholarly journals is an example to illustrate trends in their publications.

In the next two uses, the researcher attempts to compare the content materials coming from different sources. He may be interested either to disclose international differences in communication content or to compare media or "levels" of communication. Cartwright *(1970, p. 426)* has cited two studies comparing Germany and the United States. Herbert Lewin *(1947)* made comparable categorization of the literature of the Hitler Youth and the Boy Scouts of America in terms of their goals and justification. Mc Granahan and Wayne (1948) compared the major themes of the most popular dramas appearing in Germany and America in the year *1927* and *1910*. Cartwright *(1970)* points out that substantially similar differences were found between the two countries. He has reported that other studies comparing different countries have been made in terms of such media as radio, newspapers, and text books, and a few comparable interviewing surveys have also been conducted in different countries. It may be pointed out that in making such cross-national comparisons, the researcher may face problems of sampling and of translations. But such types of studies have produced useful comparative data for understanding national differences.

In the fifth use the researcher may be interested in studying the role of various mass media in moulding public opinion. For example, differences in partisanship among newspapers, journals, radio and T.V. in the role of a certain voluntary organization in the *National Literacy Alission Programmes* may be studied by some researcher to identify which media favour more the role of the organization in comparison to other.

In the sixth use of the analysis of characteristics of systematic material, the observed substance of communication content is evaluated against standards adopted by the researcher. Studies are conducted to evaluate the social contributions of the media of communication. Comparing actual performance against some specified explicit and precise standards such as "fairness", "objectivity" or "balance" can make such an evaluation. In a study of evaluating performance against standards by British Royal Commission of the Press (1949), a list of major facts concerning the first year's progress of the National Coal Board was prepared by the research group. The group then checked the reporting of these "actual events" in various newspapers and found insignificant coverage of what they regarded as socially important information

Cartwright (1970) has pinpointed three other uses of content analysis in which the focus of the researcher is upon the *form* of the content. The first of these is concerned with the content analysis of propaganda so as to reveal the ways in which the propagandist pursues his objectives of influencing the public. The ways may include the themes or appeals employed by the propagandists. An analysis of the content of British and German propaganda in World War I by Lasswell (1927), for example, concluded that British stressed humanitarian ideals much more than did the Germans.

In the second use, the main concern of the researcher is to measure the *readability* of communication material. Grading such material on the basis of their difficulty of comprehension may do this. Educators undertake such type of studies to make textbooks fit the age and mental level of different groups of students using various schemes. Flesch (1951) used (i) reading ease and (ii) human interest as the two major components of readability. "Reading ease" is measured by number of syllables per 100 words and by the average length of sentence, and "human interest" is measured by the percentage of *personal words* and *personal sentences*.

The third use confines to the discovery of the stylistic features or characteristics of literary products. The study by Miles (1951) pertaining to ratio of verbs to substantives in poetry since sixteenth century is an example of such type of content analysis.

(ii) Producers or Causes of Content

In the second major approach, the researcher attempts to draw valid inferences about the nature of the procedures of the content or the causes of the symbolic material from the characteristics of the material itself. In some situations where the researcher cannot study the producer of the content (communicator) directly, but has access to the communicated material (content), this approach is used to make valid inferences about the nature of the producer of the content. In other situations, where a researcher can persuade an individual to produce symbolic behaviour as a response to standard conditions, the characteristics of such behaviour are generally taken as a very acceptable indication of the individual's own characteristics. Cartwright (1970) has highlighted four uses of content analysis which illustrate various ways in which researchers have tried to construct a picture of the communicator from his symbolic materials or products. The first use in confined to a number of studies in which intentions and attitudes of communicators have been inferred from an analysis of their communications. As illustration of this type of content analysis is the study of Leites et al. (1951) of speeches delivered in 1949 by members of Soviet elite in celebration of Stalin's birthday. These speeches were analyzed so as to know the attitudes of the speakers towards Stalin.

It was found that sharp differences existed in the image of Stalin as revealed by the old Bolsheviks and by other speakers.

Assessment of psychological state of persons or groups using contents of clinical interviews, protective tests, biographies, autobiographies, diaries, letters and other personal documents illustrates second important use of content analysis. For example, Baldwin (1942) studied the motivational and ideational clusters in a writer's personality after recording frequencies with which certain themes were contiguous to another within a sample of letters written by him. To detect the existence of propaganda or to obtain political and military intelligence illustrate other two uses of content analysis. For example, during the World War II the United States Department of Justice, making use of content analysis developed by Lasswell (1949), revealed remarkable similarities between allegedly native-fascist propaganda and the propaganda of Nazis. During war time, there is need for intelligence (political or military) about the activities of hostile nations. For this, methods using content analysis of various communication material, have been developed.

Audience and Effects of Content

In the third major approach to content analysis, the researcher interprets the content so as to reveal something about the nature of its audience or its effects. He takes the content material as a basis for drawing inference about the characteristics of the *audience* for whom the material (content) is designed, or about the effects of communication. This approach is illustrated by the following three uses of content analysis.

Some studies of the content of mass media assume that the material communicated through these media reflect the feeling or thought of the group or population existed at that time. For example, Hart (1933) analyzed the content of popular magazines in the United States over a period of years from 1900 to 1930. He found what he took to be evidence for a decline in the status of religion and an increase in tolerance of sexual freedom during this period.

In the second use of content analysis, it is assumed that there is a more or less approximate correspondence between the content of the mass media and the cognitive behaviour of the audiences exposed to the media. If a particular theme is stressed in the media at some place and time, it is assumed that this theme will be prominent in the thinking of the audience or population. A researcher, for example, may study that day time TV programmes deal predominantly with the themes concerning personal problems rather than public affairs.

Studies dealing with the description of attitudinal and behaviour responses to communications illustrate 'the third use of content analysis. Berelson (1942) points out three ways in which content analysis has been used to study the effects of communications. The first consists in analyzing materials which were produced in response to some specific communication. A researcher, for example, may study published reactions to a book on a theme highlighting *Indian Culture.* In the second kind of analysis, a researcher may attempt to show empirical relations between the content of a communication and responses to it. To illustrate, a researcher may attempt to trace a relationship between the frequency of arguments concerning "Privatisation of Higher Education" in the various media and the number of university teachers who could recognize the argument. The third kind of analysis attempts to make a direct inference to the effect of content without any reference to response data themselves. Using this type of approach, Lasswell and Blumenstok (1939) analyzed the themes employed by communists in Chicago in 1930's and concluded that their propaganda was relatively ineffective because it was not in line with fundamental values of citizens to whom it was addressed.

STEPS IN CONTENT ANALYSIS

The preceding discussion was confined to the details about the objectives of content analysis and its uses. The following section describes the steps involved in the process along with some issues relating to this operation.

1. Defining the Unit of Analysis

The unit (material) may be confined to single words, to phrases, to complete sentences, to paragraphs, or to even larger amounts of materials such as articles or to complete books. Either of these can be considered as an entity whose specified characteristics can be determined and analyzed. Hayman (1968, p. 80) suggests that the unit should be comprehensive enough to provide meaning through some content at least, but small enough not to allow subjectivity in its use.

2. Specifying Variables and Categories

Once the unit is defined, the researcher conducts its analysis so as to create reproducible or objective data for scientific treatment and generalization beyond the specific set of symbolic material analyzed. For converting symbolic material into objective data, it is necessary to specify the "variables" explicitly, in terms of which descriptions are to be made. The variables are sometimes referred to as "dimensions" or "types of attributes". A few examples of such variables are: *number of words, percentages of personal pronouns, attitude towards privatisation, attractive traits of teachers, degree of confidence in a friend.* etc. After the selection of some variable, viz., degree of confidence in a friend, there are many ways in which this variable may be broken down into categories as: (1) Unqualified confidence, (2) Qualified confidence, (3) Confidence and mistrust equally balanced, (4) Qualified mistrust, (5) Unqualified mistrust, (6) Question not asked by interviewer, (7) Question asked, but answer not classifiable in above categories. A second classification of categories of the same variable may be: (1) High, (2) Low, (3) Not classifiable in either. It may be pointed out that if two independent persons were to code the same material, one using the first set of categories and the other using the second, they would come out with different descriptions of the same material. Hence, explicit specification of the system of categories used with each variable is necessary for reproducible analysis.

There is need for framing explicit rules specifying what features of the content are to be taken as indication that it falls in one category rather than another. A statement of these rules constitutes the operational definition of the category. These specific rules are helpful in arriving at an agreed system of coding if two or more independent analysts conduct the analysis.

In developing such an operational definition, an analyst may begin by designating die units of analysis that are to be used. In this context, Cartwright (1970, p. 437) suggests that there are basically two kinds of units to be specified. The first of these he calls as the "recording unit" and the second as the "content unit". The recording unit is the specific segment of the content that is characterized by placing it in a given category. The content unit is the largest body of the content that may be examined in characterizing a recording unit. For example, in the coding of free-answer interviews, the answer to a single question is often taken as the recording unit and whole set of related questions as the content unit.

Another aspect of the operational definition of a category consists in specifying the 'indicators', which determine whether any given unit should fall within the category. For example, while considering the category "degree of confidence in a friend", the statement "stood by me and my brother to protect our family from armed bandits" can be taken as an indicator. Ifan analyst is coding a large content or a very large number of interviews, lie would encounter many statements or indicators for a particular category. Thus, a category consists of a range of possible indicators, all of which are given the same label and are therefore treated equivalently in all the subsequent analysis.

3. Frequencies, Direction and Intensity

Once the unit is defined and the variables along with their categories to be employed specified, the analyst will classify units, in the material to be analyzed, according to frequency, direction and intensity.

For frequency, the analyst merely counts the number of units, which fall into each of his categories. Cartwright *(1970, p. 440)* refers to it as "unit of enumeration". The "unit of enumeration" and "recording unit" are not necessarily the same. But when the analyst merely counts the number of recording units, which get a certain categorization, the recording unit is exactly the same as the enumeration unit. For example, in the analysis of public speech by an economist, the number of times "privatisation of higher education" may be employed as an "argument" for a certain policy of government. In this case an "argument" is taken both as the recording unit and the enumeration unit.

In another example, suppose an analyst analyses an editorial on "Privatisation of Higher Education" for its favourableness or unfavourableness. For purposes of quantification, he counts the number of column inches of the whole editorial. In this case, a column inch would be the unit of remuneration, whereas the editorial as a whole would be the recording unit and hence the two units are not identical.

In certain situations, it is useful to further classify the units according to direction and intensity. Direction refers to whether the reference was favourable, unfavourable, or neutral. It might be pleasant-unpleasant, interesting-uninteresting, threatening-non-threatening. Intensity indicates the emotional impact of the units anal zed is it large or small, and in what direction'?

Judging direction and intensity is more subjective than merely counting for frequency.

4. Contingency Analysis

The contingency analysis aims at considering the content within which the unit is found. A researcher should consider the favourableness or unfavourableness of a single unit in the light of the remainder of the communication so that its real meaning might not be lost.

5. Sampling

One of the major and practical problems in content analysis is sampling. The unit, which a researcher analyses must be representative of the total material with which he is concerned, so that the results can be generalized. Invariably a researcher undertakes the analysis of a specific content in order to reveal something about the universe of data than just that symbolic material with which he deals.

Cartwright *(1970, pp. 449-450)* points out that:

> In considering the problem of generalization, it *is* convenient *to* distinguish two rather different types of inference which may be involved in the process. The first type rests upon the assumption that the materials analyzed are a representative sample of some specified universe of (actual or potential) materials. The need to make this kind of inference derives from practical considerations of conducting research. Money and time will be saved if the description of a small sample can be taken *as* a safe description of the complete universe. The second type of inference rests upon the assumption that the 'discovered' relations between certain conditions and certain consequences are universally true. In this type of generalization, it *is* asserted

that whenever and wherever the specified conditions obtain, there will follow the specified consequences, and no assumption need be made that the quantitative incidence of certain conditions found in the sample will also be found in the universe.

In any given study, the universe *of* symbolic materials that should be selected will depend upon the purposes of the investigation. If, for example, the objective is to compare the editorial content of "The Times of India" against some established standard or norm, the universe under consideration should be all editorial content appearing in all issues of "The Times of India" over a certain period of time. After the specification of the universe, proper procedures for drawing a representative sample of that universe must be employed.

6. Constructing the Content Analysis Outline

Cartwright (1970, pp. 454-460) has suggested the following six steps for arriving at a satisfactory content analysis outline:

Step 1. Specify Needed Data

In laying out a satisfactory analysis outline, a researcher should clearly specify the data that are required by him in the total research design so that he may face fewer difficulties in the long run. The specification *of* needed data is helpful in planning the final tables, which the researcher may use at later stages of content analysis.

Step 2. Map out Plans for Tabulation

A researcher can avoid a number of problems if he makes explicit plans for the tabulation of coded data. He should decide in advance whether the coded data are to be punched on cards for machine processing or to be tabulated by hand.

Step 3. Lay out the Skeleton of the outline

The researcher should list the variables in terms of which the content is to be coded. Fcr example, if the study pertains to analyzing interviews, these variables will be used to classify not only various features of the answers to questions about the psychological make up of the respondent but also such matters as his age, income, marital status, and other demographic and behavioural characteristics. In listing the variables to be included in the outline, the researcher should ensure that all information needed on the punch cards is placed on some variable. The outline should contain provision for coding the name of the study, the number of each enumeration unit (interview, issue of journal or newspaper, etc.), the name of coder, and any other relevant information.

The researcher may make use of the following list of variables summarized by Berelson (1952) under two broad headings of "what is said" and "How it is said"

(i) What is said

1. Subject matter: what is the communication about?
2. Direction: Is the treatment favourable or unfavourable towards the subject'?
3. Standard: What is the basis on which the classification of direction is made?
4. Values: What goals are explicitly or implicitly revealed?
5. Methods: What means or actions are employed to realize goals?
6. Traits: What characteristics of persons are revealed?
7. Actor: Who initiates actions?
8. Authority: In whose name are statements made?
9. Origin: What is the place of origin of the communications?
10. Target: To whom is the communication particularly directed?

(ii) How it is Said

1. Form of communication: Is it fiction, news, television, etc.?
2. Form of statement: What is the grammatical or syntactical form of the unit of analysis?
3. Intensity: How much strength or excitement value does the communication have?
4. Device: What is the rhetorical or Propagandistic Character of the Communication?

Step 4. Fill in Categories for Each Variable

A researcher should use a system, which is exhaustive with mutually exclusive categories. The system is exhaustive if there is a category in which to place every relevant item, which may be found in the content. Its categories are mutually exclusive if there is one and only one place to put an item within that system of categories. After defining all the categories in a system, a manual of instructions should be prepared with operational definitions of the categories.

Step 5. Establish Procedure for Unitizing Material

It is essential for a researcher to establish a procedure for unitizing material. Cartwright (1970, p. 458) is of the opinion that specific working definitions to be used in the content analysis should be formulated in such a way that various coders can all unitize the same material in the same way. These definitions should be written down as a part of the coding instructions.

Step 6.

(i) Tryout the Analysis Outline and Unitizing Procedure

The analysis outline and unitizing procedure on a sample of material should be given a tryout in order to discover what modifications are need ed. This trying out of the coding procedures is also used as training for those who are to do the final coding.

(ii) Selection and Training of Coders

After constructing the analysis outline, the researcher should select coders who are able to use the analysis outline as intended and in a standardized manner. It is assumed that several coders are involved in actual coding. The number of coders who are able to use the analysis outline in a standardized manner will depend upon the volume of material (content). If the volume of material to be analyzed is large, several coders will do the actual coding. In case the volume of the content is too small, the researcher may act as the coder himself. However, in such situations it is desirable to have an independent coder also so that the whole procedure can be objectified.

Whatever the case, certain skills and abilities are essential far satisfactory coding. According to Cartwright (1970, p. 461):

> The coder must be a sensitive person, well differentiated in respect to symbolic materials. He must be able to detect subtle differences of meaning but also to neglect differences that do not make a difference for a specific purpose. In other words, he must be able to make use of the genotypic categories required by the analysis outline. In most social-psychological research, this means that the coder must have some acquaintance with the concepts of social psychology. If the analysis outline requires only phenotypic categories or categories defined in terms of everyday usage, the coder may well be an intelligent layman. A reasonably good level of intelligence is the minimal requirement for any content analysis.

The successful and meaningful use of a well-developed outline depends upon the selection of efficient coders and their effective training in the outline being used under good supervision so that the proper procedures of coding are followed. If the content to be analyzed is large, the process of coding involves the repetitive application of the analysis outline to the material. It demands same operational definition of categories, the same frame of reference, the same degrees of differentiation, etc. throughout the entire coding operation. In such cases, a person who is easily satiated with repetitive work should not be selected as a coder.

After the selection of efficient coders, it is necessary to train them in the use of analysis outline so that they have a full understanding of the objectives of the project.

7. Mechanics of Coding

A good analysis of material requires that regularized procedures be established for their storage, assignment to coders, and recording. It is convenient to package together a collection of material and get the package coded. When the coded package is returned to a central storage place, a new package is taken. In the distribution of material to coders, it is desirable to randomize the material so as to eliminate any systematic biases among the coders. This will also ensure that all the material gets coded once and only once. The same precautions should be taken in collecting and storing the sheets upon which coding has been recorded.

At the stage of final coding, the coder can add new categories to some of the variables of the outline if he comes across a recording unit for which there is no category. However, the merit of adding a new category should be assessed by determining whether the new category would be meaningful within the rationale of the system of categories. It is also desirable to hold periodic discussions among the coders to ensure that same frame of reference and operational definitions of categories are maintained throughout the coding period.

Cartwright (1970, p. 465) has suggested the procedure of "Check Coding" for assessing the reliability of coding. In this procedure, a "Check Coder" who is taken as a sort of "Criterion" independently records a certain percentage of the content. The records of disagreements as a result of check coding should be maintained and tabulated in various ways.

The records should be tabulated separately for each coder and the interpretation of differences among coders should be taken into consideration in the final results.

INDUCTIVE ANALYSIS

Inductive analysis means that patterns, themes, and categories of analysis emerge out of the data. In this analysis, researcher looks for natural variation in the data. According to Patton (1982, p. 306):

> For evaluators, the study of natural variation *will* involve particular attention to variations in programme processes and how participants respond to and are affected by programmes. Two ways of representing the patterns emerge from analysis of data. First, the analyst can use the categories developed and

articulated in the programme studied to organize presentation *of* particular themes. Second, the analyst may also become aware of categories or patterns for which the people in the programme did not have labels or terms, and the analyst develops terms to describe these inductively generated categories.

Patton describes these approaches as: (i) Indigenous typologies, and (ii) Analyst-constructed typologies. "Indigenous typologies" approach is called as the "emic" approach to analysis in anthropology. In this approach, cultural behaviour is studied in terms of the inside view of human events rather than imposed from cross-cultural classification of behaviour. In order to understand the thoughts and views of a particular group of people, it is necessary that the whole analysis of experience must be based on their concepts. Hence, indigenous typologies approach requires an analysis of the verbal categories used by the sample group or participants of the programme so that complexity of reality is broken into meaningful parts. The `verbal categories' used by the participants or others who are associated with a particular programme are `labelled' and given names so that one can be separated from others. Once these labels have been identified from an analysis of what participants in the programme have said, the next step is to identify and list the characteristics or attributes that distinguish one from the other. At a later stage, these categories become "themes" which are important throughout data study analysis and in the final report.

Suppose a study aims at enhancing the achievement level of slow learners studying in eighth grade of a high school. In observation and interviews at the selected high school, it is necessary to understand the ways in which teachers categorize students with regard to problems of low achievement in unit tests, absenteeism, and irregularity in the completion of home assignments. The teachers may label students as either "extremes" or "borderlines". One teacher may describe the extremes as the ones who fail in almost all the unit tests and never complete their home assignments. Another teacher may mark them as irregular in almost all teaching periods and in class tests. The borderlines, on the other hand, may be described as the ones who fail in more than half of the unit tests. Another teacher may characterize them as different from extremes but their performance in the unit tests being far below than that of other students.

Not all teachers use the same criteria to distinguish "extremes" from "borderlines", but all of them use the same labels in talking about them. In order to study the impact of any, remedial programme activities on the achievement of slow learners, it is important to understand the differences in programmes between the "extremes" and "borderlines". Moreover, it is not possible to analyze fully the situations in the programme as understood by teachers and experienced by students without understanding the indigenous typology of "extremes" and "border-lines". This typology will have immense implications-or how the programme activities were organized and the extent to which different strategies are to be developed to deal with the "extremes" and "borderlines". Finally, these categories become themes, which are important throughout the data analysis and in the final report.

In the "analyst-constructed typologies" approach, the researcher looks for patterns, categories and themes for which the participants of the programme do not have labels or terms, and the researcher himself constructs typologies to explain variations and contrasts in activities, participants and others associated with the programme. However, the researcher must take utmost care that such constructed typologies are accurate and make sense when presented to the people. The main objective of these typologies is to make descriptions based on an analysis of the patterns that appear in the data so as to make interpretations about the nature of the programme.

The patterns in qualitative data are converted into meaningful categories. Guba (1978), quoted by Patton (1982, pp. 311-312), suggests several steps for converting field notes and observations about issues and problems into systematic categories of analysis using the principle of "convergence" i.e. "figuring out what things fit together and "divergence". Categories are further judged by two criteria: "Internal homogeneity' and "external homogeneity". The first criterion concerns the extent to which the data that belong to a certain category hold together. The second criterion concerns the extent to which differences among categories are significant and clear. The existence of a large number of unassignable or overlapping data items indicates that there are some basic faults in the category system. Using these two criteria, the researcher develops several different classification systems of categories and then establishes some priorities to determine which category systems are more important than others.

By "divergence" Guba means that the researcher must deal with how to "flush out" the categories. He suggests that this can be done by process of extension (building on items of information already known), bridging (making connections among different items) and surfacing (proposing new information that ought to fit and then verifying its existence).

The procedures suggested by Guba for analyzing qualitative data are flexible. Since identification and naming patterns, themes, and categories is a creative process, the researcher must rely on his own intelligence, experience and judgement.

LOGICAL ANALYSIS

Inductive analysis is used for representing patterns as dimensions or categories, either using participant - generated constructions or evaluator generated constructions. It is sometimes useful to cross-classify different dimensions to generate new insights about how the data can be organized and to look for patterns that may not have been recognized in the initial inductive analysis. Logical analysis aims at creating potential categories by crossing one typology with another, and then moving back and forth between the logical construction and the actual data for creating a "new typology" using cross-classification matrices.

According to Patton (1982, p. .314):

> Creating cross-classification matrices *is* an exercise in *logic.* This procedure involves creating potential categories by *crossin3* one dimension or typology with another, and then working back and forth between the data and one's logical

constructions, filling in the resulting matrix. This logical system *will* create a new typology all parts *of* which may or may not actually be represented by the data. Thus, the analyst moves back and forth between the logical construction and the actual data in *the* ongoing search for understanding through description.

The researcher must be extremely careful in using this kind of analysis. He should be sensitive to interpreting the possibility of a category of activity or behaviour that has either been overlooked in the data or that is logically a possibility in the setting but has not been manifested.

VALIDITY OF QUALITATIVE ANALYSIS

This section is concerned with the major strategies that are helpful for validating and verifying the results of qualitative analysis. Patton (1982, pp. 327-334) has listed the following seven major strategies for validation of results:

1. Rival Explanations

Once the researcher after qualitative analysis has described the patterns and their explanations, it is important to look for rival or competing themes and explanations both inductively and logically. Inductively it implies looking for other ways of organizing the data that might lead to different results. Logically it involves searching for other logical possibilities and then finding if those possibilities can be supported by the data. However, it may be noted that when considering rival hypotheses and competing explanations, the strategy to be employed by the researcher is not one of attempting to disprove the alternatives, but to look for data that support alternative explanations. In this strategy, the researcher should give due weightage to supporting evidence and look for the best "fit" between data and analysis.

2. Negative Cases

The search for negative cases and instances that do not fit within the identified pattern and their understanding is also important in the verification and validation of results.

3. Triangulation: Reconciling Qualitative and Quantitative Data

This type of triangulation aims at comparing data collected through sonic kind of quantitative methods with data collected through same kind of qualitative methods. It is highly likely that qualitative methods and quantitative methods will eventually lead to different findings and not to a single and well-integrated picture of the situation. It is because qualitatively data are commonly used for "generating hypotheses" or "describing hypotheses" and quantitative data are used to "analyze outcomes", or "verify hypotheses". However, in endorsing the notion triangulation. Trend (1978), quoted by Patton (1980, p. 330), maintains that it is useful to bring a variety of data and methods to bear on the same problem in order to reduce system bias in interpreting results of study. Supplementing qualitative approach with quantitative analysis could strengthen the findings of some studies.

4. Triangulation: Comparing Multiple Qualitative Data Sources

This type of triangulation involves comparing and cross checking consistency of data derived by different means at different times using qualitative methods. It means: (i) Comparing observational data with interview data: (ii) Comparing observational data with questionnaire data: (iii) Comparing what participants of a programme say in public with what they say in private; (iv) Checking for the consistency the opinion of the participants about a programme over a period of time and (v) Comparing the opinion of the participants of a programme with others who were associated with programme in one capacity or the other. The triangulation of data sources within qualitative methods will seldom lead to a single totally consistent picture. But such triangulation is helpful to study and understand when and why there are differences.

5. Triangulation: Multiple Perspectives from Multiple Observers

The aim of this kind of triangulation is to involve triangulating observers or using several interviewers so as to reduce the potential bias or subjectivity as a result of observation by single observer.

6. Design Checks: Keeping Methods and Data in Context

The nature of research design and methodology also contribute to distortion in results. Sampling gives rise to three type of errors. The errors may be due to: (i) distortion in the situations that were sampled for observation; (ii) distortion introduced by the time periods during which observations took place; (iii) distortion because of selectivity in the people who were sampled either for observation or interviews. Thus the researcher must be careful to limit results of his study to those situations, time periods, people, and contents for which the data are applicable.

7. Evaluator Effects

The presence of researcher during the observation or interview can distort the results of study. The distortion may be due to : (i) reactions of programme participants and others associate with it to the presence of researcher; (ii) changes in the researcher during the process of observation or interview; (iii) biases of researcher, and (iv) incompetence of the researcher. The presence of a researcher during observation or interview may create a halo effect and consequently the participants of the programme are motivated to "show off". Their deviation from the normal behaviour will lead to distorted findings. It is desirable to undertake long-term observations for minimizing the halo effect. Researcher sometimes becomes personally involved with programme participants and therefore loses their sensitivity to the full range of events occurring during the process of observation of interview. A record of the changes in the researcher, field notes and conversation with the people associated with the programme is helpful to overcome evaluator effects.

The basic objective of qualitative analysis is to provide *useful*, *meaningful* and *objective* answers to the research questions of researchers, decision makers and information users. To be useful, answers provided must relate directly to the questions that have been asked; to be meaningful the answers must be understandable and clearly presented; to be objective the researcher must demonstrate that answers (findings) will stand the test of careful scrutiny.

Quantitative Data Analysis

This chapter reflects the following purposes. First, it deals with the organization of quantitative data in terms of editing, classifying and tabulating the information gathered through the administration of various tools on the selected sample or samples. Second, it describes certain modes, which are helpful in the analysis of the gathered quantitative data. Third, it deals with the various modern computational mechanical aids, which are used by researchers in performing complex computations with speed and accuracy. Fourth, it describes briefly the language and various the researchers should keep in view while making interpretations, and formulating conclusions and generalizations.

Learning Objectives

After carefully reading this chapter, you will be able to meet the following objectives:

1. Describe the procedures used in the organisation of gathered quantitative data.
2. List and describe certain modes, which are helpful in the analysis of gathered quantitative data.
3. List and describe certain modern computational aids, which are used by researchers in performing computations with speed and accuracy.
4. State what is meant by `language' of the computer.
5. List and describe briefly the various elements of a computer system.
6. Describe the factors, which the researcher should keep in view while making interpretation of results, and formulating conclusions and generalizations.

The quantitative data collected through the administration of various tools on selected sample or samples are raw. These data need to be tabulated, organized, analysed and interpreted for drawing sound conclusions and valid generalizations.

ORGANIZATION OF QUANTITATIVE DATA

Organization of data includes editing, classifying and tabulating quantitative information. Editing implies accuracy, usefulness and completeness. Classification refers to dividing the data into different categories, classes, groups researcher is guided by the nature of the problem, the hypotheses to be verified, or by the responses or characteristics of the samples he has selected. If the problem or hypotheses, for example, involved the difference between attitudes of men and women teachers towards co-education at the secondary school stage, the categories male and female serving in government and private aided schools would be clearly indicated. In some situations when the group is sufficiently homogeneous, no breakdown into categories or subgroups is necessary and it is desirable to describe the group as a whole. However, in the situations where the group is sufficiently heterogeneous, it is desirable to divide the group into homogeneous sub groups or categories that have in common some distinctive attributes significant for the purpose of analysis.

Tabulation is the process of *transferring* classified data from data gathering tools to the tabular form in which they may be systematically examined. This process may be performed in a number of ways. In simple and less sophisticated types of research, hand sorting and tabulating procedures are usually employed. More extensive and sophisticated investigations make use of card-tabulating process.

Hand sorting and Hand-tabulation

Hand sorting and hand-tabulation require careful planning. It includes method of hand-sorting and recording on tabulation sheets in accurate marking and counting frequency tallies for differ by mathematical terms by marking and counting frequency tallies for different items on which information is sought.

The sorting of responses sheets in case of psychological tests, scales or opiniormaires in various categories case of psychological tests, scale must be done before the tabulation of responses. At times without planning, a researcher may waste his time and energy by tabulating responses first and then it might occur to him that it would be interesting sample the to compare the responses of the various sub-groups comprising under investigation. This process would require another handling of the response sheets, scales or opinionnaires and would involve re-tabulating the responses.

Card Tabulating Process

Several types of cards are used in data tabulation. They include edge marked cards, edge-notched cards, IBM punched cards and mark-sense cards. Edge-marked cards are provided with rows of numbered holes around their four edges. Each numbered space is used to record only one type of information, such as space 3 for sex and space 5 for IQ. These cards can be sorted quickly into groups, but they are suitable only for investigations that involve a small number of variables. On edge-notched cards, data are notched into punched holes spaces along the four edges of the card; For example, hole number 4 is notched if the subject is boy and not notched if the subject is girl. By inserting a long needle through hole 4, the researcher can lift out the cards of the girls and the notched cards of boys will be left. IBM punched cards serve the most efficient and rapid method of processing a large volume of data on cards for electronic computer processing. On mark-sense cards, a subject can mark his answer in the proper space on a card with an electrographic pencil. A machine is used to read these marked data and convert them into punched holes on the same card. The machine further records data on another medium or transmit them directly to a computer.

Analysis of quantitative data

Analysis of data means studying the organized material in order to discover inherent facts. The data are studies from as many angles as possible to explore the new facts. Analysis requires an alert, flexible and open-mind. It is worthwhile to prepare a plan of analysis before the actual collection of data. Good, Barr and Scates (1941, pp. 599-601) suggest four helpful modes to get started on analysing the gathered data:

1. To think in terms of significant tables that the data permit.
2. To examine carefully the statement of the problem and earlier analysis and to study the original records of the data.
3. To get away from the data and to think about the problem in layman's terms, or to actually discuss that problem with others.
4. To attack the data by making various statistical calculations.

The exploratory modes may prove very helpful in the analysis of data of any research study and no similarities, differences, trends and significant factors would go unnoticed by the researcher.

Statistical techniques have contributed greatly in gathering, organizing, analysing and interpreting numerical data. The processing of numerical data through statistics calls for competence in the use of statistical methods and for understanding of concepts that underline their development and their application. The researcher must know the strengths and the weaknesses of the statistical methods, which he uses so that he may not mislead or be mislead by such methods.

A discussion of two major areas of statistics, descriptive statistics and inferential statistics, is presented in some detail in Chapters 7 and 8. The main purpose of such discussion is to help the researcher develop an understanding of statistical terminology, and the concepts necessary to study with understanding the literature dealing with educational research. It is also to help the student develop competence and know-how to conduct investigations using simple types of statistical analysis.

MODERN COMPUTATIONAL MECHANICAL AIDS

Modem computational mechanical aids are a boon to the modern researcher. They are used to save time and effort, and to minimize 'error during organizing and analysis of research data. The increasing and popular use of these computational devices has advanced educational research in terms of both quality and quantity. The computational mechanical aids commonly used are 'desk calculators' and 'digital computers'.

Desk Calculators

The most common type of computational mechanical device available to the researcher is the desk calculator. Its principal advantages are speed and accuracy in performing addition, subtraction, multiplication and division. These operations are performed easily merely by depressing the necessary keys to enter the data and another key to begin the desired operation. Setting their order as required in computational problem can also perform the calculations involving combinations of the fundamental operations. The desk calculator provides reliable results. At times, improper input of the data or incorrect operation of the machine, or both, furnishes erroneous results.

The electro mechanical desk calculators perform the calculations by electrically operated mechanical devices called counters. On the other hand, electronic desk calculators developed recently operate electronically and perform calculations without the use of mechanical counters with greater speed. Some of these electronic calculators are capable of performing operations beyond the four basic operations of addition, subtraction, multiplication and division. These additional operations include interpolation, extraction of square roots and reciprocals.

A serious limitation with electro-mechanical and electronic desk calculators is that they require a human operator at ever,' stage of operation. However, some of the more modem electronic desk calculators with the help of an attached card reader can accept a series of instructions in the form of "programmes" and then execute these programmes automatically.

The manufacturers'-of desk calculators usually provide instruction manuals with them for the use of their operators. These manuals provide directions even for simple operations. If they are studied carefully, the user may not face any difficulty in performing any operation.

Electronic Digital Computers

Electronic digital computers have a long history. The history of their development can be traced back to the first mechanical calculator developed by Blaise Pascal in 1642. But the modem digital computer has grown out of the work of Charles Babbage; a nineteenth century English mathematician. Because of the many errors appearing in scientific tables, Babbage discovered a method of performing complex arithmetic operations quickly, accurately and cheaply. He developed an automatic calculating instrument and later conceived an even more automatic machine, which used punched cards to control and perform complex operations with a capability for printing the results. Babbage borrowed this idea from the work done in Germany by Miiller and from the work done in France by Joseph Jacquard. Late in the nineteenth century. Herman Hollerith, a director of the United States Census Bureau, devised a whole punched-card technique for the storage of data, and built a card sorter and card tabulator. The data on the card was transmitted by means of electrical contacts through the punched holes and each hole was reserved for recording a specific item of data. The punched card was a significant development as it is a very important part of modem computer data processing.

During the past thirty years, a stream of ideas for devising faster and accurate methods of processing data has created a computer revolution. In the mid 1940s, an electrical impulse computer was developed with circuits using thousands of vacuum tubes. However, these computers were very large and inconvenient to use and required a great deal of space. The heat generated by the vacuum tubes required air conditioning equipment to prevent heat damage.

Moreover, the uncertain life of vacuum tubes created mechanical difficulties. During 1950s, the use of electronic switches and replacement of vacuum tubes increased the efficiency of computers. The use of microminiaturized solid-state circuits and a host of other improvements during the 1960s greatly increased the storage capacity, speed, reliability, and range of application of computers. With these developments, modern computers can accept, store and execute more elaborate programmes and can process data four hundred times faster than the earliest one.

LANGUAGE OF THE COMPUTER

A computer is an ingenious and versatile machine. It can manipulate symbols that represent information, have the ability to remember or store these symbols, and can restore them later. However, it cannot determine how to solve a problem. It can only follow direction provided in the form of a "programme". The programme provides instructions about what data to process, how to process the data, and how the results are to be shown.

The instructions are written in a language or code that the computer is able to `read'. A binary code is the most commonly used code within computers. It uses only two digits, 1 and 0, and each of these two digits is called a bit-short for binary digit. The language is important because the electronic parts within a computer can respond only to two states.

(1) Current on, or (2) Current off;

(1) a switch is opened, or (2) it is closed;

(1) a magnetic material is magnetised in one direction, or (2) in the other.

The binary code differs from the commonly used decimal system. The decimal system is based on the power of ten: when we move a digit one space to the left and add a zero, its worth is increased ten times. The binay system is based on the power of two; when we move a number to the left, its worth is increased two times.

100,000	10,000	1,000	100	10	1	Decimal: Successive powers of ten
32	16	8	4	2	1	Binay: Successive powers of two

There are various ways for converting binary number to decimal number. However, there is a short cut method for such conversion, which consists of doubling and adding. Starting at the left, copy the value of the first position, double it, and add the value of the next position; take this sum, double it, etc.

→	1	1	0	0	1	0	0
	1	3	6	12	25	50	100

The researcher must understand the binary code to know the working of a computer; but he no longer has to use the binary code when writing a programme for the computer. At one time, if he wanted the computer to add something, he might have had to provide the following binary instruction: 101 10101 1101 0001. He may now merely use a "shorthand language" for "add", and the computer will automatically translate the symbol into the correct binary instruction. Today the researcher can learn enough of a shorthand language, such as FORTRAN, to write a programme.

ELEMENTS OF A COMPUTER SYSTEM

The computer system consists of physical equipment, called hardware, and combinations of instruction, called programmes or software.

Hardware of a Computer System

The essential elements of a computer system with regard to hardware are:

1. Input devices,
2. Central processing unit,
3. Main storage, and
4. Output devices.

Figure 6.1 illustrates the functional organization of these elements:

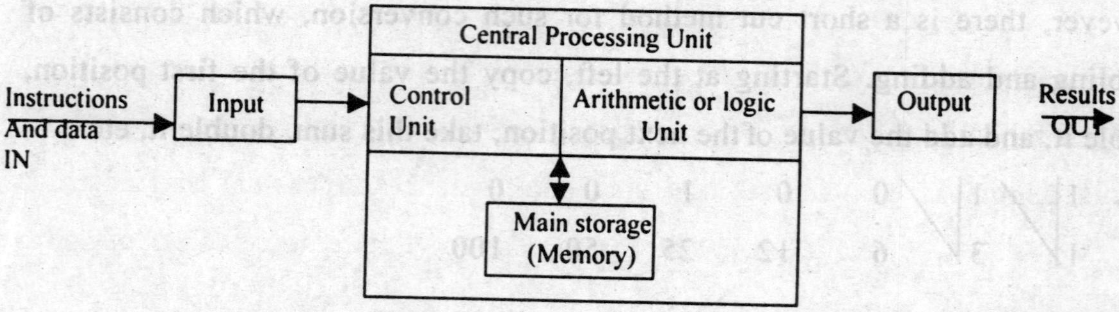

FIG. 6.1 Functional Organization of a Computer.

1. Input. It refers to the transferring of data from an external storage medium into the internal storage of the computer. Information or data are entered into the computer through the use of card reader, mark sense cards, or optical character readers that translates printed page information to punched cards or magnetic tape.

Card reader. This is one of the most common input devices. It reads into the computer system data that have been punched into cards. The data are punched into cards by means of a keypunch. The punched card is divided into the zone section and digit section. Digits are represented by a single punch in the digit section, while alphabetic and special characters are usually represented by more than one punch in the same column. To facilitate handling and statistical computation, data are usually coded before they are placed on the punch card. The area or space on the punch cards meant for recording a particular data is called `card field'. The arrangement of data card fields is referred to as the 'card format'. Once the card format has been established for the programme, data can be read quickly and conveniently into the system; and then various manipulations of the data involving summarizing, listing, selecting, etc. with maximum accuracy can be achieved with a minimum of effort.

Mark sense cards. Another device of preparing data for input into a computer system is through the use of mark sense cards. Marks are put in specific locations on a mark sense card. The card is read and the data get automatically punched into the card.

Optical character readers. This is a quicker means of preparing data for computer input. A rotating drum that transports documents past an optical scanning station provides the principal operating action. When the pattern of the optically read character agrees with a character pattern in the reader's character-recognition circuits, the character is recorded in input form, that is, punched on cards or recorded on magnetic tape.

Optical character readers can perform an additional function called mark reading. In this function, marks can be made with an ordinary pencil in specific locations and recorded for input into computer system.

2. **Central processing unit.** This unit controls and directs the entire computer system. It also performs the data treatment functions of addition, subtraction, multiplication, division, shifting, moving, comparing, and storing. The central processing unit consists of the arithmetic or logic unit and the control unit.

The arithmetic or logic unit possesses the capability to make calculations and makes logical decisions about data. At the time of decision making or making calculations, data are sent to the arithmetic or logic unit, processed, and then sent back to be stored for later use or to be used as output.

The control unit supervises and controls all the elements of the system, which must work in perfect coordination. Input data must be entered, stored, and processed as prescribed by the programme. Data must be moved in and out of storage and the input/output devices coordinated by the control unit for maximum efficiency. The control unit performs as it is instructed to perform. It is provided with a series of number codes to initiate and carry out a number of basic operations.

3. **Main storage.** The main storage of the computer system is that storage which is directly accessible to the central processing unit. The data are represented in the main storage by small ferromagnetic rings called 'cores'. The cores are very small in diameter and gets magnetised easily. They retain their magnetic state until

reversing the direction of the current deliberately changes it. These two opposite magnetic states, as represented by the direction of current, can be used to represent 0 or 1; yes or no; plus or minus; or on or off conditions.

The main storage unit of a computer is like a block of post *office* boxes. Each box has its own identifying number called an address, and each box contains one fact or one instruction. This address may be as signed by the programmer or automatically by the control unit of the system.

The main storage capacity of the computer system must be considered by the researcher in relation to the size of sample, the number of variables, and the complexity of the calculations involved in the study.

4. Output devices. The output unit receives data in machine language from the storage unit and translates it into a language, which a human being or a machine can understand. The devices of output are used for intermediate and final output. A cardpunch, paper tape punch, or magnetic tape unit may be attached to a computer to perform an intermediate output operation. The cards or tapes that are produced for output can in turn be used as input for a later computer operation. The computers make use of printers, graph plotters and visual display equipment for producing output that can be read or interpreted directly by people. The operation 'of the output device is controlled by the control unit, which operates, according to the instructions entered into the computer system. These instructions specify the medium, nature and format of the output.

Software or Programme of the Computer System

A computer system operates in accordance with specific instructions. Each instruction defines an operation to be performed. It also specifies the data, device, or mechanism needed to carry out the operation. These instructions are referred to as a programme. A computer is useless until a programmer writes a detailed set of instructions to be loaded into its internal storage (memory) unit.

The following are the main six steps involved in writing a programme:

(i) To break down the problem into a sequence of elementary steps that the computer can perform.

(ii) To make sure that all the necessary steps are included and have been placed in the proper sequence by writing a flow chart, which shows graphically how all parts of the programme fit logically together.

(iii) To write the programme in the form of detailed list of instructions on a programme or a coding sheet.,

(iv) To punch the shorthand language programme on a deck of cards.

(v) To translate the shorthand language programme into a machine language programme such as binary language.

(vi) To check the major parts of the programme for eliminating any errors.

With the development of shorthand languages and translators like the symbol languages (AU TO CODER and BAL) and the procedure or problem-oriented languages (FORTRAN and COBOL), the work of programmers has been greatly simplified. Prepared programmes are now available in the libraries at different computer centres in our country for practically all the statistical techniques that researchers are likely to employ in the analysis of data.

INTERPRETATION OF RESULTS

Once the research data have been collected and the analysis has been made, the researcher can proceed to the stage of interpreting the results. The process of interpretation is essentially one of stating what the results show: What are their meanings and significance'? What is the answer to the original problem? Interpretation is not a routine and mechanical process. It calls for a careful, logical and critical examination of the results obtained after analysis, keeping in view the limitations of the sample chosen, the tools selected and used in the study. There is always an element of subjectivity and the researcher generally commits certain errors while interpreting results of his study.

LIMITATIONS OF FINDINGS

Ignoring Unstudied Factors in Interpretation

In any type of educational research, the researcher is generally guided by the factors or variables, which he has studied during the research process. He totally ignores the influence or effect of unstudied factors while interpreting the results of his study. To totally ignore the unstudied factors and ascribe the findings or results of the research to the occurrence of studied factors alone may be misinterpreting the actual truth, for the findings in any research are conditioned not by one of two but innumerable variables. It is truer in case of experimental or causal-comparative type of research in which the researcher studies a very limited number of variables. For example, if a researcher, who finds that as group of eighth class students following programmed instruction material in social studies has performed better in comparison to another group of students of the same class taught through lecture method, ascribes the better achievement to the method alone and ignores the, other possible determining factors like high general mental ability, high achievement motivation, better study habits, interest in the subject and better socio-economic conditions found among the high achieving group, will be misinterpreting the truth

Ignoring Selective Factors in Interpretation

A researcher may grossly misrepresent the truth if he ignores the selective factors. This is more evident in the studies where a selective group is made the subject of investigation or where a particular factor is operating in the situation studied. For example, if a researcher finds that the boys of a particular tribe are mostly low in intelligence and then concludes, therefore, that the boys of all tribes have a low intelligence, is ignoring the fact that there exist outside the particular tribe, many tribal boys with average or high intelligence. Similarly, to find that in a particular secondary school, the number of the tenth class students failing in mathematics is greater than the number of students failing in other subjects and to conclude from this that mathematics is comparatively more difficult than other subjects of studs is ignoring the fact that the students in mathematics did not receive good instruction in mathematics.

Interpreting Expected Results

While interpreting the expected results, the researcher has to keep in mind that he does not go beyond his data support and that he does not forget the limitations of the study. The researcher has to be cautious in reporting all such factors, which could account for the results.

Interpreting Negative Results

Researchers often on arriving at results contrary to what they had hypothesized jump to develop a sort of defense mechanism by making a cry of all factors that could have possibly vitiated the results. They often list shortcomings in terms of the use of inadequate tools or sample fluctuations. These things may be true and there is no harm in reporting all such factors, which come in the way of making the study precise. Nevertheless, it is not always correct to get results that confirm hypotheses.

Hypotheses arise out of guess work and cannot be accepted as right in the beginning without testing them for confirmation. After the research is completed, the researcher is in a position to declare his results with certainty. When the results contradict, the original hypothesis of the study, the interpretation and discussion of results should include the researcher's re-consideration of the original hypothesis in the light of his findings. At times, researchers are reluctant to interpret and discuss results that contradict the existing known facts. This attitude is not fair and is likely to impede the progress of research. It must be noted that the hypotheses are tentative and results can differ from them.

Interpreting Results When the Null Hypothesis is Retained

A retained null hypothesis may occur for several reasons:

(1) There may be no relationship between the variables: or the experimental variable may not be more effective than the control variable.

(2) The null-hypothesis is false, but the internal validity problems of the data contaminated the investigation so badly that the actual relationship between variables could not be established.

(3) The null-hypothesis is false, but the research design lacked the power to reject it.

Since the researcher is not aware of any of these facts, he could not interpret the results of his study by claiming any one of them as the explanation of his results. Hence, it is not always correct to present a retained null hypothesis as evidence of no relationship between the variables under study.

Interpreting Results When Null Hypothesis is Rejected

If a null hypothesis is rejected and the variables other than the variables under study, that were likely to affect the results were well controlled in the study, the researcher may say that the behaviour of the variables mentioned in the research hypothesis, which was converted into the null hypothesis for being tested, my be taken to hold good, with a risk of 5 per cent or 1 per cent according to the different levels of significance at which the null hypothesis gets turned down.

Interpreting Unhypothesized Relationships

Any Unhypothesized relationship that the researcher may observe during the conduct of a study should not be ignored. It should be recognized and analysed thoroughly. Such results should, however, be viewed with more suspicion than the results based on hypothesized relationships. Unhypothesized relationships have greater possibility of being spurious. Such relationships should be reported, but the researcher should consider them as incidental to the main thrust of investigation. They may provide basis of further research.

FORMULATION OF CONCLUSIONS AND GENERALIZATIONS

In the light of the interpretation of data, the researcher has to use all care and caution in formulating his conclusions and generalizations. This final step of research process demands critical and logical thinking in summarizing the findings of the study and compares them with the hypotheses formulated in the beginning. The researcher should not draw conclusions, which are inconsistent among themselves or with external realities. The generalizations drawn on the basis of research findings should be in agreement with-facts and should not conflict with the known laws of nature. The suggestions for the application of research findings in practical settings and suggestion of problems for further research may also be provided with conclusions and generalizations.

1. Validity. By validity we mean the degree to which- a test or examination measures what it is intended to measure. In geography if the aim is to test the reasoning power of the student, the questions should be framed in such a manner as to elicit replies which may assist in judging the reasoning and argumentative power of the student. Spelling or handwriting should not be taken into account while assessing the paper. Perhaps this factor of validity is the most baffling one in regard to our essay type of examinations.

Following points regarding validity may be noted:

(i) The validity of a test cannot be reported in general terms.

(ii) No test can be said to have `high' or `low' validity in the abstract. Its validity must be determined with reference to the particular use for which the test is being considered.

(iii) The validity pertains to the results of a test or evaluation instrument and not to the instrument itself. We sometimes speak of the validity of a test for the sake of convenience but it is more appropriate to speak of the validity of the test results or more specifically of the validity of the interpretation to be made from the results.

(iv) Validity is a matter of degree. It is best considered in terms of categories that specify degree such as higher validity, moderate validity and low validity.

Types of validity. There are four main types of validity.

(i) Content Validity

(ii) Productive Validity

(iii) Concurrent Validity

(iv) Construct Validity.

(i) Content Validity. The content validity relates to the degree to which a test samples the content area, which is to be measured. The test items must adequately cover all major aspects of the content area and they must be in the correct proportions.

(ii) Predictive Validity. It refers to the extent to which a test can predict the future performance of the students/learners. This type of validity is important for those tests, which are used for classification and selection purposes. The degree to which a test can credit the future performance of the individuals depends upon the degree of relationships between the two variables - the test and the criterion. The higher the relationship between these variables, the greater will be the predictive validity of a test. The most important and difficult task in this method is to determine the criterion, which is the index of future performance. Predictive value is reported through a coefficient of correlation obtained when predictor and the criterion data are correlated.

(iii) Concurrent Validity Concurrent validity refers to the relationship between scores on a measuring tool and a criterion available at the same time. It differs from predictive validity only on time factor. Concurrent validity is appropriate for those tests, which are employed for diagnosis of existing status of the individual rather than predicting about his future outcome.

(iv) Construct validity. Construct validity refers to the extent to which a test reflects constructs presumed to underlie the test performance and also the extent to which it is based on theories regarding these constructs.

Factors Influencing Validity Index

Validity index of test is influenced by several factors some of the important factors are listed here.

(1) Length of the test (2) Method of estimating validity index (3) Criterion of validation (4) Speeded ness of the test (5) Homogeneity of the sample (6) Difficulty values of items (7) Response set and (8) Ambiguous instruction.

(1) Length of the Test : By homogenous lengthening of a test not only increase the reliability but also the validity of the test. The longer the test, the more reliable and valid it becomes. But validity as compared to reliability does not change rapidly with increase in the length of the test. The increase in validity index is estimated by homogenious lengthening. The following formula is used.

$$r_{nx}(y) = \frac{r_{xy}}{\sqrt{\left(\frac{1 - r_{xx}}{n} + r_{xx}\right)}}$$

Validity of a homogecious test increased n times length.

Since the homogeneous lengthening of a homogeneous test increases its reliability, in accordance with the Spearman Brown Prophecy formula, it will also increase its validity.

r_{xy} = Coefficient of correlation with test x and criteriyn y score.

r_{xx} = Reliability of the test x.

n= Ratio in the change of length of validity.

r_{nx} (y)= New validity index by lengthening the test.

If we require certain index of validity, the ratio of new length of the test is calculated by the following formula.

$$n = \frac{1 - r_{xx}}{\frac{r^2_{xy}}{r^2_{nx(y)}} - r_{xx}}$$

(Ratio) of new length of test for required validity)

Example. A test has validity coefficient .50 and reliability .80. It is lengthened four times in its present length. Calculate its new validity.

$$r_{nx(y)} = \frac{r_{xy}}{\sqrt{\left(\frac{1-r_{xx}}{n}+r_{xx}\right)}}$$

$$= \frac{\cdot 50}{\sqrt{\left(\frac{1-\cdot 80}{4}+\cdot 80\right)}}$$

$$= \frac{\cdot 50}{\sqrt{(\cdot 85)}} = 0{\cdot}55$$

Same test increases the validity 0·55 *i.e.* by .05

If we calculate the new reliability of the same test, the following 'Brown Prophecy Formula' is used.

$$r_{nn} = \frac{nr_{11}}{1+(n-1)\, r_{11}}$$

$$= \frac{4 \times \cdot 80}{1+3\times \cdot 80} = \frac{3{\cdot}20}{3{\cdot}40}$$

$$= 0{\cdot}94$$

The new reliability is 0·94, which is increased by ·14, if we compare the increase of reliability index with validity. It is approximately three times of reliability (increase of reliability is ·14 and validity is ·05).

(2) Method of Estimating Validity Index : There are several method and forms of expressing validity of a test. Some of the methods have been discussed in this chapter. Cross-validation is the most popular method of estimating validity. Each method yields different index of validity. The expectancy table providing an approximate index of validity. There is several methods correlation, which are used for correlating test scores with criterion scores. Each method of correlation yields different index of validity. The Pearson's method correlation is most popular and widely used for this purpose, but it has several procedure of calculating the correlation coefficient.

(3) Criterion of Validation. Correlating the test scores with the external criterion performance validates a test. There may be several criteria but all the criteria cannot be used. Each criterion would yield different) index of validity. *A teacher aptitude test* can be validated against the criteria-teacher ratings, theory and practical marks, and job success. The test scores can be validated either of the criterion, each criterion would yield different index of validity. Some time pooled criteria are used to generalize the validity index.

(4) Speededness of the Test : The speeded ness is very closely associated with the validity of test. If we increase the duration of a test so that most of the examinees may reach to the last item of the test. Thus, the speededness will decrease and validity index will also increase. The validity index is inversely proportional to speeded of a test. A power test has usually the high validity index. The speededness has the influence on validity of a test.

(5) Homogeneity of the Sample: A test is administered on a sample to estimate the validity of a test. If the sample of examinees is homogeneous in ability, the validity of the test scores is likely to be lowered. When the examinees vary widely in their range of ability or the sample of examinees is hetrogeneous one, validity of the test is likely to be high.

(6) Difficulty value of Items : Difficulty value of items is an important factor in validity of a test. When the items of the test are homogeneous with regard to their difficulty value, the validity of the test scores is lower. When the items vary widely in their range of difficulty values, the validity of the test will be high.

(7) Response Set : There is scope in responding correctly by guessing in objective type items. Guessing factor in an objective test is important source of constant error. Guessing has important effect upon total test scores. It tends to raise the validity coefficient too high. Therefore, `correction for guessing' formula should be used or multiple choice items should be included in the test to minimize this. effect on validity.

(8) Ambiguous Instruction : Usually some instructions are given in administering a test. If these instructions are ambiguous it has the effect on the performance of examinees. The validity of the test is directly influence by the instructions. There should be uniformity and clarity in the instructions. The instructions are standardized of a good test.

(9) Discriminative Value : When the test consists. of discriminating items, the validity index is likely to be high. When the items do not discriminate well between high and low groups, the validity is low. The items difficulty value and item reliability or item validity contribute to validity of the test.

(10) Assumption in defining Validity: Theoretical validity is defined as proportion of common factor variance.

$$r_{xy} = \frac{\sigma_{cf}^2}{\sigma_x^2} = \frac{\text{Common factor variance}}{\text{Test scores variance}}$$

If item variance is considered, the validity index is high

$$r_{xy} = \frac{\sigma_{cf}^2}{\sigma_x^2 - \sigma_i^2} = \frac{\text{Common factor variance}}{\text{Test scores variance} - \text{Item variance}}$$

RESEARCH PROPOSAL OR SYNOPSIS

After the formulation of hypotheses, the researcher should write out a proposal, synopsis, or plan for research including a statement of the problem and hypotheses, the research procedures, the sample to be selected, the tools to be selected or developed for the collection of data, and the quantitative or qualitative techniques to be used for the analysis and interpretation of data.

The preparation of a research proposal is a prerequisite in the research process. In many institutions, a researcher is required to submit a proposal of the research project for approval. This serves as a basis for the determination of the feasibility of the project and provides a systematic plan of procedure for the researcher to follow. It also gives the research supervisor (if any) a basis for guiding the researcher in his pursuit of study.

The research proposal is a systematic plan, which brings to focus the preliminary planning that will be needed to accomplish the purpose of the proposed study. It is just like a blueprint which the architect prepares before the construction of a building starts. The initial draft of the proposal is subject to modification in the light of the constructive criticism,. comments and suggestions of the experts in the field. These experts include researcher's supervisor, colleagues, research and statistical specialists, or other experienced researchers who act as members of the research committee of an institution or organization. The research proposal always goes through the developmental phases, and therefore, deficiencies, if any, may be corrected by discussing the same with the experts. An acceptable research proposal, therefore, is usually the result of several modifications, and as such, there should not be any haste on the part of a researcher in its preparation.

Types of Research Proposal

Research proposal can be broadly classified into three groups. This classification is based mainly on the type of the research study to be undertaken and its purpose.

1. The most common proposal is of the type that is prepared by those who wish to undertake research for their master's or doctoral degree in education. Submission of a research proposal is a general requirement in most of the universities for beginners in research. The proposal is evaluated by a committee of experts to determine the feasibility of the study.

2. The second type of research proposal is one that is submitted by a researcher to a private or governmental agency for financial assistance. Such an assistance is given on the recommendation of a panel of experts who evaluate the proposal.

3. Finally, in the third category is the research proposal that is submitted by a university or a college teacher to some research organization, such as university, the Indian Council of Social Sciences Research, the National Council of Educational Research and Training, the University Grants Commission, or any other autonomous research organisation. Since at present more funds are earmarked by such organizations for research, more teachers are taking interest to investigate problems in the areas of concern in the field of education at the school, college or university levels.

Preparation of the Research Proposal

There are certain specifications that are essential to good research and, therefore, all such specifications should appear in each plan. A worthwhile research study is likely to result only from a carefully planned and well designed proposal. The following categories of information should appear in the research proposal.

INTRODUCTION

The introductory part of the proposal should include the following information:

1. The Title

The title of the research proposal should do no more than name the topic. It should be so worded that it suggests the theme of the study. In selecting a title, the researcher should consider two things:

(a) The title should not be burdened by pompous words and should not include terms of unscientific; rhetorical, argumentative, emotional, or biased nature. The language in the title should be professional in nature but not pedantic.

(b) The title should not be too lengthy or too involved. It should be specific to the area of study. An adequate title for a study is one which represents a reasonable restriction and implies an objective approach. It must be noted that the proposed study cannot be completely presented in the title; but it should be so worded that it would give sufficient information about the nature of the study.

2. Statement of the Problem

Statement of the problem is not exactly the same as the title of the thesis. It has a definite place in the introductory chapter and is an attempt to focus on a clear goal. Statement of the problem should primarily be an expansion of the title. It should be either in question form or as a declarative statement. The major question or statement may be followed by several minor questions or statements and explanations.

3. Review of Related Literature

The theoretical and empirical framework from which the problem arises must be briefly described. Both conceptual and research literature are to be reviewed for this purpose. The latest research trends pertinent to the problem should also be mentioned in this section. The researcher has to make it clear that his problem has roots in the existing literature, but it needs further research and exploration. A brief resume of related studies found in journals, magazines, abstracts, and reports should be made. This provides evidence that the researcher is familiar with what is already known and also with what is unknown and unproved. An analysis of the previous research eliminates the risk of duplication of what has been done, and provides a basis for formulating hypotheses.

4. The Hypotheses

Questions that the research is designed to answer are usually framed as hypotheses to be tested on the basis of evidence. This step establishes the problem and the logic underlying the research study. It gives direction to the data gathering procedure. It is in the light of the hypotheses that the relevance of data to be collected is judged.

The formulation of the research hypotheses is typically determined by the implications of the related literature and the deductive logic of the problem under investigation. They should meet all the seven criteria discussed earlier.

5. Significance of the Study

A research proposal should show the worth and urgency of the study. It should indicate clearly how the results of the research can influence educational theory or practice. The need for undertaking a research study can be shown in several ways.

One way of establishing a need for a research study is to show the time lapse between the earlier study and the present one; and therefore the new knowledge, techniques, or conditions indicate a need to replicate the study.

A second way of justifying the need for a study is to show that there are gaps in the knowledge provided by previous research studies and to show how the present study will help to fill in these gaps and add to the quantum of existing knowledge.

A third way to justify the need for a study is to show the lack of information about a problem by presenting the supporting statements of other research studies.

A final way to justify the need for a study is to relate it to the existing social issues and to priority areas in the context of national and international educational developments.

6. Definition of Terms and Concepts

It is necessary to define all unusual terms and concepts that could be misinterpreted. The technical terms or words and phrases having special meanings need to be defined operationally. We seldom come across unanimous definition or modes of measurement *for* certain concepts and terms, such as intelligence, motivation, achievement, etc., and in such situations, it becomes obligatory on the part of the researcher to provide an operational definition of such terms or concepts by stating how the variables will be measured and interpreted. The *Dictionary of Education,* edited by Carter V. Good; the *Comprehensive Dictionary of Psychological and Psychoanalytical Terms,* edited by Horace B. English and Eva C. English; and the *Dictionary ' of Sociology,* edited by H.P. Fairchild are valuable sources for definitions of technical terms.

7. Delimitations of the Study

Boundaries of the study should be made clear with reference to *(a)* the scope of the study by specifying the areas to which the conclusions will be confined, and *(b)* the procedural treatment including the sampling procedures, the techniques of data collection and analysis, the development of measuring tools and their use in the study.

8. Basic Assumptions

Assumptions are statements of ideas that are accepted as true. They serve as the foundation upon which the research study is based. According to Turney and Robb (1971, p. 29):

> They are written to reveal what the researcher, and others, theorize to be true in the study to be conducted; moreover, they are also written to indicate those factors affecting the study that are necessarily unalterable.

The researchers in writing their proposals should select their basic assumptions with care and be particularly aware of certain common errors. Turney and Robb (1971, p. 30) have listed these errors as under:

1. The first error is failure to state all of the basic assumptions that are relevant to the study. This situation usually occurs in questionnaire studies, in which necessary assumptions are taken for granted without being designated as basic assumptions of the study.

2. The second error concerns irrelevant assumptions. Such assumptions are neither applicable nor necessary to the study.

3. The third error is that of selecting unsubstantiated assumptions which cannot be defended by any logic, empirical evidence (objective data), or authoritative sources.

PROCEDURES FOR COLLECTING DATA

In this section the details about sampling procedure and the data collecting tools are described. It may be noted that in historical and philosophical researches the nature of the data and their treatment is different from other types of researches.

1. Sampling

In research situations the researcher usually comes across unmanageable populations, wherein large numbers are involved. In such cases, the researcher may use different sampling methods, such as random, systematic, multistage, stratified, cluster judgement, or quota sampling depending upon his requirement. The researcher should be well informed about the scope and limitations of each one of these sampling methods before he thinks of his own sample in the study. A research proposal should clearly define the population from which the researcher will draw his sample, and describe the procedure he will use to select the sample.

2. Tools

In order to collect evidence or data for a study. the researcher has to make use of certain testing and non-testing tools such as intelligence tests, aptitude tests, achievement tests, personality inventories, observation, interview, questionnaire, rating scales, etc. The researcher must be well versed in the development and use of these tools and fully aware of their merits and demerits.

The research proposal should explain the reasons for selecting a particular tool or tools for collecting data. The proposal should also include the reported evidence of the reliability and validity of the standardized tools for the purpose of the study. The researcher should take help of *Mental Measurement Year Books (Buros), Indian Mental Measurement Year Book* (NCERT), and other similar literature on test development for the selection of appropriate standardized tools. If he is developing his own tools, he should outline the procedure to be followed in their development.

A detailed discussion on sampling methods and on tools and techniques of data collection may be found in Chapter Five.

PROCEDURES FOR TREATING DATA

In this section the researcher describes how to organize, analyse, and interpret data. The details of the qualitative and quantitative (statistical) techniques and the rationale for using such techniques should be described in the research proposal. In case of historical research, it is necessary to throw light on the methods of internal and external criticism that are to be adhered to in the analysis of data: In documentary studies, mode of content analysis should be explained in the research proposal.

BIBLIOGRAPHY

In each research proposal, the researcher should give a list of books, journals, and other documents that he has used in selecting the problem and which he may use during the tenure of study.

TIME SCHEDULE

The researcher should also prepare a realistic time schedule for completing the study within the time available. Dividing a study into phases and assigning dates for the completion of each phase helps the researcher to use his time systematically.

BUDGET SCHEDULE

The research proposals which are submitted to government, private or autonomous agencies for financial assistance should also include a budget proposal estimating the funds required for travel expenses, typing, printing and cyclostyling, purchase of equipment, tools, books and other materials.

10. Writing Research Report

The researcher is obligated to give a completely detailed account of all his experience and thinking involved in the method of the research so as to carry the reader with him from identification and definition of the problem, formulation of hypotheses, collection of data' as evidence, analysis and interpretation of data, to testing of hypotheses and drawing out of conclusions. Such a complete and detailed account of research experience is called a research report. A comprehensive coverage of research experience and an appropriate communication of the results may be possible only when the researcher possesses requisite knowledge of the procedures involved in writing a research report. A knowledge of the rules and principles involved in writing a research report will help the researcher to write better theses, dissertations and journal articles.

GENERAL FORMAT OF THE RESEARCH REPORT

For the purposes of presentation of a research report, several style manuals are available which provide guidance to the researcher as to the specific rules on style and format to be followed in reporting findings of his research. Some universities, research organizations or journal boards have established their own format to which their theses, dissertations or research papers must conform, but all formats are somewhat similar to the following outline which comprises of three main sections: (1) the preliminary section; (2) the body of the report or text; and (3) the reference section. Each main section consists of several sub-sections.

Preliminary Section

1. Title page
2. Preface, including acknowledgements (if necessary-)
3. Table of contents

4. List of tables (if any)
5. List of figures, maps or illustrations (if any).

Body of the Report or Text

(a) Introduction

1. Statement of the problem
2. Analysis of previous research
3. Relation of present problem to theoretical position of the previous research
4. Significance of the problem
5. Delimitations of the study
6. Assumptions underlying hypotheses
7. Statement of hypotheses
8. Definition of important terms.

(b) Design of the study

1. Procedures employed
2. Sources of data
3. Data gathering instruments
4. Sampling and methods of gathering data.

***(c)* Analysis and interpretation of the data**

1. Text
2. Tables (if any, are usually included into the text)
3. Figures (if any, are usually included into the text).

(d) Summary and conclusions

1. Brief restatement of problem and procedures
2. Principal findings and conclusions with their practical implications (if any)
3. Suggestions for further research.

Reference Section

1. Bibliography
2. Appendix
3. Index (if any).

Preliminary. Section

1. Title page. Several pages of preliminary material are presented prior to the body of a research report. Generally it contains the following information:

(i) Title of the study.

(ii) Name of the institution to which the report is being submitted.

(iii) Name of, the candidate (if desired. previous academic degrees may he listed after name)

(iv) Date of submission of the report.

2. Preface. The preface usually include a brief statement of the purpose and scope of the report. A preface should also include thanks for those who gave the researcher substantial guidance or assistance in the conduct of the study. If the researcher has little to say about the contribution of his research work, the preface can easily be omitted. In such situation, the page should be labelled `Acknowledgements' rather than `Preface'. Acknowledgements should be brief and simple. A long list of effusive Acknowledgements full of flattery is not in good taste. The brief statement of acknowledgement should sincerely recognize the persons and institutions to whom the researcher is indebted for providing academic guidance, administrative facilities and financial assistance.

3. Table of contents. The table of contents includes the major divisions of the report; the introduction, the chapters with their sub-sections, the bibliography and the appendix. Page numbers for each of these divisions and sub-divisions are given. The titles of chapters and sub-divisions within chapters should correspond exactly with those included in the body of the report with correct page citation. The preface or acknowledgements, list of tables and list of figures are also entered in the table of contents. The table of contents provides reader a birds' eye view of the report and enables him to locate quickly each section of it.

Body of the Report

The main body of the research report ';usually contains four logical divisions: (1) an introduction; (2) design of the study, (3) analysis and interpretation of the data; and (4) summary and conclusions. In a thesis or a dissertation these divisions comprise chapters, while in a research paper they may consist of sections with suitable headings.

1."Introduction. The introduction of a research report should be lucid, complete and concise. It should introduce the research problem in a proper context, and arouse and stimulate the reader's interest. If introductions are dull, confused, and lacking in precision, direction and specificity, there is little incentive for the reader to continue reading the research report.

In the introduction the researcher defines, analyses and states the nature of the problem. He also reviews the related studies so as to lay a foundation for research. The review of the results of previous researches brings out areas of agreement and disagreement, and shows how the present study arose from contradictions or inadequacies of earlier investigations. The introduction also includes the significance of the problem and the need for conducting the investigation. After reviewing the background of the problem, its scope and delimitation, the researcher presents his hypotheses and the assumptions on which the hypotheses are based. He then defines the terms used in the study that have a special meaning or significance for the investigation.

2. Design of the study. This section explains the design of the study in detail. It includes a detailed description of the manner in which decisions have been made about the type of data needed for the study, the tools and device used for their collection; and the method by which they have been collected. A researcher may present definition of the population; the size of the sample 'and the rationale for the size of the sample; the method of sampling; the number of individuals who declined to participate and weeded out, or did not participate in different phases of study and why, where, when and what types of data were collected; the tools and devices used for collecting data along with their reliability and validity; the design and method of conducting the experiment giving full details about the assumptions, classification and manipulation of variables, and nature of treatments; directions given to the subjects; the characteristics of interviewers or observers and the type of training provided to them; the types of data analyses made; the statistical methods employed and reasons for selecting such methods; and how the data will be organized and presented for analysis and interpretation.

3. Analysis and interpretation of the data. This section is the heart of the research report. The data analysis and interpretation may either be presented in separate chapters or may be integrated and presented in one chapter. The data is presented in tables and figures accompanied by textual discussion. The tables and figures should be constructed and listed in such a way that they clarify significant relationships and become self explanatory. Tables which are complex and lengthy should be placed in appendix, otherwise the continuity of textual discussion gets broken. In the textual discussion. of the data, the report should not repeat all the detailed information that is provided in the tables and figures. It should only point out important facts and relationships to give meaning to the data and make certain generalizations about the data.

The formulae and statistical procedures which were used in the analysis of the data should be clearly specified and explained in detail. Statistical information may be presented in the form of sums, ratios, proportions or percentages; frequency distributions: means and variances or standard deviations; coefficients of correlation, and prediction. The reasons for selecting a particular test of significance, the assumptions underlying its use and the confidence levels chosen in arriving at the results must be presented carefully. All the unexpected developments in the form of unanticipated relationships or unforeseen trends should be reported fully. Any weakness in the research design, tools, techniques, or population that have come to light during the conduct of study should be discussed frankly. along with the manner in which factors may have affected the findings of the study.

4. Summary and conclusions. This section includes a brief re-statement of the problem, a description of the procedures used, and discussion of findings and conclusions of the study. The conclusions are presented concisely and related directly to the hypotheses that were tested. They announce whether the findings of the study accept or reject the hypotheses. Conclusions are answers to the questions raised and suggest modification in the existing theory. In addition, the researcher may list unanswered questions that have occurred in the process of study and which require further research beyond the scope of the problem investigated. If no further research would appear to be advantageous in the area investigated and a new approach to the problem is needed, the researcher should make suggestions. In short, the discussion -and presentation of the conclusions should leave the reader with the impression of completeness and of positive gain.

The summary and conclusion section is the most widely used part of the research report because it reviews all the information that has been presented in its previous sections. Most readers scan this section of the report first to get an overview of the study and to determine its utility to them. If the study is of some utility to them, they go through the remaining chapters also.

In addition to summary, some institutions and research journals require a researcher to submit an abstract of study. This abstract serves as a synopsis that gives relevant information to a reader to judge whether he wishes to read the complete research report.

Reference Section

The reference section includes bibliography and appendix. The bibliography, which will be discussed in detail later in this chapter, follows the main body of the report. In a research article the heading `references" is used in place of bibliography The bibliography is a record of those sources. and materials that have been used for the study If the number of references is large, the researcher may divide the bibliography into various sections, one for books, one for periodicals and journals, and possibly one for' reports and special documents.

An appendix follows the bibliography. All the relevant supporting unwieldy materials, that are important but not essential to the understanding of the report, are presented in the appendix. These materials include questionnaires, copies of covering letters used, evaluation sheets, checklists, courses of study, long quotations, documents, tests, interview forms, and raw data.

If a study is of major importance and is to be published in book or monograph form, the researcher also prepares an index in alphabetical order which follows the appendix

Evaluation of a Research Report

The evaluation of a research report is a valuable exercise for the student of educational research. Using a pattern such as the one suggested, the critical analysis of the many aspects of another researcher's report helps the student to develop competency in his own research and reporting skills. The evaluation aspect is much more useful even to a guide or supervisor for instructing his research scholars in preparing a research report.

The following questions are suggested relating to the various aspects of research report as a possible structure for the analysis:

1. The Title : - (a) Is it clear and concise ?

(b) Does it promise no more than the study can provide ?

2. The Problem : - (a) It is clearly stated ? (b) Is it properly delimited? (c) Is its significance recognized . (d) Are specific questions raised and hypoheses are clearly stated ? (e) Are the assumptions and limitations stated ? (f) Are important terms defined ?

3. Review of Related Literature:- (a) Is it adequately covered?, (b) Are important findings noted ? (c) Is it well organized ? .(d) Is an effective summary provided ? (e) Is the researcher commented adequately? Has he justified that his study is related to the studies and has the deviations from earlier studies.

4. Methodology used for conducting the study : -

(a) Is the research design describe in detail ?

(b) Is the method adequate ?

(c) Is the population defined properly ?

(d) Is the sample described ?

(e) Are the relevant variables recognized ?

(f) Are appropriate controls provided ?

(g) Are data collecting tools appropriate ?

(h) Are validity and reliability established ?

(i) Is the statistical treatment appropriate ?

5. Data Analysis : - (a) Is appropriate use made of tables and figures ? (b) Is the textual discussion clear and concise ? (c) Is the analysis of data relationships logical and perceptive ? (d) Is the statistical analysis accurately interpreted ?

6. Conclusions and Suggestions: - (a) Are the results discussed at length adequately ? (b) Are the inferences stated appropriately ? (c) Are the limitations of the findings enumerated clearly (d) Are the applications of the findings suggested adequately ? (e) Are some suggestions for further studies proposed appropriately ?

Apart from these aspects of research report, its literary presentation should be worth for publications. There should be minimum or no typing errors. The researcher should have the confidence and competency to define his work clearly and should be aware of the limitations of his study.

NOTES

NOTES